D0817407

always up to date

The law changes, but Nolo is on top of it! We offer several ways to make sure you and your Nolo products are up to date:

 Nolo's Legal Updater
We'll send you an email whenever a new edition of this book is published! Sign up at **www.nolo.com/legalupdater**.

 Updates @ Nolo.com
Check **www.nolo.com/update** to find recent changes in the law that affect the current edition of your book.

 Nolo Customer Service
To make sure that this edition of the book is the most recent one, call us at **800-728-3555** and ask one of our friendly customer service representatives. Or find out at **www.nolo.com**.

please note

We believe accurate, plain-English legal information should help you solve many of your own legal problems. But this text is not a substitute for personalized advice from a knowledgeable lawyer. If you want the help of a trained professional—and we'll always point out situations in which we think that's a good idea—consult an attorney licensed to practice in your state.

1st edition

The Work Less, Live More Workbook

Get Ready for Semi-Retirement

by Bob Clyatt

FIRST EDITION	SEPTEMBER 2007
Editor	CATHY CAPUTO
Cover design	SUSAN PUTNEY
Proofreading	ROBERT WELLS
CD-ROM preparation	ELLEN BITTER
Index	SONGBIRD INDEXING SERVICE
Printing	CONSOLIDATED PRINTERS, INC.

Clyatt, Bob.
   The work less, live more workbook : get ready for semi-retirement / by Bob
Clyatt. -- 1st. ed.
       p. cm.
   ISBN-13: 978-1-4133-0695-8 (pbk.)
   ISBN-10: 1-4133-0695-0 (pbk.)
   1. Retirement income--Planning. 2. Finance, Personal. 3. Retirees--Finance,
Personal. I. Title
   HG179.C6519 2007
   344.024'014--dc22

                              2007013013

For information on bulk purchases or corporate premium sales, please contact the Special
Sales Department. For academic sales or textbook adoptions, ask for Academic Sales. Call
800-955-4775 or write to Nolo, 950 Parker Street, Berkeley, CA 94710.

Acknowledgments

My thanks to the many semi-retirees who shared their stories and insights to help others on the semi-retirement journey. Particular thanks to the folks at www.early-retirement.org who are always ready to help, 24/7.

Tom Orecchio, of Greenbaum and Orecchio, an advisor approved to sell Dimensional Fund Advisors (DFA) funds, has enthusiastically helped refine and test my ideas about the Rational Investing Portfolio and turn it into something worth sharing.

Paul Fendler, my friend and accountant, reviewed the book's tax and insurance information and continues to provide me with a ready sounding board for new strategies to help semi-retirees.

My finance professors at MIT's Sloan School taught me the foundations of Rational Investing long before I knew how valuable I would find it one day.

Dave and Karol Dondero, my old friends who asked for this workbook, helped with numerous comments and suggestions along the way.

My editor Cathy Caputo, layout designer Terri Hearsh, and the entire Nolo team, whose calling is to create clear, empowering books.

My yoga teachers who keep me clear to write and sculpt.

And last, to my family, who are my supporters and companions in the semi-retirement journey.

JoAnn Cancro Photography

About the Author

Bob Clyatt semi-retired at age 42, leaving a career as an information technology entrepreneur. In semi-retirement, he uncovered a love for sculpting and has time to pursue long-held interests of writing and yoga. He lives with his wife and two sons in Westchester County, New York. Contact Bob at www.workless-livemore.com.

Table of Contents

Appendixes

Your Semi-Retirement Companion

Retirement will never be the same: Those of us who created hula hoops and popularized organic food are not going to hang up our spurs at age 65 for shuffleboard in West Palm Beach. In fact, many of us have decided we won't even wait until age 65 to begin enjoying a better life than our hyper-stressed full-time careers seem to allow. Semi-retirement is proving the perfect way to match our dreams and our needs. We get plenty of free time for leisure, fitness, and adventure, while a sensible amount of work—done on our own terms—gives us the income to make ends meet and provides the challenges and connectedness we need to feel fully engaged in life.

But making all this work can sometimes seem overwhelming. Will you really be able to afford to cut back on work? What will you do all day? What steps should you take now to be able to semi-retire? How will you know when you're ready? To move forward into this unknown territory we look for new guidelines and examples to help give us confidence that we're on the right track.

This workbook, a companion to *Work Less, Live More: The Way to Semi-Retirement*, is designed to give you some of those guidelines and examples. Drawing on the accumulated experience of hundreds of semi-retirees, you'll find advice here that is tailor-made to help you step through all the planning and preparation to achieve a safe and satisfying semi-retirement.

The first goal of this book is to give you the tools to responsibly plan and manage your finances, both before and during semi-retirement. You'll see where your money is going and build a workable budget to start saving more. You'll track your progress toward your semi-retirement date. And you'll learn a safe, proven, low-risk way to invest for the long run, and how to sensibly tap your savings. You may be pleasantly surprised to see how your income taxes will likely drop dramatically in semi-retirement. Spreadsheets and worksheets are included on the enclosed CD-ROM, so you can customize everything to your own situation and play with different possible scenarios.

Just as important are the other tools provided in this workbook, designed to help with the emotional and psychological preparation you'll need to ensure that your semi-retirement is fulfilling and doesn't self-destruct. Semi-retirement often comes in midlife, a time when old priorities are drawing to a close, old habits are being questioned, and a new structure for life's second half starts to take shape. Understanding this process so that it can be approached with a sense of adventure—not fear—is the second goal of this book.

Most people find their health, relationships, and stress levels all improve when they semi-retire. Your outlook on life may shift from one of simple survival and endurance to one of possibilities—you'll have the time to create and experience the life you've always dreamed of and to find the satisfaction that comes from fulfilling your sense of purpose. This is life the way it was meant to be, life beyond quarterly numbers, stuffy conference rooms, and endless meetings.

Semi-retirees are discovering their true work as artists, writers, small business owners, community organizers, yoga teachers, high school counselors, and fashion photographers. Or they are shifting to part-time roles in their former careers and using their free time to travel, volunteer on environmental projects in developing countries, assist in archaeological digs, learn to surf, sail across the ocean, or start nonprofit organizations.

With the tools, examples, support, and resources in this book, you too can take control of your future and begin writing the next chapter of your life.

Are You Ready for Semi-Retirement?

A century or two ago, most people expected to live only into their 30s or 40s and probably felt little need to be concerned about life's second half. Now, we increasingly have a choice about how much and how long to work. A quarter of American families headed by someone between the ages of 45 and 64 could enter semi-retirement today and live at or above the national median income, according to the most recent Federal Reserve Board Survey of Consumer Finances.

If you're one of that group, are you ready to take advantage of your situation? Some of us yearn and plan for retirement and know exactly what we'll do when that happy day arrives. But most of us need help transitioning from our busy working lives into the less-structured—and saner—pace of life in retirement.

The 20th century's image of retirement as a leisure-only, 65-and-older lifestyle increasingly doesn't fit our needs or match our self-images or dreams. The term semi-retirement may seem awkward, but it is the best I've found to describe what most people who leave full-time careers eventually find themselves doing. (You may prefer to call yourself early retired, partially retired, or even transitionally retired.) Your activities may feel nothing like Work—that four-letter-word variety that you gladly left behind—and they may not even be paid. But if you're finding your way to a congenial blend of responsibilities, challenges, and rewards balanced with plenty of leisure time, then you've discovered semi-retirement and are part of an emerging trend.

I made that change at age 42 and learned a number of valuable and humbling lessons, which are collected in my first book, *Work Less, Live More: The Way to Semi-Retirement*. This companion workbook was created in response to requests from readers who wanted to apply the principles from that book to their own situations. The hands-on exercises and spreadsheets in this workbook will help you calculate your financial readiness for semi-retirement, rebalance your portfolio, track your fund management expenses, and ensure that your spending stays within the amount you can safely withdraw each year from your savings. You'll find nuts-and-bolts spreadsheets and worksheets to help you ensure that your savings are prudently invested and tapped to meet your financial needs over the long haul.

But no less important are the non-financial chapters, filled with worksheets, encouragement, exercises, and resources to help you tap into your fullest potential for creating a fruitful semi-retirement, whatever form it may take. Many people entering semi-retirement experience a giddy sense of freedom slipping out from the routines, priorities, and commitments that have too long governed their lives. Good planning helps ensure that when the euphoria fades, you'll have plenty of new interests to keep you from feeling bored or homesick for the structure and sense of accomplishment you enjoyed in your old career.

Two of the things I've enjoyed most about semi-retirement have been meeting the many people whose stories are recounted in my books and feeling the encouragement of an extended community of early- and semi-retirees. This workbook offers tips and advice that have helped me—tips from people who've made this transition themselves, that speak to its triumphs and pitfalls, help you analyze your financial fitness, or help you find your life's calling. Those who've taken the plunge want to share what they have learned and help you join in the adventure. "The water's fine," they are calling. "Here's how to swim, here's where the rocks are, and when you're ready, come on in!"

Running a Business That Leaves Time to Enjoy Life

Ever wonder who buys season tickets to major league baseball games and actually has the time to show up dozens of times a year to watch the team? One of the regulars at Oakland A's games is a semi-retiree named Mike. Mike's path to semi-retirement started in college where, to help pay his tuition and expenses, he washed windows. After graduating with a business degree, Mike capitalized on his experience in the trenches and began working as an account representative for a large cleaning services company. Eventually, Mike spun off the window washing portion of that business and began running it as his own company.

Over the years, Mike earned the respect and loyalty of a close-knit group of family members and long-term employees who now keep the business running smoothly. As a result, he's cut work back to about ten hours a week. Though he may work more from time to time on certain projects, once things are stable he cuts his hours again. Mike's business generates steady profits, and he'd rather have more free time than more money and employees.

Mike's typical weekday includes a couple of hours of paperwork in the morning, an hour jogging around the lake with his dog, a leisurely lunch with his wife, and an afternoon of projects improving his home and garden. He remains "on call" for business matters but generally confines work to the morning. Not only does that leave him plenty of free time to see friends and family, but it also leaves afternoons and evenings free for ball games. Mike enjoys running a profitable, high-quality, family-friendly business and sees himself continuing in this manner for many years to come.

How Ready Are You?

In the following questionnaire you'll find a wide range of questions based on the experience of semi-retirees. The questions deal with both the carrots that might be luring you on to a dynamic second half of life (wanting to spend more time traveling or with your family, for example) and the sticks that might be painfully urging you to stop whatever you're doing now and find a better way (stress at work, for example). The questionnaire is in two parts—one section asks you about your stress levels and job satisfaction, and the other section focuses on your financial preparedness.

Taking this test gives you a chance to see how you compare to people who are already semi-retired, or well on their way there. You may be pleasantly surprised to learn that you're already taking the steps that many semi-retirees before you have taken. Or you may see that you are still working toward the kinds of personal finance and personal development goals that will help you prepare to leave full-time work behind.

Though no test can tell you exactly where you stand, this test's questions, scoring, and methodology have been extensively validated by people at each stage of the semi-retirement journey, coming from many different backgrounds and perspectives. Overall, their experience can give you a good indicator of where you are on your path to semi-retirement.

When answering the questions, choose the answer that most closely describes where you are today.

Is Semi-Retirement Right For You?

1. Check the statement that best describes your feelings about your full-time career work.

   ☐ a. I love my work and would consider taking a pay cut if necessary.

   ☐ b. Although I enjoy my job, I'm really motivated by the money.

   ☐ c. I'm satisfied with my work, though problems and stress are a regular part of my job.

   ☐ d. Most days I would rather be somewhere other than work.

   ☐ e. I'd be happy to retire tomorrow.

   ☐ f. I don't work full-time.

2. My sense of self-worth is tied to my career success.

   ☐ Usually   ☐ Sometimes   ☐ Never

3. My age is (check one): ☐ under 30   ☐ 31 to 40   ☐ 41 to 50   ☐ over 51

4. If I had a whole month free, I would (check all that apply):

   ☐ a. Go stir crazy.

   ☐ b. Take a vacation.

   ☐ c. Take care of lots of chores around the house.

   ☐ d. Try something new I've always wanted to do.

5. Check the statement that best describes your experience of work-related stress:

   ☐ a. I am under constant grinding pressure at work.

   ☐ b. Sure there's stress, but that's because my work is challenging and creative.

   ☐ c. My work isn't too stressful.

   ☐ d. I could deal with more stress—my job is dull and I am seeking more challenge.

6. I have a clear idea of things I would like to do in semi-retirement.

   ☐ Yes   ☐ Somewhat   ☐ No

7. I want to spend much more time with my partner and family or friends.

    ☐ Yes   ☐ Somewhat   ☐ No

8. My spouse or partner and I have a shared goal and vision about shifting to semi-retirement.

    ☐ Yes   ☐ Somewhat   ☐ No   ☐ I'm single

9. I am very interested in socializing with my work colleagues.

    ☐ Yes   ☐ No

10. I feel there is much more I need to do with my life, but can never find the time.

    ☐ Usually   ☐ Sometimes   ☐ Never

Do you have the means to semi-retire?

11. I have saved money most years.   ☐ Yes   ☐ No

12. My financial assets (including home equity I could access if I moved to a smaller home) are equal to:

    ☐ a. 0 to 5 times my annual spending (the amount I spend each year for all my living expenses—excluding my pension)

    ☐ b. 6 to 10 times my annual spending

    ☐ c. 11 to 20 times my annual spending, or

    ☐ d. more than 20 times my annual spending.

13. I generally replace a car after owning it:

    ☐ a. 1 to 3 years

    ☐ b. 3 to 5 years

    ☐ c. 5 to 10 years

    ☐ d. 10 or more years

    ☐ e. I don't have a car.

14. The total amount of my unpaid credit card or consumer debt (aside from debt I pay in full each month on a mortgage or car payment) equals more than one month of my living expenses.

    ☐ Yes   ☐ No

15. I have a budget that I follow every month.   ☐ Yes ☐ No

16. My mortgage will be paid off:

    ☐ a. it's already paid off

    ☐ b. in less than 5 years

    ☐ c. in 5 to 15 years

    ☐ d. in 15 or more years

    ☐ e. I don't own a house, or

    ☐ f. I could pay it off tomorrow but choose to invest the proceeds instead.

Scoring

Give yourself the points indicated below for each question, and then add up your total.

1. a. −5
   b. 0
   c. 1
   d. 3
   e. 4
   f. 5

2. Usually: 0
   Sometimes: 2
   Never: 4

3. under 30: −4
   31 to 40: −2
   41 to 50:   0
   over 51:   2

4. Count each checked answer
   a. −5
   b. −2
   c. 1
   d. 2

5. a. 4
   b. 0
   c. −1
   d. −3

6. Yes: 3
   Somewhat: 1
   No: 0

7. Yes: 3
   Somewhat: 0
   No: −2

8. Yes: 5
    Somewhat: 2
    No: −2
    Single: 2

9. Yes: −1
    No: 3

10. Usually: 3
    Sometimes: 0
    Never: −2

11. Yes: 3
    No: −3

12. a. 0
    b. 4
    c. 7
    d. 10

13. a. −10
    b. −2
    c.   1
    d.   3
    e.   0

14. Yes: −3
    No: 4

15. Yes: 3
    No: −3

16. a.   2
    b.   0
    c. −3
    d. −5
    e.   0
    f.   2

What your score means

15 points or less: You have some way to go. You are probably in the early stages of your planning for semi-retirement. You may simply need to continue building your savings. Use the exercises in this book to start thinking about what you'd do if you weren't required to work full-time, and to budget and add to your savings.

15 to 29 points: You're getting close. You are well on your way to being ready to semi-retire, but there is still more to do. This workbook will help you budget and continue to save and invest wisely.

30 points and above: You are ready. Life has brought you a long way and if you aren't already semi-retired, you are certainly thinking like someone who is. Your transition into semi-retirement should be relatively comfortable when you choose to take that step. This workbook will help you fine-tune your investment allocation and rebalance your portfolio, along with helping you figure out your likely taxes.

Whether you're close to semi-retirement or have a long way to go, this workbook can help you reach your goals. Read the chapters in order because each chapter builds on the previous one. You'll review your current budget and pull together spending and saving into a concise, informative picture (Chapter 2). You'll learn how to apply the principals of Rational Investing to your portfolio and how rebalance your portfolio annually (Chapter 3). You'll see how you can safely withdraw from your savings to fund your living expenses in semi-retirement (Chapter 4). You'll evaluate your tax situation (Chapter 5). And, you'll take steps toward creating the life you desire (Chapter 6).

On the Road to Semi-Retirement

Sue and Sean are both about 40 years old and hope to semi-retire in the next ten years. They have been saving conscientiously for the past ten years, ever since reading *Your Money or Your Life*, by Joe Dominguez and Vicki Robin (a book that advocates a frugal life with careful attention to how money is earned and spent).

Long-term international postings with Sean's engineering firm gave the couple a taste for extended foreign travel, and they have made some important lifestyle choices to get closer to their goal. Though they own a home in the Southeastern U.S., they rent it out and travel together on Sean's project assignments. Living in hotels and short-term rentals may not be for everyone, but they make the dollars stretch and live almost completely on Sean's per diem compensation for travel expenses. This lets them save his entire salary.

Sue does part-time contract work in each new location, which leaves her plenty of free time to be with Sean and pursue her own interests. As a physiotherapist, her skills are very portable, and local rehab centers are happy to hire her on a short-term basis. When the couple recently moved to Colorado, Sue had a job within a few days of arriving in town. As an experienced part-time independent contractor, she now earns roughly as much as her coworkers make from their full-time salaries.

Connecting to Your Dreams and Talents

What does semi-retirement mean for you? The closer you can come to tasting that, to feeling almost exactly what an ideal day or month would feel like in semi-retirement, the straighter you'll be able to steer toward that result.

Try Something New

Are you in a rut? How often do you do something in a new way—go out of your way to meet someone new, visit a new store, try a new product, read a book on a new topic or in a new genre for you, make a new dish, or rearrange your furniture? We all like our routines, and frankly they can be an efficient way to conduct life. After all, having found a favorite café with great coffee and atmosphere, do you really need to keep trying all the other places in town? Still, if we let routine rule all aspects of our lives we can grow stale.

Whether it's trying a new restaurant, finding new part-time work, or discovering a new avocation, early- and semi-retirees have the time to uncover new things. Develop the habit of staying open to fresh experiences—it can lead you toward new activities that may become immensely satisfying. If you close yourself off to new possibilities, you may well find yourself back at your old job muttering about how semi-retirement is boring or a waste of time. Though discovering your new second-half-of-life avocations can take time and patience—even sleuth work—it's worth the effort. The whole point of early and semi-retirement is to reclaim your time, and then do something particularly fun and rewarding with it.

Turning a Hobby Into Paid Work

Sometimes figuring out what to do in semi-retirement is as easy as just doing your hobby. Doug was a partner in a major consulting firm that was acquired by IBM. Three years later, the buyout offer came and Doug, at age 50, took it, knowing that the pension would cover his family's core expenses. He had been puttering around his own woodworking shop for years and longed to be able to work with high-end designers doing woodworking every day.

Luckily, Doug was connected. One of the other parents at his child's school was a well-known furniture designer whose creations regularly grace the top design magazines and the homes of Manhattan's wealthy. Doug worked out an arrangement to work side by side with master furniture craftsmen three days a week during the school year. Now, he is paid as a craftsman and offers marketing and business advice, too, when needed. The other two days a week, Doug works in his own shop on his own projects. He spends summers at the family's weekend home (which also has a wood shop, of course).

Doug relishes the no-stress work atmosphere and the chance to rub shoulders with some of the country's best craftspeople and designers as a peer. For a guy who spent his career in offices and meeting rooms, Doug feels he has finally arrived at the perfect work-life balance.

Take a Look at Your Sense of Self

Do you secretly get a charge out of answering the question, "What do you do?" or "Who do you work for"? If so, does the charge come because you are enthusiastic about your firm or work, or is it from knowing that your answer is likely to impress the person who is asking? When you pull out your business card, do you expect the company logo to impress the recipient and make you appear more successful, intelligent, or talented?

Most of us like to associate with winners, and successful organizations use that to attract and retain talented people. But if you let your identity become too bound up with that of your employer, you risk allowing your sense of self and self-esteem to become too tied to your work. Though identifying with an employer and being part of its success is doubtless a good thing for a while, it can eventually make it hard for you to move on to more independent pursuits. And it can keep you tied to an organization long past the time when you should leave. A well-developed sense of self, based on internal values and priorities, will better prepare you for the independent life of a semi-retiree.

Let Your Creative Self Emerge

Here are some tips and techniques I've learned to help get in touch with your creativity. Some of them may sound silly, and they will certainly feel different or even uncomfortable at first. Allow yourself to be silly, just for a few minutes. You may find out something about yourself that you never expected to learn. After all, until we change our thinking, it can be very hard to change anything else about our lives. And semi-retirement is a big change.

Tip 1: Use your nondominant hand

Try doing routine tasks with your nondominant hand for a few minutes or hours each day. If you're a righty, brush your teeth with your left hand. Or try eating with your nondominant hand. Not only will you learn to break long established muscle patterns and habits, but your actual brain and neurocircuitry will get a useful stir. Out of this, new pathways to new ideas have a chance to get started.

Tip 2: Listen carefully to music

Get a set of headphones. With eyes closed, listen intently to a new or favorite piece of music. Follow a single instrument, preferably one that is in the background. Concentrate deeply on that single instrument. This exercise trains your concentration skills in a way that is fun and comfortable. Concentration skills also build new brain capacity—meditation, a formal type of concentration, actually creates new gray matter. If you've spent years only half-listening to music, it can be a revelation to finally notice what's been there all along. This is a powerful metaphor that can be applied to other parts of our lives—from relationships to behaviors, or physical environments.

Finding Success in a Creative Field

Many semi-retirees find meaning and challenge in second careers where they can use long-dormant creative or artistic skill and talent. Not everyone who wants to be a professional photographer or painter can actually earn a living in the field. But with financial resources to fall back on and the skills and dedication it took to be successful in their first careers, some semi-retirees are able to break through and achieve noteworthy success a second time, even in highly competitive fields.

Stefan is in the middle of this process. After a financially successful career in the business side of design and film, Stefan longed to move over to the creative side, which always seemed like more fun. Finally heeding his own motto: "When this stops being fun, I'll do something else," Stefan began pursuing his long-held dream of being a professional photographer. He enrolled in photography classes.

Stefan recently held his first one-man show of original photographic works (landscape and still-life), and several works sold. With his strong sense of design, he found himself drawn to the world of fashion photography.

Stefan clearly has creative talent, but he has gone further: By beginning to see himself as an artist instead of a business person, and by devoting time and effort to develop his talent, he has started to make real success in a creative field.

He is beginning to get contracts from companies to shoot advertising and catalogue work and looks forward to one day having a steady flow of plum assignments. When that happens, the financial rewards are built-in, which should allow him to systematically reduce the amount he draws from savings for covering living expenses and provide an additional measure of long-term financial security. In the meantime, he experiences real joy in the work, a sense of freedom, and immense satisfaction from having listened to his heart and taken action to follow his dream.

The Emerging Neuroscience Behind Creativity and Personal Growth

Solid scientific research is beginning to find that changing thoughts and actions can change what goes on in the brain and support continued personal growth. Developing your brain's potential through mental training is being seen as akin to developing your cardiovascular system through aerobic exercise. Whether in learning to moderate emotion, developing a part of the brain to take over for damaged regions after a stroke or other brain injury, or simply altering the pattern and frequency of the brain's electromagnetic waves, brain training regimens are demonstrating clear effects.

Like a muscle that gets stronger with use, neurochemical circuits widen and trigger more readily with use, improving memory, skilled performance, and emotional response. This in turn supports our efforts to make durable changes in our lives in the way we think, create, and respond to life's ups and downs.

Though scientists are still in the early stages of these explorations, this research may lead to a dramatic shift in our understanding of human potential.

Useful resources for further inquiry in this area include:

- Edward Taub, Professor in the Dept. of Psychology, University of Alabama, Birmingham, a leading researcher in brain plasticity, the brain's ability to rewire itself to use undamaged brain areas for motor or sensory control following brain injury.
- Richard Davidson, Vilas Professor of Psychology and Psychiatry, University of Wisconsin, Madison, who in addition to studying brain function of people with affective disorders, monitors brain function of Tibetan monks to discover how their mental training enables them to consciously and dramatically alter their brain's neurochemical and electromagnetic activity.
- The Mind and Life Institute (www.mindandlife.org), provides forums for collaborative research between neuroscientists and contemplative practitioners.
- *Train Your Mind, Change Your Brain: How a New Science Reveals Our Extraordinary Potential to Transform Ourselves*, by Sharon Begley, provides a comprehensive yet accessible overview of many of these research topics.

Tip 3: Sketch

If you're not already an artist, try your hand at sketching. It's another way to get new neural pathways going in the brain. Sketching is good because it can be done sitting down with minimal equipment, it is humbling to people who are used to being masterful in everything they do, it is fun, it teaches you to really start observing, it connects you to childlike stuff, and it slows you down. And as an added bonus, you just might come up with something you like. No one needs to see your efforts unless you want them to. My own sketches are generally lopsided. Over time, sketching may help you start to see differently—to really notice things that have been staring you in the face all along. This can help you find creative solutions to daunting questions whose answers may be right in front of you.

Get a sketch pad or blank sheet of paper, sharp pencil, and eraser and start with something simple. Sketch by looking carefully at a still-life subject, and then work to get each line down on your page in the correct relationship to other lines and parts of the subject. Try shading darker areas to give a sense of three-dimensional form. If you are sketching a person, study closely how each area of the figure connects to the whole. What makes that person unique? How are his or her hands or eyes different from someone else's? What does an eyelid really look like?

Tip 4: Notice your internal chatter

Listen to the internal chatter or dialogue in your head. Notice any themes that emerge. Are you nice to yourself; hard on yourself; hard on others? If someone else said the same things to you, how would you react? If your dialogue is consistently negative, work to replace some of those thoughts with more constructive and kind ones.

Tip 5: Pay attention to your daydreams

Notice things that draw your mind back again and again—places, people, or experiences. What emotion connects you to that place or time? Is there something there to learn? If possible, go back to those places with sufficient time and clarity of mind to see if any fresh ideas come to you there. This practice can link you more closely to deeper feelings that are unconsciously informing your attitudes and behaviors today.

Tip 6: Notice when you're in the flow

In which activities do you sometimes feel a state of "flow," where time and distractions disappear and you are just deeply immersed in the activity itself, in the moment? Is it possible to organize your time to spend more time doing these kinds of activities?

Tip 7: Make a life list

Make a list of the top ten or 11 things you'd like to accomplish in your life if you had more time and post it somewhere visible. When you semi-retire, your list will be a handy guide for how to fill those days when you realize you have nothing scheduled to do the entire day. Your list will keep you on track like a map and compass, guiding the small steps to create a life that reflects your dreams and values.

Tip 8: Remember your dreams

When you were 18 or 22 years old, what did you love doing or think you might want to be "when you grew up"? If you had all the time in the world, would you want to pick up some of those threads again?

Tip 9: Use your imagination

Imagine a perfect weekend. Where would it be? What would you be doing? Who would you be with? What would be your state of mind? Write down these answers in as much detail as possible. Now do the same thing for an imagined typical week in semi-retirement.

Tip 10: Whom do you admire?

What type of person do you admire? What is it about them or their life, their work, or their activities that appeals to you? Do you wish you could hang out with them or be like them? What steps might be required to get from here to there? How can you learn more about the persons you admire or the activities they are involved in?

Tip 11: Write

Write down fragments of ideas, thoughts about any of these tips, long stream-of-consciousness entries about how you're feeling about work or politics or relationships or the next chapter in your life. Writing down your ideas is a time-honored way to get things moving around you— either to process and get past something that has been bothering you or to start weaving the threads together for something new and useful to happen. Whether or not anyone reads what you write doesn't seem to matter—it's the act of writing that counts. Pictures, diagrams, and scribbles are all nice additions to plain old words.

Tip 12: Ask yourself for help

Before falling asleep, frame a question that is puzzling you, from "What should I do with the rest of my life?" to "How can I learn more about welding?" Keep a notebook handy and write down any ideas that come to you during the night or first thing upon waking in the morning. Follow up on those ideas.

Tip 13: Retreat and renew

Go on a silent retreat in a monastery or spend a few days hiking and camping at high elevation. Try to give yourself a little free time upon returning, with a notepad or sketchpad handy. New ideas and perspectives typically come to people after such experiences.

Tip 14: Give yourself encouragement

Cultivate confidence in your new ideas—take them seriously by writing them down, acting on them, talking about them with others, or otherwise tending them as if they were seedlings in a garden. Some will wither away, but others, with time and care, can grow into something of substance. Look for inexpensive ways to explore and expand on your ideas until you see which ones have the potential to grow. For instance, rather than jump straight in and open an art gallery as your first step in semi-retirement, try visiting with art gallery owners, volunteering at a local co-op gallery, or even getting a part-time job or internship in an established gallery. None of these steps are expensive or difficult, and you can learn a lot about your dream of owning a gallery without breaking the bank or becoming emotionally distraught if things don't work out.

Tip 15: Take the long view

Figure out how to salvage something of value from any so-called "failure," and give yourself plenty of slack if an idea doesn't work out. Who knows when or how today's failure will set up tomorrow's inspired success? Practice framing any disappointments along the way in positive terms.

Tip 16: Ask for help

If you have a spiritual tradition, access its prayerful or contemplative element. You may be surprised at how powerful and helpful this simple practice can be. Or, try asking other people for help instead. Frame your question clearly and ask someone you trust to help you.

Tip 17: Try yoga

In additional to traditional sports or workouts, I've found that a well-rounded yoga practice can bring physical exercise, diet, spiritual practices, and meditation into focus and provide a solid foundation for personal discovery. Yoga is now a mainstream activity and local classes can be found almost everywhere. If yoga doesn't appeal to you, look into other low-impact exercises with a spiritual and reflective dimension (such as tai chi). In any case, try paying attention to your breathing—working to lengthen and deepen your breaths when possible.

Tip 18: Look to art

Any creative work or artist you feel drawn to can be great inspiration for your own creative journey, even if your path will have nothing to do with fine arts. Whether it's painting, music, writing, dance, or drama—make exposure to creative works part of your life.

Putting It All Together

I'm the type of person who usually reads through lists of useful suggestions and never actually stops to do the exercises. But I am going to nag you gently to do better. In fairness, at one time or another I have actually done all the things in the list above.

So pull out a sheet of paper and pick one or two of the above tips to develop. Next week or tomorrow try a different tip. When you brush your teeth tonight, which hand will you use to hold the toothbrush?

Here's a worksheet that might help you (also on the CD-ROM included with this workbook—open the "Get Going" file). It's designed to get you thinking in action steps—coming up with concrete activities and committing to doing something. But we all know that the best intentions don't always make it to fruition. That's why the final column gives you a chance to draw a picture, describe a memory or feeling, or make any other reference that pops into your head about the task and actions you're hoping to accomplish. By tapping the creative and unconscious, you can help unblock or build resolve in support of an action that might otherwise be swept aside in the swirl of good intentions and overriding priorities. Images and poetry hooked to your goal can keep it coming back for you, against all odds.

Get Going: Accessing Your Creativity

	What tip will you try?	When?	What are your next steps?	Memory, activity, sketch, poem...
Example	Tip #5: daydreams	Tomorrow	Visit pond (bring sketch pad)	Ice skating—age 8 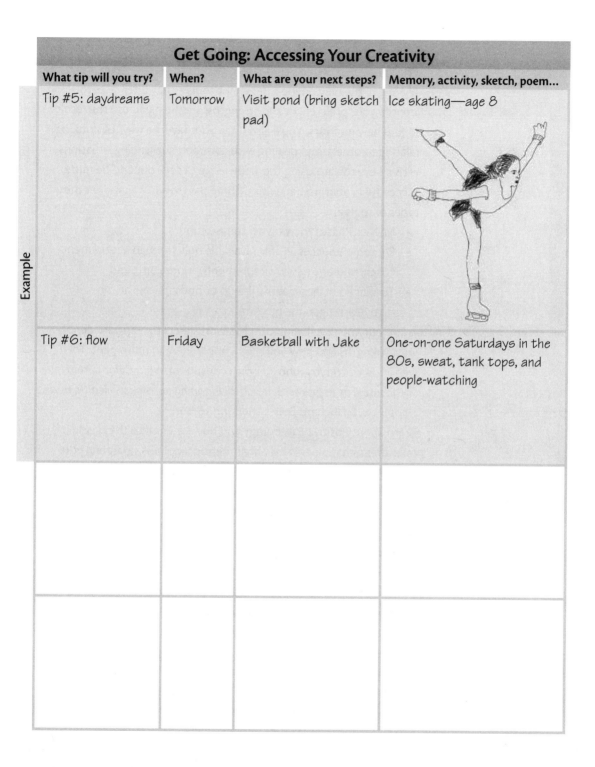
	Tip #6: flow	Friday	Basketball with Jake	One-on-one Saturdays in the 80s, sweat, tank tops, and people-watching

RESOURCE

For more help in making the transition from work to retirement.

- Try one of the new online assessment tools—they offer tests to identify your preferences and strengths, and help you use the results to find new interests. You'll also learn your favorite ways of thinking, relating to others, and dealing with common challenging situations, with an eye toward using this knowledge to seek out and be more successful in your new activities. Three paid services that offer these types of tools are:
    - MyNextPhase (www.mynextphase.com)
    - RetirementSuccessProfile (available only through a retirement coach; find one at www.retirementoptions.com), and
    - TurningPointsNavigator (sign up or find a course at http://turningpointsinc.com).
- www.retirementwellbeing.com has worksheets to help you identify your strengths and how you might apply them in retirement. The website is written by John Nelson, coauthor of *What Color is Your Parachute? For Retirement: Practical Planning for Money, Health, and Happiness*, by Richard Bolles and John Nelson.
- Learn about Positive Psychology and how you fit into the classic measures of happiness at www.authentichappiness.sas.upenn.edu.
- Learn how to live long enough to enjoy your reengineered life with the longevity calculator at www.eons.com.
- Take a Meyers-Briggs personality test at www.humanmetrics.com/cgi-win/JTypes2.asp.
- Find your personality type on the Enneagram of Personality by taking the free test at www.enneagraminstitute.com/dis_sample_36.asp.
- *Don't Retire, REWIRE!*, by Jeri Sedlar and Rick Miners, is full of strategies, case studies, and encouragement for making the transition to avocation in semi-retirement.
- *A Whack on the Side of the Head*, by Roger Von Oech (with great illustrations by George Willett) is a perennial favorite for boosting creativity. The title is drawn from the Zen tradition of whacking a

How Sculpture Found Me

Soon after I started early retirement, I made a list of ten things I wanted to accomplish. In addition to more time devoted to family and health, the list included "writing" and "sculpture." Though I had always enjoyed writing, I'm still not sure how "sculpture" made it onto the list.

More than once, I came close to crossing this item off the list as somehow mistaken, but one day, a few years into my own semi-retirement, my son asked for help on a school project. He needed to make a Minotaur from clay. Because parents were allowed to help and I had the time, I said "Sure!"

I set about "helping" the next day while he was at school. In a burst of creative fervor, I spent a thoroughly enjoyable morning pushing and pounding clay around into a credible-looking Minotaur. No one was more surprised than I with the results—my son was delighted and my wife instantly told me that I had to start taking classes at a local arts studio. Within months I was enrolled and starting new sculpture projects.

I'd hoped to learn how to make busts that didn't crack and that looked vaguely like the person they were supposed to represent. For the first few years, I took a class every Friday afternoon, slowly building my skills. By the third year, with a home studio and more skills under my belt, friends began asking me to create sculptures of their kids, which began to blossom into a perfect semi-retirement-friendly little business. New commissions followed and one loyal patron has even begun making regular studio visits to see each new piece in case she should want to add it to her collection. Recently, I've started displaying my work at art fairs and juried competitions and applying my old marketing skills to selling art.

Family vacations now include a visit to a museum or public sculpture. The garage is overflowing with finished and half-finished pieces, molds, armatures, and so forth. Hours spent working on a new piece fly by, and I've made lots of new friends in the sculpture world. Whenever things get a little too crazy, I remind myself to slow down well before it starts to feel like work.

ready and willing student on the shoulder as a way to give birth to satori—a sudden moment of enlightenment.

- *What Color Is Your Parachute?*, by Richard Bolles, helps people find their way to the vocation or avocation of their dreams. It includes lots of self-assessment exercises. At some point, you may decide that finding your calling is a lot of hard work, and that maybe a whack on the side of the head is easier!

- *The Artist's Way* and its related workbooks, by Julia Cameron, help people find the artist within through a careful step-by-step process. She places a big emphasis on keeping a journal and doing new activities in support of personal transformation. Her approach is helpful to anyone making a life change, not just artists.

With ideas about what you'd like to do in retirement now percolating, let's turn to the next chapter, where you'll start to figure out the financial side of semi-retirement and the financial steps you can take now to semi-retire on schedule. ●

Budgeting for Your Early Retirement

I f you're serious about retiring early, it's time to roll up your sleeves and get a solid handle on your spending and saving. Even if the numbers show that semi-retirement is a way off, you'll have a good handle on the choices and trade-offs you can make to speed you toward that happy day, and a clear idea of how long you'll need to work toward your goal.

In this chapter, you'll:

- track your monthly spending
- learn ways to save more money
- calculate your expenses in early or semi-retirement, and
- learn whether you have enough money to retire early.

If you're already semi-retired, you may not need to go through these exercises, but you do want to make sure your finances stay on track. So this chapter also introduces a very practical spreadsheet that will help you take a quick financial snapshot any time you want—after a major market move, for instance—to reassure yourself that you are still on course.

The tools in this chapter will also help you use your current financial information to look at your first year in semi-retirement, assuming that it will be similar to the remaining years of your semi-retirement. (Chapter 4 covers long-term planning, where market returns and your spending may vary.) For now, though, you'll walk before you run and work out exactly how to become financially ready for your first year in semi-retirement.

Tracking Your Spending

To find out where you're going, you first need to know where you are right now. To do this, I'd like you and your spouse or partner to keep track of all of your spending for two months. The point isn't to change your spending habits right away, but rather to simply hold the mirror of reality up for you to see clearly what you are doing. Later, if changes are warranted, you can decide what to do from a position of knowledge. The phrase "penny wise and pound foolish" was coined to describe the process of spending inordinate amounts of time and effort working on the wrong problems—in this case, trying to save money in places that won't make much difference. A good baseline analysis will help you sort out where and how you might start to make meaningful changes in your finances.

If you're one of the many people who use cash-back credit or debit cards for many of your monthly purchases, you'll have a convenient, consolidated record of where you spend your money. I recommend using these types of cards as a good way to get the raw data you need to track your expenses (and you'll get 1% or more of your spending refunded to you at the end of the month or year).

SKIP AHEAD

You may be able to skip ahead.

- If you use personal budgeting software such as *Microsoft Money* or Intuit's *Quicken*, then you should already have much of the data you need to determine your spending habits and monthly averages. You can skip ahead to "Using What Your Monthly Budget Exercise Tells You," below.

- If you're simply looking for an estimate of annual spending for your long term semi-retirement planning, you'll find a quick way to compute that in "What Will You Need to Spend in Semi-Retirement?" below.

What Do You Really Spend?

Now it's time to set up a system to track what you really spend every month and every year.

For monthly expenses, you'll keep track of each expense and group your expenses into categories (groceries, entertainment, or child care, for example) to see where your money goes.

Tracking Day-to-Day Expenses

Cash: Carry a small notebook with you and jot down each transaction.

Checks: Write detailed descriptions in your check register so you'll know later what the expense was for.

Credit cards: Write down what each purchase was for and keep receipts in an envelope.

If you spend money any other ways (automatic withdrawals from your checking account, for example) pay close attention and make sure you record all expenses.

Later in this chapter, you'll enter your annual expenses or other items that you pay a few times per year (car insurance or property taxes, for example). Don't include them in your monthly expenses for now.

Do it now: You'll need eight plain envelopes to start tracking your spending—you'll use four each month for the next two months to keep your receipts and other spending information. I suggest you go get them right now and work through this exercise as you read the book. Write today's date on four of the envelopes and label them as follows:

- Credit card statements
- Cash expenditures
- Checks written, and
- Other.

One month from now, you'll have the necessary information to enter your data into the Month One spreadsheet discussed below.

Next month, you'll create four more envelopes with these same labels, and two months from now you'll have everything you need to analyze your spending as described below.

Here's what to do with each envelope.

Credit card statements: Collect your credit card statements during the two months of this exercise and put them here. Keep your individual credit card purchase receipts here, too, if you think they'll help you categorize the purchases later.

It's helpful to set up online access to your credit card statements (in a format that can be downloaded into a spreadsheet or into one of the personal budgeting tools like *Quicken* or *Microsoft Money).* Even if you don't choose to download your credit card transactions, online access will let you look at your spending and statements whenever you like, saving you from waiting for the next paper statement.

You can begin your first month's analysis on any day you find convenient, but it may be simplest to just track a calendar month—such as the month of March. Most bank and credit card statements don't start their cycles on the first of the month, though, so you'll typically need to piece together a whole month's purchases from two statements. This is where the online access can help fill in the missing pieces whenever you're ready to sit down and do your budget analysis, without having to wait for yet another statement to arrive. Be sure to check for any fees that may appear on your statement, late charges, annual charges, over-limit charges, and the like.

Cash expenditures: Each time you withdraw cash from the bank, make a note in your notebook or put the receipt in the cash expenditures envelope. Even though you'll track your actual spending for cash purchases, knowing the withdrawal amount lets you double-check yourself to make sure you haven't forgotten any cash purchases during the month. Each time you buy something with cash, write that amount in your notebook or put the receipt in the cash envelope.

At the end of the month, enter your cash spending (using the information from your notebook and the receipts from the envelope) into the Cash Tracking Worksheet on the attached CD-ROM (open the Chapter 2 Spreadsheets and click the "Cash Tracking" tab). When completed, your worksheet will look something like this:

Checks written: For the two months of this exercise make a habit of writing a detailed checkbook entry or writing a note in a separate section of your cash notebook to document each check you write. You'll need to know the amount and category of each expenditure (the categories are discussed in Categorize Your Expenses, below). Be sure

Cash Tracking

Date	Amount of Withdrawal	Amount Spent	Description / Notes
6/1	$ 200		ATM withdrawal
6/1		$ 25	Lunch
6/1		$ 5	Book
6/2		$ 55	Housekeeper
6/2		$ 5	Coffee
6/3		$ 15	Exercise class
6/4		$ 15	Groceries
6/5		$ 20	Kids' allowance
6/6		$ 75	Gardener
6/8	$ 200		ATM withdrawal
6/9		$ 20	Charitable donation
6/10		$ 20	Birthday present
6/10		$ 15	Exercise class
		$ 270	Total spending
		$ 125	Plus cash on hand
Totals:	**$ 400**	**$ 395**	**Total cash accounted for**

		$ 5	Cash not accounted for (error/change/fudge factor)

to include checks from all checking accounts you have, not just your primary one.

Other: If you spend money any other way (direct deductions from your checking account, for example), record it here. Also put your paycheck stub in this envelope—it will show any funds directly deducted from your paycheck, such as health insurance. Also, your state and federal payroll taxes (the amounts withheld from your paycheck) belong here. Any expenditure that isn't captured in the other envelopes should go here. Also, if you receive money from any source, record it here—withdrawals from a savings account, cash taken from a part-time business, the sale of personal items, personal checks, or payments you receive and use for spending cash.

At this point, you don't need to track any deposits into your savings. Saving is very important—in fact, this whole analysis is designed to help you spend less and save more—but for now, just track outflows to third parties, not movements of funds between your various accounts.

Categorize Your Expenses

After you've tracked your spending for one month, you'll be ready to categorize your expenditures to see where your money is going. Your expenses will be grouped into monthly and annual expenses.

Annual Expenses

We'll start with your annual expenses. To begin, click the "Annual Expenses" tab in the Chapter 2 Spreadsheets. Thumb back through your pay stubs and checkbook for the past 12 months to find any expenses that you don't pay monthly.

Then sort them into these categories:
- property tax
- Social Security/Medicare
- medical insurance
- auto insurance
- home insurance
- travel

- financial management, and
- other.

Enter the amount you pay per year for each of these items in column B, beginning on line 5. The spreadsheet will automatically calculate the monthly cost. For example, if you pay an alarm service once a year to monitor your home's alarm system, enter the full annual amount you pay in column B, and the spreadsheet will automatically divide the amount by 12 to be included in your monthly budget.

If you have annual expenses that don't fall into one of these categories, enter those expenses on one of the "other" rows (starting on line 11). Some things you might put in the "other" category include:

- life insurance
- taxes—if you pay income taxes in addition to what's withheld from your paycheck (either due to under withholding or perhaps on investment income) add that amount to one of the "other" rows
- memberships and dues, and
- recurring charitable donations, such as to a church or favorite charity.

Your annual expenses spreadsheet will look something like this:

Track Your Spending
Annual Expenses

Annual Expenses	Per Year	Per Month Equivalent
Property tax	$ 2,000	$ 167
Social Security / Medicare	500	42
Medical insurance	1,200	100
Auto insurance	600	50
Home insurance	1,000	83
Travel	2,000	167
		-
		-
		-
Totals:	$ 7,300	$ 608

Monthly Expenses

You'll assign your monthly expenses to these categories:

groceries	gardening/home	mortgage/rent
clothing	phone/tv/video	child care
entertainment	utilities	income tax
restaurants	charities	other
miscellaneous	gas/car/commuting	

After you have collected receipts for one month, click the "Month 1 Expenses" tab in the Chapter 2 Spreadsheets to begin entering your data. Go through each of your envelopes and enter each expense next to the appropriate heading starting on line 5. The spreadsheet will total each category of expenses, and those numbers will appear in column B. If you have any items that don't fit in the existing categories, add them to the bottom of column A. Your spreadsheet will look something like this:

Track Your Spending

Month One Expenses

Category of Expense	Totals	Enter individual expenses in the rows below:				
Groceries	$ 167	50.00	25.00	60.00	32.00	
Clothing	$ 100	100.00				
Entertainment	$ 77	25.00	52.00			
Restaurants	$ 114	100.00	14.00			
Miscellaneous	$ 36	12.00	24.00			
Gardening / home	$ 318	18.00	300.00			
Phone / TV / video	$ 96	96.00				
Utilities	$ 70	30.00	40.00			
Charities	$ 75	50.00	25.00			
Gas / car / commuting	$ 160	40.00	40.00	40.00	40.00	
Mortgage or rent	$ 2,000	2,000.00				
Child care	$ 800	800.00				
Income tax	$ 300	300.00				

After the second month, do the same thing with that month's expenses (into the "Month 2 Expenses" tab, beginning on line 5).

Using What Your Monthly Budget Exercise Tells You

Once you have entered your annual and monthly expenses, the numbers will automatically transfer to the Total Expenses spreadsheet where you can compare your expenses for months one and two and see your average monthly spending. Click the "Total Expenses" tab to see your results.

Having tracked your spending for two months, you'll have a good idea of how much your household's expenses vary month to month, which in turn tells you how closely you can rely on these numbers to anticipate your future expenses. If the two months are very different, look for possible mistakes or clues to your spending habits.

EXAMPLE 1: Reena and Jo were puzzled to find that their March spending was about 15% higher than their February spending. A close look at the figures revealed the culprit: airline tickets purchased in March for an annual vacation were not pulled out of the March totals. Reena and Jo had counted this as an annual expense when they set up the spreadsheet in February, so a portion of this money was being automatically accounted for in each month's budget. So when the actual charge occurred in March, it needed to be deleted from that month's expenses.

EXAMPLE 2: Gunther was concerned that his Month One expenses seemed high compared to his Month Two expenses. A look at the detailed transactions simply showed a rash of entertaining and gifts in Month One that were not typical of his monthly expenses. He decided to run the exercise for three months to get a more accurate average.

EXAMPLE 3: Ianna found that her August expenses were significantly higher than her September expenses, but concluded that the difference could be almost entirely explained by her effort to pay off a credit card balance in August. Because this payment was not a typical expense, she subtracted the amount from her August expenses and found that the resulting spending totals were within a few hundred dollars of each other. She concluded that was a closer estimate of her actual monthly spending.

If your two months of data were reasonably similar, you now have a good indication of your spending. You can see your average monthly expenses on line 28 of the Total Expenses spreadsheet. Line 29 transfers the monthly amount of your annual expenses to this spreadsheet. And on line 30 you can see your total monthly expenses including the monthly portion of your annual expenses.

Now it's time to give some thought to your spending habits.

- What category of expense surprised you the most?
- What expense was higher than you thought it would be?

- What expense was lower than you thought it would be?
- How do your expenses compare to your income?

Use your answer to the last question to calculate your personal savings rate. First, subtract your total expenses from your income to get your total savings (verify this number against the amounts you think you have added to savings during the year—it is a useful way to see whether you're saving as much as you could be). Second, to get your personal savings rate, simply divide your total savings by your total salary income.

EXAMPLE:

A. Income over the two months	$ 12,500
B. Spending over the two months	$ 10,780
C. Savings over the two months (A–B)	$ 1,720
D. Savings as a percent of income (C/A)	13.76%

Americans as a whole have a negative savings rate, but many people on the path to semi-retirement save much more. A savings rate of 20% would put you in the ranks of elite savers in the U.S., but some people on their way to semi-retirement save as much as 50% of their take-home pay, living, for example, on one spouse's salary while saving the other's or putting large annual bonuses directly into savings.

Earnings and gains from investments are not counted as savings in the U.S. government's personal savings statistics, although they do represent a potentially powerful way for you to augment your savings each year. But the key to achieving an early semi-retirement for most people is regular saving.

In *Your Money or Your Life*, Joe Dominguez introduced a concept that I try to follow: In an ideal world, each additional dollar spent would garner an equal amount of benefit. That means that money you spend in one area of your budget should bring you roughly equivalent benefit or value as does the money you spend in other parts of your budget. But after tracking their spending, many people find that a certain part of the budget seems to be taking up a lot of extra dollars without actually delivering much satisfaction or benefit. Though there may be good reasons for this, or little you can do about it in the near term, it's worth thinking about ways you can change your spending habits. Semi-retirement offers the chance to make bigger changes that can bring your budget into better balance by, for example, moving, downsizing, or making bigger lifestyle changes that bring your spending more in line with your values.

EXAMPLE 1: After tracking their spending, Russ and Carol found that travel was among the biggest items in their budget, at a time when there were few funds left over each year for savings. They enjoyed travel, but they realized that they were putting their personal travel standards on a par with the business travel that Russ did for his employer on an expense account. This realization helped them choose less expensive hotels and restaurants during vacations with an eye toward saving more money.

EXAMPLE 2: Susan and Ted realized that their tax bill took up a large percentage of their total budget. Because they were already considering early retirement, they were open to lifestyle changes (including moving) that would reduce their taxes. This helped them decide to move to a state with lower state income and sales taxes. The move, along with their shift to self-employment, helped them reduce their overall tax bill to a small percentage of its previous level.

EXAMPLE 3: Recent empty-nesters George and Liz did the math on the costs of maintaining, heating, and cooling their home in an expensive northeastern suburb. Lawn care, taxes, utilities—it all added up to over $30,000 a year. A modern town house in the center of a gentrifying mid-Atlantic city cut these recurring charges in half, while freeing up home equity for investment and living expenses.

Comparing Your Expenses to Your Values

Here, write down your five biggest categories of expenses. Include the monthly share of your annual expenses if those are among the five largest expenses.

Expenses	Rank
Example: mortgage expense	1 (because my home is very important to me)
1.	
2.	
3.	
4.	
5.	

Now, rank these five areas in order of their value or importance to you ("1" for the one you feel is most important, "2" for the one that is next-most important, and so on). Assigning these rankings to your expenses is a very personal decision. Only you will know which expenses provide you with the most satisfaction or value.

See if your rankings correspond to the amount of money you're spending on an item. Is a less-expensive item giving you more satisfaction? If so, can you imagine any ways to rearrange your life to spend less on an expensive item that gives you less value? Ask your spouse or partner to also rank spending areas this way and use this exercise to start a conversation about budget matters.

> **EXAMPLE 1:** Phil enjoyed flying and owned a private plane. Over the years, he used it less and less, especially after he and his partner became parents. Meanwhile, his hangar rental and maintenance charges were mounting. After this budgeting exercise, Phil realized the plane cost as much as the family spent on food each month, and was the family's most costly expense

aside from taxes and home utilities. Phil sold the plane and now rents a plane when he wants to fly.

EXAMPLE 2: Rita and Les live in an expensive suburb with high taxes, which makes the property tax portion of their budget stand out. They ranked this as an important item, though, because the property taxes pay for great schools for their children and a high level of community services. They consider their high tax bill to be a good value, yet they wonder if they will feel the same way in the years ahead when their children are out of the local schools.

Take Another Look at Your Expense Categories

Is your spending out of step with your priorities? Take another look at the expense categories below and write down your thoughts about each category. Can you see ways to rethink your spending in these areas? If your spending is not in line with your priorities and values, what can you do about it?

Take Another Look at Your Expense Categories

1. **Miscellaneous expenses.** If your miscellaneous expenses are large, try breaking them down into smaller subcategories. For example, how much do you spend monthly on restaurant lunches, espresso bar visits, unreimbursed business expenses, or soft drinks? If you were to bring your lunch, make espresso at home, and curb the trips to the vending machine, how much would you save? Take a look at your parking and commuting expenses—is there a cheaper way to get to work?

   _____

   _____

   _____

   _____

2. **Phones, television, video.** If you're paying multiple vendors for these services, try shopping around to see if materially better deals are available. Some telecommunication companies offer packages for phone, mobile phone, Internet connection, and cable television at quite a savings. If you subscribe to a DVD rental service, consider borrowing movies from the library instead.

   _____

   _____

   _____

3. **Energy.** How careful are you about turning off lights when they are not in use, or in reducing the heat (or air conditioning) in areas of the house you're not using? Is the house properly insulated? Do you leave lots of chargers and similar items plugged in which are quietly drawing energy 24/7? How is your driving style—if you have a lead foot, your engine efficiency and gas mileage can be decreased by ¼ or more. Can you group errands together and spend less time on the road, saving both gas and stress?

   _____

   _____

   _____

   _____

4. **Insurance.** Take a few minutes and shop around for auto insurance to see if a better price is available for similar coverage and service. Examine your life insurance options to see whether inexpensive term insurance for a specific number of years may meet your needs. If your employer is not providing your health insurance, consider whether a high-deductible health insurance plan combined with a health savings account (HSA) could be a better value for you.

_____

_____

_____

5. **Recurring charges.** Are you paying recurring credit card charges that you no longer need—for example, fees for Web storage space or Web pages? Get rid of any credit cards that charge you an annual fee, unless they give you frequent flyer miles or points you feel are worth the price. (Be sure to use up any accumulated points before you cancel the card or you could lose them when you leave. Some cards will also let you redeem miles for gift certificates to home supply or clothing stores.) Consumer-friendly credit or debit cards—often from credit unions—are now available with cash rebates, low penalty fees, and no annual fees. If you pay in full each month through automatic withdrawal, there will be no late fees or finance charges. (Some banks charge egregious per-transaction or overdraft fees on debit card purchases, so be sure to shop around.) Does your bank still charge you a monthly fee for your checking account? Free services are now widely available— ask your bank manager to drop your fee before switching to another bank. If you are running a credit card balance or line of credit balance and paying interest on it, roll that balance over to a zero-interest card if you can (being careful to watch the fine print so you don't get caught with a late payment or other breach of the terms and find yourself suddenly paying hefty fees or interest) or pay off this expensive consumer debt as soon as possible.

_____

_____

_____

_____

6. **Car expenses.** Keeping your car a long time is one significant way to save money. Cars should be able to last at least ten years with normal use and proper maintenance. Buying a used car is also generally a good way to save money, as long as you are not the one stuck with it when it starts to need major repairs. Even if your car is less than ten years old, a hybrid or high-gas-mileage car may be worth the switch early if your gas-guzzler is not otherwise meeting your needs. Remember also that unless you lease a car (which I don't recommend), your car expense isn't just your car payment. It includes the amount of your car's depreciation plus any interest charges on a loan, supplemented, of course, with any repair or maintenance charges. To help calculate your actual expense, see "Should You Buy or Lease a Car?" below.

7. **Restaurant expenses.** How often did you eat out during the two months you tracked your expenses? What was your least expensive lunch or dinner? What was your most expensive (comparing lunches to lunches and dinners to dinners)? If the more expensive meal cost twice as much as the lower-cost one, did you enjoy it twice as much?

8. **Charitable giving.** What percentage of your monthly or annual spending goes to charities? What percentage of your income? Are you comfortable with this level? Are you happy with the organizations or people you support? In his *Automatic Millionaire* books, David Bach makes a compelling case for ensuring that charitable donations remain a core budget item no matter how much you are trying to save.

Earning More

One way to save more money is to earn more. Before dismissing this possibility, be sure to fully consider your earning options—either within your current position or employer or through a job or career change. Trying out a new field you hope to enter in semi-retirement could both provide extra income and let you explore and transition into a field you like better.

Once you land a raise or a job, resist the urge to upgrade your lifestyle. Instead, plow all additional earnings directly into your savings, preferably through automatic deductions from your paycheck or checking account.

If you need some incentive to save, take a look at the Savings Over Time table, below. Here you'll see the long-term value of a little self-denial today. Assume you gave up a single fancy coffee each week, saving just $20 per month. Put that into savings and deprive yourself for just the next five years. After that, you can return to your old ways or find some other use for the money, but the $20 per month you stashed away will continue to grow, earning an assumed 8% per year (5% real return, after inflation).

At the end of five years, you will have put an additional $1,200 into savings, and it will have grown modestly in value to $1,521. By the end of 40 years, however, deep into your retirement, those five years of missed coffees (just one a week, remember) will have grown in value to $22,483 or $7,361 in constant inflation-adjusted dollars.

If you can come up with something even bigger to forgo for the next five years, the numbers start to get truly impressive.

> **EXAMPLE:** Jan and Carlos decide to forgo one expensive restaurant dinner per month, saving about $100. For five years, they will save that $100 per month in a blended investment portfolio (like the Rational Investing portfolios introduced in Chapter 3), which has historically earned over 8% per year. After 40 years, they can expect to have an extra $38,404 in their pocket.

If you do some serious saving and put aside an additional $1,000 a month or $12,000 per year for the next five years, in 30 years or so you'll be able to withdraw $12,000 per year forever (in today's dollars). In other words, save a dollar this year (and each year for five years), wait 30 years, and it will have grown big enough to give you that same inflation-adjusted dollar to spend every year thereafter. Even if you are 50 or 60, the value of saving is still strong, given the trend toward longer life expectancies.

Save for Your Child's Future

Once you see the powerful impact of compound interest in generating future income, you might be motivated to help your children start life with their own chunk of savings. Granted, it's not an option for all parents. But if you have the resources, the extra years of compounding make gifts to children especially powerful. Whether through a child's Roth IRA (explained in detail in *Work Less, Live More*, Chapter 5), a trust fund, or another type of gift that helps ensure the money stays invested, a relatively small sum for a ten- or 20-year-old can ensure a very comfortable retirement or semi-retirement 30 or 40 years down the road.

Any amount you save will continue to grow and can be given to your heirs or a favorite charity when you die, and they'll be able to do the same thing in perpetuity themselves. This is as close to creating a perpetual motion machine as you'll ever see—it just takes a little discipline today, and some years of compounding, then the magic begins, creating your financial independence.

What Will You Need to Spend in Semi-Retirement?

The amount of money people need in retirement is often half or less of the amount they currently earn, which can come as a pleasant surprise.

Savings Over Time

Savings Returning 5%

This chart shows the growth of regular monthly savings at a 5% return, which is a typical real (inflation-adjusted) rate based on historical market returns.

Monthly Savings	Total Saved in 5 Years	Value after: 5 years	10 years	15 years	20 years	25 years	30 years	35 years	40 years
$ 20	1,200	1,392	1,777	2,268	2,895	3,695	4,715	6,018	7,681
$ 50	3,000	3,481	4,443	5,670	7,237	9,237	11,788	15,045	19,202
$ 100	6,000	6,962	8,886	11,341	14,474	18,473	23,577	30,091	38,404
$ 250	15,000	17,406	22,215	28,352	36,185	46,183	58,942	75,227	96,010
$ 500	30,000	34,811	44,429	56,704	72,371	92,365	117,884	150,453	192,021
$ 1,000	60,000	69,623	88,858	113,408	144,741	184,730	235,768	300,906	384,041
$ 2,000	120,000	139,246	177,717	226,817	289,482	369,461	471,536	601,813	768,083

Savings Returning 8%

This chart shows the growth of regular monthly savings at an 8% return, which is a typical nominal (non-inflation-adjusted) rate based on historical market returns.

Monthly Savings	Total Saved in 5 Years	Value after: 5 years	10 years	15 years	20 years	25 years	30 years	35 years	40 years
$ 20	1,200	1,521	2,234	3,283	4,824	7,088	10,414	15,302	22,483
$ 50	3,000	3,802	5,586	8,207	12,059	17,719	26,035	38,254	56,207
$ 100	6,000	7,603	11,171	16,415	24,118	35,438	52,070	76,508	112,415
$ 250	15,000	19,008	27,929	41,036	60,296	88,594	130,174	191,269	281,037
$ 500	30,000	38,016	55,857	82,073	120,592	177,189	260,349	382,538	562,073
$ 1,000	60,000	76,031	111,715	164,146	241,184	354,378	520,697	765,075	1,124,147
$ 2,000	120,000	152,062	223,429	328,291	482,367	708,756	1,041,395	1,530,151	2,248,293

You may be closer to achieving financial self-sufficiency than you realized.

This spreadsheet helps you estimate, based on your current spending, how much money you'll need in retirement. To see how the calculations in this spreadsheet work, take a look at the sample worksheet (click the "ER Spending" tab in Sample Worksheets on the attached CD-ROM) while reviewing the instructions below.

When you're ready to enter your data, click the "ER Spending" tab in Chapter 2 Spreadsheets.

Step 1. Enter your salary or expenses

Begin by using either the paycheck method or the spending method to estimate your spending needs. Read the descriptions below to see which method works better for you.

Using the Paycheck Method

If you don't have a budget now and aren't sure how much you currently spend each year, the paycheck method will probably work better for you.

Start by entering your current net salary—the amount that gets deposited in the bank after all payroll and income taxes are taken out. Enter it next to the line that best describes how often you are paid (weekly, biweekly, twice per month, or monthly) on line 5, 6, 7, or 8. Enter any bonuses you received last year on line 9.

Next, enter the amount of money you saved last year—that is, the amount you actually deposited in your savings. Your portfolio may have increased or decreased based on market performance, but here you are after the amount you deposited yourself. Enter it in cell B13.

Next, enter any credit card debt you incurred this year as a positive number in cell B14. If you paid off debt during the year, enter it as a negative number.

The spreadsheet will subtract the amount you saved from your earnings. The resulting amount will be the amount of money you had available to spend.

Early Retirement Spending—Paycheck Method

Paycheck Method 1—start with current salary		Annual
Enter only one of the following:		
Take-home pay (weekly)		$ -
Take-home pay (biweekly)	$ 2,450	$ 63,700
Take-home pay (twice per month)	$ -	$ -
Take-home pay (monthly)		$ -
After tax bonuses received last year	$ -	-
Net Annual Pay Last Year		63,700
Less Value of Net Savings		10,000
Deposits made to savings/investments	11,000	
New credit card debt	1,000	
Work Related Expenses		2,594
Laundry (per week)	20	1,000
Child care (per week)	0	0
Lunches (per week)	0	0
Snacks/coffee (per week)	0	0
Miles commuting (per week)	41	
Cost per mile	0.485	
Annual car maintenance		994
Commuting tolls (per week)	0	0
Parking (per week)	12	600
Work clothes budget (per year)	0	0
Less Paid Debts (by retirement date)		18,600
Mortgage payment	1,550	18,600
Car payment	0	0
Other debts expected to be paid off	0	0
Amortization		3,500
Number of cars owned @ 2,500	1	2,500
Personal residence owned (1= yes)	1	1,000
Net Other Annual Spending Changes (enter cuts as a negative number)	(3,000)	(3,000)
Income needed for spending		29,506
Expected Income Tax (3% of spending)		990
Fund Management Fees	0.0035	2,786
Total Financial Savings	796,000	
Total Spending in Retirement		$ 36,782

Using the Spending Method

If you already know how much money you spend each month—perhaps through tracking your spending as outlined in the previous section—then the spending method will be easy to use.

Enter the amount of your total monthly spending in cell F14. If you tracked your monthly expenses, you'll find this number in cell C30 on the Total Expenses tab. In the sample data, we have used $4,480 per month to provide a rough match between the two ways of calculating on this sheet.

Step 2. Subtract work-related expenses

If you used the Paycheck method in Step 1, enter the rest of your data into column B. If you used the Spending method, enter your data into column F.

Enter work-related expenses that you will no longer have to pay once you retire, including the costs of dry cleaning, child care, restaurant lunches, snacks and stress-busting treats you won't be buying anymore. Enter the amount you spend weekly next to these items listed on lines 17 through 20, and the spreadsheet will calculate the annual amount.

On line 21, enter the miles you commute to work. The spreadsheet will use the IRS standard reimbursement rate ($.485 in 2007) to calculate the average cost in gas, maintenance, and wear and tear on your car from commuting.

On line 24, enter the weekly amount, if any, you pay for tolls while commuting.

On line 25, enter your weekly parking cost, if any.

If you do not drive to work, but pay other commuting expenses, enter their weekly equivalent here. For example, if you pay for a $200 train pass each month, add $50 per week as a good approximation of your commuting costs. If you pay $300 annually for a commuter parking permit, enter it as $6 per week.

On line 26, enter any annual charges you pay that are required by your work, and that you won't need in semi-retirement, such as,

Early Retirement Spending—Spending Method

Spending Method—start with current budget		Annual
Current Annual Spending		$ 53,760
Monthly Spending	4,480	
Work Related Expenses		2,594
Laundry (per week)	20	1,000
Child care (per week)	0	-
Lunches (per week)	0	-
Snacks/coffee (per week)	0	-
Miles commuted (per week)	41	
Cost per mile	0.485	
Annual car maintenance		994
Commuting tolls (per week)	0	-
Parking (per week)	12	600
Work clothes budget (per year)	0	-
Less Paid Debts (by retirement date)		18,600
Mortgage payment	1,550	18,600
Car payment	0	-
Other debts expected to be paid off	0	-
Amortization		3,500
Number of cars owned @ 2500	1	2,500
Personal residence owned (1= yes)	1	1,000
Net Other Annual Spending Changes (enter cuts as a negative number)	(3,000)	**(3,000)**
Income needed for spending		29,566
Expected Income Tax (3% of spending)		992
Fund Management Fees	0.0035	**2,786**
Total Financial Savings	796,000	
Income needed for spending		**$ 36,844**

suits and dress clothes, memberships in professional organizations, or periodicals.

The total of all your work-related expenses will appear in line 16. This amount will be subtracted from your current spending to arrive at an estimate of what you'll spend in semi-retirement.

Step 3. Subtract debts you'll have paid off

If your mortgage will be paid off by the time you retire, enter the amount of your current monthly mortgage payment on line 29. This amount will be subtracted from your expenses. Don't enter the amount of your property taxes; if your taxes are added to your mortgage payment, deduct them before entering the mortgage amount. If your home will not be paid off by the time you retire, leave this line blank.

If you currently make monthly debt repayments that you expect to have paid off by the time you semi-retire, enter those amounts on line 30 (car payments) and line 31 (other consumer debt, such as credit cards).

Step 4. Add car and house costs

On lines 34 and 35, enter the number of cars and homes you own. The spreadsheet will automatically add $2,500 for each car you own to account for depreciation, and $1,000 for each house, to cover the annual amount of long-term recurring maintenance charges, such as painting, that you effectively use up each year. The spreadsheet will assume you will spend this much each year during semi-retirement, even if you don't actually pay for a new car or paint your house in any particular year. Note that other regular maintenance costs must simply be budgeted and paid for each year as they arise.

Step 5. Adjust for spending fluctuations

If you expect any other increases or decreases to your annual spending in early retirement—through moving, economizing, or additional travel, for example—enter those on line 37. You can also use this line to enter any other adjustments to the numbers in the model as a result of your own unique circumstances, such as the net effect of payments you expect to begin receiving or paying in the future, taxes on pensions, or Social Security or IRA distributions that may be over the amounts assumed in this model (see Step 6).

> **EXAMPLE:** Karen expects to cut her budget by about $3,000 per year by eating meals at home more often, doing her own gardening and yard care, and consolidating her phone and Internet services into one bill. She will enter $3,000 on line 37.

Step 6. Add your income tax estimate

The spreadsheet will automatically calculate your expected taxes as 3% of your expected annual spending. This number may seem surprisingly low, but is backed up by solid experience among semi-retirees who live off their investment income.

But, if you live primarily on pension income, Social Security, or withdrawals from taxable IRAs, your taxes will be higher than those assumed in the spreadsheet because these income sources are generally taxed at a higher rate. You'll need to adjust the spreadsheet to reflect your expected taxes. Use an online tax calculator (like the one discussed in Chapter 5) to estimate your taxes. Then add any additional expected taxes to the adjustments line in Step 5. See Chapter 5 for more information about taxes in semi-retirement.

 RESOURCE

A good online tax calculator for estimating your taxes from various income sources can be found at: http://turbotax.intuit.com/tax_help/tax_ calculators/tax_estimator.jhtml

Step 7. Add fund management fees

Enter your overall average fund management expense ratio, if you know it, on line 43. (You'll be able to calculate it precisely in Chapter 3.) As a guideline, investors who have carefully chosen low-fee, tax-advantaged, and index-style funds, including the funds listed in the Rational Investing portfolio in Chapter 3, will pay an average of 0.35% of their total portfolio per year in fund management expenses. The average U.S. investor, however, pays 1.3%.

On line 45, enter the amount of savings you expect to have available when you begin early retirement. (To estimate these savings, see Calculating Your Savings Over Time, below.) The spreadsheet will calculate the amount of your fees based on the amount of your savings.

> **EXAMPLE:** Tony anticipates that his total savings at the time of his retirement will be $792,000. The spreadsheet multiplies this amount by 0.35% to arrive at the total amount Tony can expect to pay in fund management fees each year ($2,786).

Step 8. Look at your results

The total on line 47 (Total Spending in Retirement) shows you the amount you'll need each year in retirement. You'll fund this from your portfolio withdrawals and part-time earnings, along with pensions or other income sources if you are fortunate enough to have them. In the rest of this chapter, you'll use this number to figure out when you'll be financially positioned to begin early or semi-retirement.

Calculating Your Total Savings Over Time

This worksheet will show you how your portfolio will gradually move toward your financial targets by showing you the effect of regular contributions to your savings each year, combined with the compounding growth of your previous savings. Knowing when you can expect to reach your required savings target can help you count down to that happy day when you'll be able to leave full-time work and begin your semi-retirement.

Think of this worksheet as a way of keeping score and watching your progress over the years ahead. Once you see this growth and compounding at work, you may want to speed it up, which can be a strong impetus to your efforts to earn more, spend less, and have more left over to add to savings. To see how the calculations in this spreadsheet work, take a look at the sample worksheet (click the "Total Savings" tab in Sample Worksheets on the attached CD-ROM) while reviewing the instructions below.

When you're ready to enter your data, click the "Total Savings" tab in Chapter 2 Spreadsheets.

Step 1. Enter the year

Enter the current year in cell C4.

Step 2. Enter expected contributions to savings

Here, enter the amounts you expect to contribute to your savings over the next several years. Enter the amount for this year in column C, and the amounts for future years in the columns to the right. Enter your IRA (including Roth IRAs), 401(k), and other tax-advantaged savings for both you and your spouse on line 6 for each year. If you still expect to have additional savings each year after putting the maximum possible into your tax-advantaged accounts, then they will be regular taxable savings, in regular brokerage or bank accounts. Put those on line 7 for each year. Don't include any amounts you're saving for your children's college—that money won't be used to support you in retirement.

Tax-Advantaged and Taxable Accounts

The government wants to help us save for retirement. All of the various flavors of IRA or 401(k) offer great tax advantages, and everyone should attempt to use these plans, either through employers or independently, to the full extent allowed by the law. Your benefit will be maximized if you can make your contributions as early in the year as possible, as they will start growing in a tax-advantaged manner that much sooner.

Once you have contributed the maximum each year to tax-advantaged plans, additional savings of after-tax dollars will simply go into regular taxable brokerage, mutual fund, or bank accounts.

In this book, you'll see these two types of savings described as tax-advantaged (IRAs and 401(k)s) and taxable (brokerage or mutual fund accounts) savings plans. Most semi-retirees find they need both types to accumulate a large enough nest egg to fund their semi-retirement. Because the tax-advantaged plans restrict your ability to withdraw from them before age 59½, it often helps to have taxable savings that allow you full access to your funds, if needed, during your 40s and 50s. You can, however, withdraw your IRA funds penalty-free before you reach traditional retirement age, although the process leaves very little room for flexibility. It is a technique known as annuitizing your IRA into substantially equal periodic payments (SEPP). The law that allows this is Section 72(t) of the Internal Revenue Code.

To learn more about IRAs, read *IRAs, 401(k)s & Other Retirement Plans: Taking Your Money Out*, by Twila Slesnick and John C. Suttle (Nolo), or visit www.retireearlyhomepage.com/wdraw59.html, to read about withdrawing money from your IRA before age 59½.

Step 3. Enter current financial assets

In column C, enter the amount of all of your current assets next to the appropriate type of asset. Start with the current balances of all of your IRAs and other tax-advantaged investments, such as 401(k)s, or other employer savings plans—enter these on lines 9 and 10. Next, enter the current balances of all of your taxable savings accounts and other

Total Savings Over Time

		This Year 2008	Projected 2009	Projected 2010	Projected 2011
Expected Annual Contributions to Savings					
IRA/401(k)/Roth Contributions		7,000	7,000	7,000	8,000
Additions to Taxable Savings		6,000	6,000	6,000	6,000
Current Financial Assets (Savings)					
IRA/401(k)/Roth Accounts #1		35,000			
IRA/401(k)/Roth Accounts #2		48,000			
Total IRA/401(k)/ Roth Accounts	0	83,000	97,200	107,326	122,246
Taxable Savings Account #1		37,000			
Taxable Savings Account #2		187,000			
Taxable Savings Account #3		127,000			
Taxable Savings Account #4		200,000			
Other Assets					
Total Taxable Assets	0	551,000	601,560	625,787	669,694
Total of all Financial Assets (year-end)	0	647,000	698,760	733,113	791,940
Expected Market Return			8%	3%	6%
Average Market Return (over all years)			**6.7%**		

Projected 2012	Projected 2013	Projected 2014	Projected 2015	Projected 2016	Projected 2017	Projected 2018
8,000	10,000	10,000	12,000	12,000	13,000	13,000
8,000	8,000	8,000	8,000	8,000	9,000	9,000
151,085	156,252	172,902	201,544	224,221	265,687	298,195
786,125	770,301	809,433	891,002	943,952	1,067,307	1,151,648
937,210	926,554	982,336	1,092,546	1,168,173	1,332,994	1,449,844
16%	(3%)	4%	9%	5%	12%	7%

assets on lines 12 through 16. Your taxable savings accounts include your regular mutual fund and other savings accounts. You can find the amounts of these investments on your brokerage statements. I've left room for two nontaxable accounts and four taxable accounts, but feel free to add more rows if you need them. I suggest you change the names in column A to the actual names of your accounts to avoid confusion.

The spreadsheet assumes your funds will not grow this year. But the totals for next year and the following years assume that your savings will be growing—from both new contributions and from interest earned at a projected growth rate that you will enter in Step 4, below. You may wish to enter, as this year's numbers, the value you expect your funds to have reached by year-end.

You can take a moment now, if you like, and fill in data for last year's balances in the same way, just to make your spreadsheet's historical record more complete. Use your past brokerage statements from December or January to locate the correct year-end amounts. You can add these numbers in column B.

At the end of each year, you can replace your projected data with your actual investment results, and after a few years you'll have an investment record that will show you how well you're progressing toward your goals. The future year's projections will continue to display correctly; they will simply now key off your actual results instead of projected results. For example, if your base year in column C is 2008, then the spreadsheet will create projections in column D for 2009. At the end of 2009, you can simply write my actual 2009 results into the correct cells of Column D, and the projections for 2010 and beyond will be based on these new actual 2009 results.

Step 4. Enter expected market return

Here, enter what you expect to earn on your investments. Historically, the Rational Investing portfolios have returned over 9.5% from a broadly diversified portfolio of assets held in low-fee funds. You can set each year's return to this average, or, if you feel strongly that markets will under- or over-perform these averages in future, enter a lower or higher number.

The 9.5% returns earned by the Rational Investing portfolios are not adjusted for inflation. Over many decades, inflation has averaged about 3% per year. You can choose to make this spreadsheet reflect real— meaning inflation-adjusted growth—by simply subtracting 3% from your projected growth rates. For example, 9.5% returns would translate to a 6.5% real return. If you use an inflation-adjusted figure on line 19, all your projections will be in inflation-adjusted dollars. This can be useful in determining when a future savings target will be met, based on your need to have a certain amount of income in today's dollars.

Step 5. Look at your results

Look at line 18 to see how your assets will grow and when you might have enough to think about semi-retirement. The next spreadsheet will help you calculate that target amount, so that together, these two sheets will tell you when you can reach a state of financial independence from full-time work.

Calculating Your Savings, Income, and Expenses in Retirement

This Savings, Income, and Expenses Worksheet ties together all the financial information you'll need to find out whether and when you'll be able to break through to financial independence. It is the central spreadsheet that all semi-retirees need to plan their retirement.

The spreadsheet consists of two sections. Section 1 gives a complete look at savings; Section 2 summarizes income and expenses. By adding up all of your savings and applying a Safe Withdrawal Rate (discussed in detail in Chapter 4), you'll find how much income your savings will produce annually over the long run.

To see how the calculations in this spreadsheet work, take a look at the sample worksheet (click the "S, I & E" tab in Sample Worksheets on the attached CD-ROM) while reviewing the instructions below.

Here you'll enter a few more pieces of data, including two key amounts from the previous two spreadsheets. When you're ready to begin, click the "S, I & E" tab in Chapter 2 spreadsheets.

Step 1. Enter total savings

Enter the amount of your total savings, including IRAs and 401(k)s, at the start of early retirement on line 4. If you completed the previous spreadsheet (in the "Total Savings" tab), use the results from line 18 from the year you hope to retire. This figure should be in today's dollars. (As discussed in the previous section, the amount on line 18 of the Total Savings spreadsheet will be in today's dollars if you reduce the projected annual growth by 3% to give a real, inflation-adjusted expected growth rate for savings.)

Step 2. Enter any deductions

Next, make sure this number is clean—for example, that you have not inadvertently included your children's college savings and that you have adjusted for any personal debt that needs to be paid off or for major expenses just around the corner.

Outstanding personal debt

On line 5, enter the amount of any consumer debt that you expect to owe when you retire. This includes most credit cards, car loans, or other consumer debt. Don't include your mortgage if you expect to continue holding a mortgage in semi-retirement and have budgeted for your regular mortgage payments. High-interest consumer debt, however, should be paid off as soon as possible—it's unlikely you will earn a rate of return on those borrowed funds higher than the interest payment you'll be making.

Children's college savings accounts

On line 6, enter the amount of any children's college savings accounts that you included in your total savings amount. These funds will not be available to you to fund your semi-retirement.

Savings, Income, and Expenses

Total Savings

FINANCIAL ASSETS or TOTAL SAVINGS (insert amount from "Total Savings" tab, line 17 for desired year)	$	792,000
DEDUCT outstanding personal (nonmortgage) debt		-
DEDUCT children's college saving accounts		-
DEDUCT additional parent contributions to children's college savings		-
DEDUCT known/planned major capital expenditures		-
Net Value of Savings:		792,000
ADD value of personal property you would sell for cash		50,000
ADD net value of other planned downsizing steps (e.g. home)		-
Adjusted Value of Savings:	**$**	**842,000**
Safe Withdrawal Rate	4.30%	
Annual Safe Withdrawal Amount	**$**	**36,206**

Income and Expenses

Income	Monthly		Annual	
Safe withdrawal amount (from line 15 above)	$	3,017	$	36,206
ADD pension income		-		-
ADD expected work income		500		6,000
ADD other expected income/gifts		-		-
Total Income	**$**	**3,517**	**$**	**42,206**
Expenses				
Annual Spending in Early Retirement (insert amount from "ER Spending" tab, line 51)		3,583		43,000
Net Shortfall or Surplus	**$**	**(66)**	**$**	**(794)**

Additional parent contributions to college savings

If you expect to contribute additional money to your children's college expenses, enter that amount on line 7. This is not an annual amount, but the aggregate sum of additional money you expect to contribute to your children's education that has not already been set aside in one of the accounts listed on line 6. Again, because this money is earmarked for your children, it will not be available to help fund your semi-retirement.

Major capital expenses

If you plan to do any remodeling or other large projects, enter the anticipated amount on line 8. These funds will be leaving your portfolio in the near future and will not help fund your semi-retirement. This is not an annual number, but the total amount you expect to be spending in a lump sum.

Step 3. Add any increases to savings

On lines 10 and 11, enter any amounts that could increase your savings. You can include any adjustments you feel are warranted—for example, the cash you could pocket if you sold your house and moved or personal property you are prepared to sell if needed. You can also add funds you expect to inherit, though these numbers may end up being smaller or arriving later than you anticipate due to taxes and a variety of other factors outside your control.

> **EXAMPLE:** Mary and George own a home that they could sell for $500,000, on which they owe a mortgage of $150,000. They could buy a new home in a less expensive area for $250,000, and are willing to do so if it becomes necessary to round out their retirement nest egg. They add $100,000, (the difference between their home equity of $350,000 and the $250,000 they'll need to spend on a new home) to the value of their savings, which they use to calculate the amount of money they can safely withdraw during retirement, on the assumption that if and when they need to they can make the move and raise the actual cash.

Bear in mind, though, that this type of supplement to your savings—while useful for planning purposes—is not the same as real cash until you actually make the sales and have the proceeds in hand. Together these adjustments give you the adjusted value of savings on line 12.

Step 4. Enter your Safe Withdrawal Rate

On line 13, enter your Safe Withdrawal Rate—the percentage of funds you plan to withdraw from your portfolio each year for living expenses. Withdrawals of between 4% and 4.5% are generally considered the maximum safe levels over the long run, with 4.3% a good compromise. If you are over 70, however, and aren't concerned about leaving funds to your children, a larger withdrawal rate—up to 6% or 7%—should be safe, though purchasing an inflation-adjusted annuity would be even safer, and potentially offer an even higher annual spending stream. See Chapter 4 for more information about Safe Withdrawal Rates.

Step 5. List your income

If you expect any pension income either from an employer or from Social Security list it on line 18. However, do not list income you hope to withdraw from your IRAs or 401(k) plans—these are part of your savings, and withdrawals from them are already included in your safe withdrawal amount. On line 19, enter the amount you expect to be able to comfortably earn each year from part-time work or other activities. If you expect any gifts or other steady income sources during retirement, enter them on line 20. (Enter annual amounts and the spreadsheet will automatically compute monthly amounts for you.) More worksheets in Chapter 4 will help you refine the expected value of your work income—for now, just enter your best estimate.

Step 6. Subtract your expenses

Using the results from line 48 of the Early Retirement Spending spreadsheet (the "ER Spending" tab), enter the annual amount of your spending needs during early or semi-retirement, or choose another number that you feel best reflects your expected spending in today's dollars.

Step 7. Look at your bottom line

Check the last line of the spreadsheet (line 24). If the numbers are positive or only slightly negative, congratulations! You should be able to support your spending in semi-retirement from your blend of income sources. Though these specific numbers apply only to your first year of semi-retirement, future years will likely be similar. To see how different market returns, macroeconomic assumptions, asset sales, and spending changes might affect your semi-retirement finances over time, see the multiyear tools in Chapter 4.

If the numbers on line 24 are negative, then you are still working toward financial independence. Experiment with changing variables—try increasing the amount of your savings or projected income from part-time work or decreasing the amount of your projected annual spending. These changes should help to bring your bottom line closer to positive territory.

Try not to be discouraged or impatient. All semi-retirees have worked through the long years and decades to save enough to achieve their financial goals. Just keep working through the exercises and see what suggestions help you to make progress, and each year you'll find yourself moving steadily closer to your goals.

If You're Already Retired

If you're already early or semi-retired, you can use the Snapshot of Annual Finances in Retirement spreadsheet any time to see where you stand.

If markets slump, your part-time income dips, or your spending changes, it is normal to worry a bit. You may wonder if you're still being fiscally prudent to spend at your beginning-of-year Safe Withdrawal Rate. Or you may want to see what would happen if you changed your safe withdrawal amount today based on your current portfolio's value. With this information in hand, you can then start casting around for possible ways to cut back your budget and be that much more prepared for next year's new financial realities. On the other hand, if markets have been particularly kind, or you've had a financial windfall and augmented your savings, you might have the pleasant task of wondering how much of a raise you might be able to expect next year, if good conditions continue and you could reset your new annual budget around that new higher portfolio value. In any of these cases, this spreadsheet will quickly pull all the numbers together and let you know whether you're still living within your means, giving you the sort of quick sense of reassurance that comes from knowing exactly where you stand.

I recommend setting your safe withdrawal just once a year, using the new value of your portfolio to set your new annual safe withdrawal amount, and then maintaining those levels throughout the year. The extensive historical testing on the Safe Withdrawal Method for semi-retirees outlined in Chapters 3 and 4 of this book and in *Work Less, Live More* show that this is possible and safe.

You'll see that the spreadsheet is broken up into two sections: Portfolio and Income on the right, and Spending on the left. In the example below, the positive net of $350 in the lower right corner quickly shows that the person in this example is on track, with expenses covered by various income sources.

To see how the calculations in this spreadsheet work, take a look at the sample worksheet (click the "Annual Snap" tab in Sample Worksheets on the attached CD-ROM) while reviewing the instructions below.

When you're ready to enter your data, click the "Annual Snap" tab in Chapter 2 Spreadsheets.

Let's go step-by-step through this spreadsheet.

Step 1: Enter portfolio and income figures

This is where you'll enter the amount of your current portfolio and any income you receive from work or other sources. All of the numbers will be entered in column B.

Portfolio Value

On line 4, enter the total of your financial savings. To find this number, add up the totals from your recent brokerage statements or online services. If you are unsure of what to include, see Step 1 of the Savings, Income, and Expenses spreadsheet, above.

Adjustments

On lines 5, 6, and 7, enter any adjustments to your overall savings you feel are warranted, such as home equity you could free up through a planned downsizing of your home, or major assets you would be prepared to sell to raise cash if needed. (Read more about these sorts of adjustments in Step 3 of the Savings, Income, and Expenses spreadsheet, above.) The spreadsheet will subtract these adjustments from the portfolio value you entered above, and the result will appear on line 8. This number is your Total Assets—the value of all your assets on which you can draw to support your annual spending.

Safe Withdrawal Rate

I recommend a maximum Safe Withdrawal Rate of 4.3% for people who have a widely diversified portfolio similar to the Rational Investing portfolios discussed in Chapter 3, and who expect to withdraw from their portfolio for at least 25 more years following the Safe Withdrawal Method outlined in Chapter 4. So for now, I suggest that you enter a withdrawal rate of 4.3%—you can change it later if you wish, after reading the next two chapters. Enter your withdrawal rate on line 9. The spreadsheet will calculate the amount you can safely withdraw from your portfolio each year, and the result will appear on line 10.

Work and Other Income

On lines 11 and 12, enter the amount of income you expect to receive from part-time work. Use the two lines either for two different sources of income or to enter income for each member of a couple. On line 13, enter any other income you expect to receive (such as from royalties, planned estate planning gifts, or trust distributions).

Snapshot of Annual Finances in Retirement

Portfolio and Income			Spending		
Portfolio Value	$	1,050,000	Basic Monthly Spending Annualized	$	38,500
Adjustment #1		50,000	Annual Expense #1		3,000
Adjustment #2			Annual Expense #2		1,500
Adjustment #3			Annual Expense #3		8,000
Total Assets		1,100,000	Charitable Contributions		2,250
Safe Withdrawal Rate		4.30%	Income Taxes on Work & Withdrawals		1,000
Safe Withdrawal Income		47,300	Amortization		3,500
Work Income #1		10,000	Fund Management Fees		4,200
Work Income #2		5,000	Average Fees Across Portfolio		0.40%
Other Income			Total Annual Spending	$	61,950
Total Annual Income	$	62,300	Net: (Income less Spending)	$	350

Total Annual Income

The spreadsheet will automatically calculate the total annual amount you can safely spend given the current values and conditions you have entered. This number will appear on line 14. Later on, you can compare it to your spending, which you'll complete in the next section.

Step 2: Enter how much you expect to spend

This is where you'll enter the amount of your expected spending. All of the numbers will be entered in column E.

Basic Monthly Spending, Annualized

Here, enter the amount of your core monthly spending as an annualized number (12 times the average monthly number). If you tracked your spending for two months as suggested earlier in this chapter, you can find your monthly spending amount in line 30 of the Total Expenses tab. If you haven't completed that exercise, estimate your monthly spending and multiply it by 12 to arrive at the annual amount. Another way to get this number is to simply look at the amount you routinely deposit in your checking account to cover basic monthly expenses, if that is how you manage your finances. Enter the amount on line 4.

Annual Spending

On lines 5, 6, and 7 enter the various types of one-time annual spending for taxes, insurance, or other expenditures such as those found in column B of the Annual Expenses tab. Even if you didn't complete that exercise, you probably already have a good idea of your annual expenses (which aren't included in your monthly budget) and you can list them here. If you pay annual expenses from a particular account—your money market checkbook, for instance—look in your records for insurance, taxes, club dues, or other similar annual payments you don't typically pay from your everyday checking account. The idea is simple—between your basic monthly spending in Step 2 and your annual or one-time expenses here in Step 3, aim to cover the full spectrum of your spending for the year.

Charitable Contributions

On line 8 enter the amount of your expected charitable contributions for the year if it isn't already included in your annual spending amounts above.

Income Taxes on Work and Withdrawals

On line 9 enter the amount of your expected state and local income taxes for the year, both from any self-employment income as well as your capital gains, dividend, and interest income. You can use the calculator and worksheets in Chapter 5 to get a good idea of these amounts, or use your last year's tax number if your situation is roughly similar to last year's.

Include only those taxes you incur to generate your income for the year from your pension, part-time work, and withdrawals from your investments—that is, the tax attributable to the funds you actually free up and spend during the year. Your total tax bill may be higher. In particular, if you owe large capital gains taxes from rebalancing or unexpected mutual fund distributions, or if you owe taxes from a Roth conversion, don't include these taxes as part of your budget. Think of those extra taxes as decreases in the size of your portfolio—rather than as increases in spending—because they don't reflect your regular, ongoing spending. They must be accounted for somehow, of course, and they are: Because of these occasional tax payments that reduce your portfolio's value, you will automatically receive a slightly diminished annual withdrawal from your savings in the years ahead.

 SEE AN EXPERT

Consult an adviser. If you need help figuring out which portions of your taxes are attributable to your pension, work income, and withdrawals from your portfolio, consult an accountant or tax adviser.

Amortization

Here, enter costs for car and home maintenance, spread out over a number of years. For each car you own, allow $2,500 per year (or find a more accurate number using the Lease vs. Buy tool at the end of this chapter—use the number in cell B16, Net Cost Per Year).

If you own a home, add an amount that represents this year's allowance for such long-term maintenance jobs as painting the house. For example, if you must paint your house every seven years, and painting can be expected to cost $7,000, then you would budget $1,000 each year for the value of those occasional paint jobs.

Add the various car and home amounts together and enter the total on line 10.

Average Fees Across Portfolio

This item represents the average fund management fees you pay across your entire portfolio. You can calculate it using the Portfolio Management Fees spreadsheet in Chapter 3. Most semi-retirees find they can keep this number in the 0.35% per year range by investing in low-cost, no-load mutual funds, exchange-traded funds, CDs, and other low-cost investment vehicles. Enter your fund management fees expressed as a percentage on line 12. If you don't know the exact amount, enter an estimate for now. Later you can enter a more exact number after you've completed the Portfolio Fees spreadsheet in Chapter 3. The spreadsheet will calculate the total amount of your fees, which will appear on line 11.

Total Annual Spending

The spreadsheet will calculate your total annual spending and enter this number on line 13. This number includes all the expenses you incur each year.

Your Bottom Line

The net amount on line 14 shows you your total income less your total spending. You want this number to be positive or only slightly negative. In that range, you're still living within your safe withdrawal levels despite whatever unfavorable income, spending, or market levels you may have recently experienced and recorded in the spreadsheet.

If you show a negative net amount, then you are spending more than would be safe on an ongoing basis. Though things might get better by year-end, you at least know where you stand. It's likely that even a significant decline in the markets will not lower your safe withdrawal amount significantly, and you'll realize that you are still relatively close to having your budget balance. This can be reassuring and help you avoid becoming overly concerned with the inevitable ups and downs of the financial markets.

Once you are pretty familiar with your numbers for each of the items in this spreadsheet, you'll find you can leave most of them in place and simply change one or two items when you have any material changes in your portfolio, income, or spending. Once you've completed this spreadsheet, you can update it in less than a minute to see how you're doing at any point throughout the year.

More Personal Budgeting Tools

Worksheets and calculators—such as college tuition planners and inflation adjustment tools—help you make financial decisions. Here are links to some very good tools that are available on the Web. I've also included a simple and helpful calculator to help decide whether to buy or lease a car.

Should You Buy or Lease a Car?

In general, leasing a car isn't a good idea if you're interested in long-term savings. Buying and keeping a car for ten years or more is still the hands-down best deal, at least until major repairs become necessary.

Other lease vs. buy calculators compare costs over a three- or four-year period and compare between two methods of financing cars. In those cases, the lease vs. buy decision is often quite close. People who pay cash and keep their cars a long time need a different way to compare, which this following tool provides.

But note that the comparison is not completely fair because the person who leases a car typically gets a new lease every three years, and so is always driving a relatively new car. The car buyer ends up driving an increasingly aged car in the last years of ownership.

In the example below, we calculated the cost of leasing vs. buying a 2007 Prius, with a purchase price of $27,000 plus $1,000 in various fees, and including a full-service maintenance contract similar to that of a leased car. Over ten years, it costs almost twice as much to lease the car as it would to buy it.

Buying vs. Leasing a Car: Comparison Over Ten-Year Period

Buying a Car				Leasing a Car	
Purchase price (including fees but excluding sales tax)	$	28,000	$	28,000	Purchase price (including fees but excluding sales tax)
				7.15%	Interest rate used for lease
Sales tax rate		7.50%		0.00298	Money factor (interest rate divided by 24)
Sales tax on purchase		2,100		15,400	Value at the end of 3 years (or apply percentage if known)
Total purchase price with sales tax		30,100		350	Part I: Depreciation / 36 (assumes a 3-year lease term)
				121	Part II: Money Factor x (capital cost + depreciation)
				7.50%	Sales tax rate
Payments		30,100		35	Sales tax on lease payment
				506	Total monthly lease payment (Part I + Part II + Sales Tax)
Residual value after 10 years	$	5,000		60,757	Total of 120 lease payments over 10 years
				6,076	Annual cost to lease (divide total payments by 10)
Net cost		25,100		1,120	Less initial purchase price invested at 4% (the safe withdrawal rate) (because capital not tied up in car can be invested)
Net cost per year (net cost/10 years)		**$2,510.00**		**$4,955.75**	**Net cost per year**

Notes:
Lessee is assumed to have three or four sequential and similar leases over the 10-year period.
Money Factor and Residual Values are found by shopping local or current market conditions.
In most states, lessee does not pay sales tax on purchase, but pays sales tax on full value of each lease payment.
Lease calculations assume that the car is turned in at the end of each lease, and a new lease is signed.

To begin, click the "Buy-Lease Car" tab in Chapter 2 Spreadsheets You'll need to enter only five numbers to see whether it's more cost-effective to lease or buy.

Under *Buying a Car* (column B), enter the following:

Line 4: the purchase price of the car.

Line 6: the local sales tax rate.

Line 13: the car's value after ten years. Use www.edmunds.com for current estimates, or look at current prices for equivalent models that are ten years old, with similar mileage, and in similar condition.

Under *Leasing a Car* (column D), enter the following:

On line 6, enter the "Money Factor" (the interest rate divided by 24). You can get this number from the dealer. One truly odd aspect of leasing is that the money factor is applied to the sum of purchase price and the depreciation over the life of the lease.

On line 7, enter the value of the car at the end of the three-year lease term. Again, use www.edmunds.com for an estimate. Sometimes the residual value is given as a percentage, for example 55%. This means the car at the end of the lease is presumed to have trade-in value of 55% of the initial price. In that case, depreciation is 45%, or the difference between the initial price and the residual value.

Note that in line 15 of the Leasing a Car column, I have added an amount that represents the extra income you would have available to spend each year if you leased and kept the purchase price of the car in your portfolio, available to invest.

On line 16, you can see the net cost per year of leasing a car compared to buying it.

College Financing Calculator

The best calculator I have found to estimate college costs is the T. Rowe Price college planning tool (www.troweprice.com). Look under the Individual Investors and the Investment Planning and Tools tabs. Not only does this tool give you the option of choosing specific colleges from a comprehensive list (to get the most up-to-date data on tuition and fees), but it also has an optional investment advisory segment on the best mix of investments to meet your goal. Most calculators just use simple averages to give you the target amount you'll need by the time your child is ready for college.

Inflation Calculator

These calculators incorporate historical data to allow you to compare prices accurately in time, based on the U.S consumer price or producer price indexes. A good one (accurate and up-to-date) is available online from the Minneapolis Federal Reserve Bank, the people who calculate the inflation rate for us, at http://woodrow.mpls.frb.fed.us/research/data/us/calc.

Health Care Cost Calculator

A calculator from Blue Cross gives national averages for all the various costs associated with a wide range of medical conditions and procedures. For those who choose to self-insure this can be sobering, but given the source of the information it may be designed to be. Find it at www.bcbsnc.com/apps/cost-estimator.

RESOURCE

- *The Automatic Millionaire, The Automatic Millionaire Workbook,* and *Smart Couples Finish Rich,* by David Bach, offer excellent advice and encouragement and good exercises.
- *Get a Life: You Don't Need a Million to Retire Well,* by Ralph Warner (Nolo), offers advice for both financial success and developing areas of your life that will truly make a difference in retirement.
- *Making the Most of Your Money,* by Jane Bryant Quinn, is an encyclopedic reference on all things related to personal finance.
- *Your Money or Your Life,* by Joe Dominguez, has great personal finance tips for the true bare-bones approach to living off savings.
- *Wall Street Journal Guide to Understanding Personal Finance,* by Ken Morse, is graphically rich and easy to understand.
- *Live Well on Less Than You Think,* by Fred Brock, gets inside the semi-retiree mindset with plenty of detailed information on making the shift from high-cost full-time work in an expensive area of the U.S. to low-cost semi-retirement in the heartland.
- *The Complete Tightwad Gazette,* by Amy Dacyczyn, is the bible of frugal living and extreme saving.

Put Your Investing on Autopilot

nvesting for the long run has become a lot easier than it used to be. Using flexible, low-cost investments and related Information services, you can sidestep many of the pitfalls that reduce investor returns. Using the Rational Investing method discussed here you can allocate your assets among a diverse set of investments, hold them for the long term, and buy or sell only during your annual portfolio rebalancing. By following these steps, not only will you beat the performance of the majority of experts, but you'll turn investing from a major headache into something easily managed.

This chapter will give you the tools for implementing the Rational Investing method. You'll start with a simple questionnaire to test your tolerance for risk, and a number of tables to educate and inspire you to save and invest in a way that supports your long-term semi-retirement goals. Next, you'll be introduced to the Rational Investing portfolios: two simple yet effective ways to implement Rational Investing for yourself.

A key aspect of the Rational Investing approach is making sure your investments are rebalanced every year to provide an optimal overall return. At the end of each year, some of your investments will have increased in value, while others may have fallen. Rebalancing is the process of selling some of the appreciated investments and buying more of the investments that have fallen in relative value, in the right quantities such that your overall portfolio is brought back into its original mix of investments. The spreadsheets in this chapter help you decide exactly how much of each investment to buy or sell.

Another important aspect of your portfolio's performance is to use low-fee funds whenever possible. You'll calculate the total amount of fees you pay each year to the financial intermediaries who manage your savings.

What Is Rational Investing?

Although I didn't invent the idea of Rational Investing—it has been used by institutional investors for years—I have tailored it to the specific needs of long-term semi-retirees, and suggest it for its unique ability to meet the needs of early and semi-retirees who must count on their savings to supply them with a safe income stream for life.

Rational Investing has three tenets:

- **Allocate your investments widely.** By allocating investments across several carefully chosen asset classes, you can reduce the volatility of your portfolio without giving up investment performance.
- **Rebalance your portfolio regularly.** By reviewing your investments and restoring them to their original target allocations periodically (rebalancing), you'll automatically buy low and sell high without any of the worry and second-guessing that normally accompanies investment decision making.
- **Keep management fees low.** Paying high fees can wreak havoc on long-term investment performance. By keeping fees low, you can maximize your return.

The Rational Investing approach allows an individual investor, working without expensive advisers, to mimic the investing strategies of large institutions and foundations. Universities, for example, need to invest their funds so that they will grow long into the future, yet still provide income each year for scholarships, new buildings, salaries, operations, and other expenses. Early and semi-retirees also need a portfolio that will keep up with inflation, continue to grow, and provide regular income.

New funds introduced in the last few years have made it affordable and manageable for individuals to follow the Rational Investing approach. Index mutual funds now come in more varieties and are finally available with the low fees a long-term retiree needs. Also, a new crop of exchange-traded mutual funds, known as ETFs, has brought an increased level of tax efficiency to long-term investors.

Over the long run, investors who use the Rational Investing method find that their investment returns outshine those of all but the most uniquely talented stock pickers. If you follow this investing approach, you'll enjoy the peace of mind that comes from a simple, effective, no-hassle investing process. And you'll have plenty of time left over for the things you really want to do with your life.

Calculating Your Risk Tolerance

Do you embrace risk or run from it? Knowing your risk tolerance will help you find the balance between stocks and less-risky bonds that will be right for you and will help you make important decisions about managing your portfolio in the years to come. Typically, when you add more stocks to a portfolio it becomes riskier but may also be expected to deliver higher returns. Conversely, adding short-term reserves and bonds to a portfolio makes it less risky and generally produces lower returns.

Your acceptance of risk may change over time. If you are still working and saving, then you may find your tolerance for risk is high. Most people, as they approach retirement, choose to move toward a portfolio with less risk.

There are lots of online calculators designed to help you determine how much risk you're comfortable with, but the gold standard has been set by The Vanguard Group. With Vanguard's permission, we're including its calculator here. Vanguard's risk tolerance calculator is also available at www.vanguard.com (under the Planning and Education tab, click General investment planning and then Investor questionnaire). The calculator will ask you a series of questions that are simple and easy to complete—try completing the Investor Questionnaire, below, and see what it tells you.

If You Prefer a Moderate Amount of Risk

Most retirees with long-term investing horizons embrace a moderate amount of risk and hold something between 40% and 60% of their portfolios in stocks (equities). If that's what the Vanguard calculator tells you, you're a good candidate for Rational Investing. The Rational Investing portfolios described here and in *Work Less, Live More* are designed to offer long-term investors a moderate to conservative balance between performance and risk. They contain approximately 40% stocks, 40% bonds, and 20% alternative assets such as commercial real estate, commodities, private equity, hedged, or oil and gas investments.

Vanguard Risk Assessment Questionnaire

1. I plan to begin taking withdrawals from this portfolio in …

	Points
Less than one year	0
1 to 2 years	1
3 to 5 years	4
6 to 10 years	7
11 to 15 years	12
More than 15 years	17

2. I plan to spend the money in this portfolio over a period of …

	Points
2 years or less	0
3 to 5 years	1
6 to 10 years	3
11 to 15 years	5
More than 15 years	8

3. When making a long-term investment, I plan to hold the investment for …

	Points
1 to 2 years	0
3 to 4 years	1
5 to 6 years	3
7 to 8 years	5
9 or more years	7

4. From August 31, 2000, through March 2001, stocks lost more than 25%. If I owned a stock investment that fell more than 25% in seven months, I would … [if you owned stocks during this period, select the answer that corresponds to your actual behavior].

	Points
Sell all the remaining investment	1
Sell a portion of the remaining investment	3
Hold the investment and sell nothing	5
Buy more of the investment	6

5. Generally, I prefer investments with little or no fluctuation in value, and I am willing to accept the lower return associated with these investments.

	Points
I strongly agree	0
I agree	1
I somewhat agree	3
I disagree	5
I strongly disagree	6

6. During market declines, I tend to sell portions of my riskier assets and invest the money in safer assets.

	Points
I strongly agree	1
I agree	2
I somewhat agree	3
I disagree	4
I strongly disagree	5

7. I would invest in a mutual fund based solely on a brief conversation with a friend, coworker, or relative.

	Points
I strongly agree	1
I agree	2
I somewhat agree	3
I disagree	4
I strongly disagree	5

8. From January 31, 1999, through December 31, 1999, some bonds lost almost 9% in 11 months, I would … [if you owned bonds during period, select the answer that corresponds to your actual behavior].

	Points
Sell all the remaining investment	1
Sell a portion of the remaining investment	3
Hold the investment and sell nothing	5
Buy more of the investment	6

9. The chart below shows the greatest one-year loss and the highest one-year gain on three different hypothetical investments of $10,000.* Given the potential gain or loss in any one year, I would invest my money in …

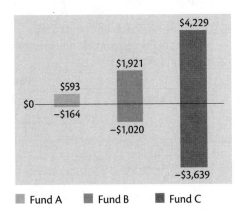

Fund A   Fund B   Fund C

* The maximum gain or loss on an investment is impossible to predict. The ranges shown in this chart are hypothetical and are designed solely to gauge an investor's risk tolerance.

	Points
Fund A	1
Fund B	3
Fund C	5

10. My current and future income sources (such as salary, Social Security, pension) are …

	Points
Very unstable	1
Unstable	2
Somewhat stable	3
Stable	4
Very stable	5

11. When it comes to investing in stock or bond mutual funds (or individual stocks or bonds), I would describe myself as a/an …

	Points
Very inexperienced investor	1
Somewhat inexperienced investor	2
Somewhat experienced investor	3
Experienced investor	4
Very experienced investor	5

Choose an Asset Allocation According to Your Score

Your Total Point Score	Suggested Asset Allocation		Average Annual Return (1960-2005)	Worst Annual Loss (1960-2005)	Number of Years With a Loss (1960-2005)
69–75 points		0% / 00%	10.5%	−28.4%	12 of 46
62–68 points		20% / 80%	10.0%	−22.7%	12 of 46
55–61 points		30% / 70%	9.7%	−19.8%	12 of 46
49–54 points		40% / 60%	9.4%	−17.0%	11 of 46
42–48 points		50% / 50%	9.1%	−14.1%	8 of 46
36–41 points		60% / 40%	8.7%	−11.3%	6 of 46
29–35 points		70% / 30%	8.4%	−8.4%	5 of 46
23–28 points		80% / 20%	8.0%	−8.2%	5 of 46
7–22 points		100% / 0%	7.1%	−8.1%	5 of 46

Source: The Vanguard Group

These are sample portfolio allocations only. Depending on your tolerance for risk or your individual circumstances, you may wish to choose an allocation that is more conservative or more aggressive than the model suggested by your score. Keep in mind that these allocations are for longer-term financial goals. You may very well hold short-term reserves for short-term goals and emergencies. For stock market returns, we use the Dow Jones Wilshire 5000 Composite Index from 1971 to 2005 and the S&P 500 Index from 1960 to 1970. For bond market returns, we use the Lehman Brothers U.S. Government/Credit Bond Index from 1973 to 2005, the Citigroup High Grade Index from 1969 to 1972, and the S&P High Grade Corporate Index from 1960 to 1968.

This Investor Questionnaire is designed to help you decide how to allocate your investments among different asset classes (stocks, bonds, and short-term reserves), but does not provide comprehensive investment or financial advice. There is no guarantee that any particular asset allocation will meet your investment objectives. All investments involve risks, and fluctuations in the financial markets and other factors may cause declines in the value of your account. As your financial circumstances or goals change, it may be helpful to fill out the Investor Questionnaire again to see if your suggested asset allocation has changed.

The returns shown include the investment of income, dividend, and capital gains distributions; they do not reflect the effects of investment expenses and taxes. Past performance is not a guarantee of future results.

If You Don't Like Risk

If your risk tolerance calculator results indicate that you would feel better keeping your percentage of stocks below 40%, think about trying to become comfortable with a bit more risk. Unless you have a very large amount of money, stock allocations below 40% probably won't provide the long-term protection against inflation or sufficient return on your investments to support a reasonable standard of living.

Some early or semi-retirees think of long-term investing as a matter of simply generating enough income from investments to meet their annual spending needs. These investors may find the whole notion of investments in stocks too risky and uncomfortable, and lean toward fixed-income investments with high annual interest payments. Although investing for dividends, rents, and interest can be a reasonable way to fund a long semi-retirement, you must approach it carefully to make sure that you keep up with inflation.

If you invest in real estate and stock, you'll get income from rents or dividends. And you'll also have underlying assets, the value of which have historically kept up with inflation. But bonds, CDs, money market accounts, and some preferred stocks and royalty trusts offer no such protection from inflation. So although you may be able to live off of the interest payments from a 20-year bond, you will find that the bond principal has not kept up with inflation at the end of those 20 years. Unless you are setting aside the first 3% or so of your return to offset inflation, a bond portfolio will not support a stable or growing standard of living over the long run.

You Can't Hide From Risk

You cannot hide from risk by investing solely in CDs or medium-term treasury bonds. Historically, it has not been possible to achieve the return you'll need (7% or 7.5%) in risk-free investments such as CDs or insured bonds. Even if CD or bond rates rose above 7.5%, those rates could not be expected to last over the long run. You'd still need to invest in riskier, higher-return assets for a large chunk of your portfolio.

Take a look at the table below. The "Real Return" column shows the returns for each asset class, adjusted down to eliminate the effects of inflation. Notice that real (that is, inflation-adjusted) historical rates of return for U.S. Treasuries are about 2%, short-term bonds and money market accounts under 1%, and corporate bonds just over 4%. And even these low rates are not guaranteed, because there is always variation in their returns over time. This means that when fixed-income returns (bonds, CDs, or savings accounts) are reduced for inflation, they provide a lower return than most semi-retirees would be comfortable living on over the long run.

So if you're trying to live on an all-bond portfolio, you run the risk of eating into principal in order to support yourself in the years ahead. This reduction in principal is what drives most long-term investors to invest some of their assets in stocks, which—though erratic and risky—have historically more than kept up with inflation over time.

When stocks are blended together with bonds, commercial real estate, and other asset classes in well-diversified portfolios, the riskiness of investing in stocks can be reduced, because the returns from these other asset classes tend to move in opposite directions to those of stocks. If you still want to avoid investing in stocks, preferring the certainty of secure income flows to fund your retirement spending, make it a point to earn those payments from investments that should also keep up with inflation, such as real estate investments, Treasury inflation-protected securities (TIPS), and even inflation-adjusted annuities.

What Different Kinds of Assets Yield: Historical Returns 1928 to present			
Assets	Return ++	Real Return *	Volatility **
U.S. Large Stocks	11.70%	8.70%	15.65%
International Large Stocks	13.00%	10.00%	16.25%
Long-Term U.S. Treasury Bonds	5.40%	2.40%	7.89%
U.S. Medium-Term Bonds	7.30%	4.30%	4.44%
Short-Term Bonds/Money Market	3.70%	0.70%	2.59%
Commercial Real Estate	16.50% +	13.50%	14.23%

++   Source: Dimensional Fund Advisors (DFA) Matrix Book
*   Assumes 3% long-term inflation
**   Source: Wilson Associates International / Advisory World, Inc.
+   1975 to present

The Rational Investing Portfolios

The Rational Investing approach offers well-researched guidelines for increasing your chances of good long-term investment performance. By blending a reasonable proportion of diverse stocks and bonds with other types of investments, such as commercial real estate and commodities, the overall portfolios will tend to fluctuate little in value and will still deliver good returns. (If you'd like to know more about the theory underlying this effect, read "Decreasing Risk" at the end of this chapter.)

Rational Investing rests on the notion that the investment returns from various asset classes move in statistically meaningful relationships, and so form the basis for profitably managing a portfolio. Rational investors care less about a given security or even mutual fund, and more about holding the right proportion of each asset class in order to best weather unknown future market conditions.

Investment Terminology

Asset class. The group or market segment into which an asset falls—for example, commodities, small U.S. stocks, large international stocks, or foreign medium-term bonds. Asset classes are widely recognized by the investment community and typically have an index that tracks their performance. Although the price of individual securities within an asset class moves up and down based on the securities' underlying merits, all investments in a given asset class tend to move up and down together often based on large forces at work in the global or national economy.

Asset allocation. The blend of different asset classes in which you are invested. Asset allocations are generally expressed as percentages adding up to 100%.

Mutual fund. A pooled investment that allows you to own a piece of many different securities, far more than you would likely be able to buy on your own. Mutual funds charge an annual management fee. Rational investors typically seek low-fee mutual funds that invest in and consistently deliver the returns of a desired asset class.

Exchange-Traded Funds (ETFs). A relatively new type of pooled investment (similar to a mutual fund) with tax advantages for long-term investors.

Portfolio rebalancing. Because assets rise or fall in value over time, you'll need to periodically rebalance your portfolio to keep your asset allocation in line with the Rational Investing portfolios. This means buying and selling assets in sufficient proportions such that your asset allocation is restored to its original or target percentages.

The Basic Principles

The basic principles of Rational Investing, when used together, form an easy-to-use investing method for semi-retirees.

Own Diverse Asset Classes

A blend of stocks, bonds, and other investments will generate equivalent or superior returns with less risk than individual securities from just a few asset classes or even a simple blend of U.S. stock and bond index funds. The mix works because modest amounts of volatile but generally high-return assets will improve overall portfolio performance with little or no additional risk.

For most semi-retired investors, the Rational Investing portfolio consists of about 40% stocks, 40% bonds, and 20% other—which includes commodities, oil and gas, market neutral hedge funds, real estate, and private equity. This allocation can be used by semi-retirees of all ages. It's designed to support steady withdrawals through all kinds of markets, with a high probability of maintaining its inflation-adjusted spending power over time.

Demand Low Fees

Your portfolio's management fees, which you can find in the fund's prospectus or by entering the ticker at www.morningstar.com, should average below 0.5% per year. Some semi-retirees get even lower, into the 0.2% per year range. Fees higher than this simply eat up too much of your expected return each year.

Use Tilts

A tilt is an investing strategy where a portfolio holds more of an asset type than it customarily would warrant. For example, if the Total U.S. Stock Market Index contains just under 7% small stocks, then a portfolio that contained more than 7% small stocks would tilt toward small stocks.

The Rational Investing portfolio tilts toward value stocks, international assets, and small stocks. The value tilt is justified by reliable academic studies showing that value stocks and value bonds—high-yield bonds—outperform the overall market over time, possibly due to their higher risk. Holding these risky assets in funds, within an overall portfolio, means the rewards can be gained while keeping the risk manageable. International stocks and bonds as well as small stocks are also attractive asset classes to tilt toward because their low correlations with other asset classes means they can reduce overall portfolio risk while delivering good returns.

Keep Volatility Low

Volatility refers to the up and down swings in the value of your portfolio. A semi-retiree, particularly a younger one, should not try to simply achieve the highest rate of return if that means an unacceptable level of volatility or risk. Choose a mix of assets to maintain an acceptable level of return at the lowest risk, which generally means holding lower levels of equity than some other long-term investing models advocate.

If You Are Still Working Full-Time

The principles of Rational Investing are appropriate for all long-term investors, and are not just for semi-retirees. If you are younger, still working full-time, or are otherwise not taking a regular withdrawal from your investments, you can probably afford to take on more risk in your portfolio by increasing the percentage of equities. A 60% or 70% allocation to equities may be appropriate for you, though any investor must understand the risk of equities. By holding a somewhat riskier portfolio allocation, you should be able to earn slightly higher returns, about 0.5% expected return for each additional 10% you add to your portfolio, though with a corresponding chance of having your portfolio decline by roughly an additional 5% over the course of an extended bear market. The other basic principles of Rational Investing continue to apply to you.

Use Index Funds Whenever Possible

Index funds deliver better returns than most actively managed funds, due to their low costs. Index funds are weighted the same as a stock exchange index in order to mirror its performance. Often, but not always, an index overlaps neatly with an asset class you want in your portfolio. If that's the case, your best choice for the portfolio will almost always be the low-fee, tax-efficient index fund or index exchange-traded fund (ETF).

> **TIP**
>
> **Not all index funds are created equal.** After years of experience in reducing trading costs while still matching the underlying index, Vanguard has learned how to often produce marginally better returns than the index, even after its fees. And Dimensional Fund Advisors (DFA) offers a variety of funds called enhanced index funds that track asset classes and tilts rather than an index per se. These will give you, for instance, funds tracking the International Small or International Large Value asset classes, making them a good fit for investors following the Rational Investing method.

Know Your Required Return

Your portfolio must remain substantially intact to withstand the triple assault of inflation (assume 3% per year), fees and trading costs (0.5% or so each year), and a 4% to 4.5% annual withdrawal. You'll need at least a 7.5% expected annual return to keep the real value of your portfolio intact each year. Between 1988 and 2006, the Rational Investing portfolio returned about 10% per year, which gives you ample breathing room to accommodate volatile and unpredictable future returns and still keep your portfolio intact.

The Portfolios

The charts and tables on the following pages show you the details of three portfolios that broadly adhere to the Rational Investing goals and could be appropriate for semi-retirees. The third and most complex portfolio, the Rational Investing portfolio, boasts the best performance with the lowest volatility, but requires somewhat more effort to implement.

The Soda Cracker: Single Mutual Fund

If you're terrified of investing or want the ultimate in simplicity, you can potentially get by with just a single mutual fund. Vanguard, along with other major fund firms, offers several packaged blends of index funds, under their Lifestyle, Balanced, and Target Retirement Date series. Some of these funds invest in a diverse mix of between 40% and 60% stocks, with the balance in bonds. Fees range from 0.25% and 0.35%. Visit www.vanguard.com for more information on their funds.

The Sandwich: An Eight-Fund Portfolio

You can achieve substantial diversification while meeting all of the Rational Investing goals with this eight-fund portfolio. The Sandwich portfolio includes most of the major asset classes in percentages roughly similar to those in the Rational Investing portfolio (discussed below). The historical return, measured since 1988, is 8.4%. Fees average 0.33% annually. And, the Sandwich portfolio is easy to implement within a single brokerage or mutual fund account. The table below shows the funds of the Sandwich portfolio.

Sandwich Portfolio		
Percent of Portfolio	Fund Symbol	Fund Description
20%	VFINX	S&P 500 (or Value Index VIVAX or VWNFX)
8%	VTMSX	Vanguard Tax-Managed Small
6%	VGTSX	Vanguard Total International Index
10%	VINEX	Vanguard International Explorer
6%	VEIEX	Vanguard Emerging Markets Index
30%	VBIIX	Vanguard Intermediate Bond Index
11%	BEGBX	American Century International Bond
5%	VGSIX	Vanguard REIT (Real Estate Investment Trust) Index
4%	VMMXX	Vanguard Prime Money Market
100%	Total	

The Rational Investing Portfolio

The Rational Investing portfolio includes 16 asset classes. Historically, this portfolio offers slightly better returns (10.2%) than the Sandwich portfolio, along with low volatility (6.86%).

Portfolio asset allocations. The portfolio asset allocation is the percentage of your total savings you invest in each asset class—or type—of fund. The table below lists the asset classes and their percentage allocations.

Rational Investing Portfolio	
Percent of Portfolio	**Asset Class**
12.0%	U.S. Large Stocks
8.5%	U.S. Small Stocks
5.0%	International Large Stocks
10.0%	International Small Stocks
6.5%	Emerging Market Stocks
4.0%	Short-Term Bonds/Money Market
4.0%	Long-Term U.S. Treasury Bonds
10.0%	U.S. Medium-Term Bonds
12.0%	International Medium-Term Bonds
5.0%	GNMA Mortgage Bonds
4.0%	High-Yield Bonds
3.0%	Oil and Gas
2.0%	Market-Neutral Hedge Funds
4.0%	Commodities
5.0%	Commercial Real Estate
5.0%	Venture Capital/Private Equity
100.0%	Total

Portfolio fund choices. Within each asset class, you'll invest in particular funds. A list of some recommended funds is included in Appendix A. Though Appendix A does not include all of the funds that you could invest in, and you may well have some other favorites, the funds included there would be strong contenders on any short list. For the less traditional asset classes, the funds listed there are a pretty good guide to the choices available.

Steady Saving Is Key

It's no secret that when it comes to saving, the best strategy is to start early. The table below summarizes savings growth over time. As a guide, the Rational Investing portfolio grew at around 10% per year (about 7% after adjusting for inflation) between 1988 and 2006.

Growth of Savings Over Time
(Initial Amount $10,000)

Year	Percentage Growth											
	1%	2%	3%	4%	5%	6%	7%	8%	9%	10%	11%	12%
1	10,100	10,200	10,300	10,400	10,500	10,600	10,700	10,800	10,900	11,000	11,100	11,200
2	10,201	10,404	10,609	10,816	11,025	11,236	11,449	11,664	11,881	12,100	12,321	12,544
3	10,303	10,612	10,927	11,249	11,576	11,910	12,250	12,597	12,950	13,310	13,676	14,049
4	10,406	10,824	11,255	11,699	12,155	12,625	13,108	13,605	14,116	14,641	15,181	15,735
5	10,510	11,041	11,593	12,167	12,763	13,382	14,026	14,693	15,386	16,105	16,851	17,623
6	10,615	11,262	11,941	12,653	13,401	14,185	15,007	15,869	16,771	17,716	18,704	19,738
7	10,721	11,487	12,299	13,159	14,071	15,036	16,058	17,138	18,280	19,487	20,762	22,107
8	10,829	11,717	12,668	13,686	14,775	15,938	17,182	18,509	19,926	21,436	23,045	24,760
9	10,937	11,951	13,048	14,233	15,513	16,895	18,385	19,990	21,719	23,579	25,580	27,731
10	11,046	12,190	13,439	14,802	16,289	17,908	19,672	21,589	23,674	25,937	28,394	31,058
15	11,610	13,459	15,580	18,009	20,789	23,966	27,590	31,722	36,425	41,772	47,846	54,736
20	12,202	14,859	18,061	21,911	26,533	32,071	38,697	46,610	56,044	67,275	80,623	96,463
25	12,824	16,406	20,938	26,658	33,864	42,919	54,274	68,485	86,231	108,347	135,855	170,001
30	13,478	18,114	24,273	32,434	43,219	57,435	76,123	100,627	132,677	174,494	228,923	299,599
35	14,166	19,999	28,139	39,461	55,160	76,861	106,766	147,853	204,140	281,024	385,749	527,996
40	14,889	22,080	32,620	48,010	70,400	102,857	149,745	217,245	314,094	452,593	650,009	930,510

RESOURCE

Timing your savings and real estate investments. A good online calculator to help you determine how long it will take you to save one million dollars (a common goal for people who want to retire) can be found at: http://cgi. money.cnn.com/tools/millionaire/millionaire.html. A simpler version that lets you determine the time needed to reach any savings target based on adding regularly to your savings can be found at: http://cgi.money.cnn.com/tools/moneygrow/ moneygrow_101.html.

Getting the Right Asset Allocation

Our three-step asset allocation tool will make determining your asset allocation or rebalancing your portfolio a snap. You'll find detailed instructions below, but here's a quick overview of the process.

Step 1: Categorize your assets. You'll start by listing all your current investments and classifying them into the right asset classes. This alone may be an eye opener for you. You may find that your investments are a hodge-podge of many different styles or types of assets or that you have most of your investments in one asset class.

Step 2: Review your current asset allocation. Once you have all your assets classified, you can evaluate your asset allocation. The spreadsheet included on the CD-ROM comes loaded with the asset allocation of the Rational Investing portfolio. You'll immediately be able to see how your current asset allocation compares to the Rational Investing portfolio target. If you have a different target allocation in mind, perhaps through other reading or through consultation with an adviser, you can easily change the percentage targets and see how your current investment mix stacks up to your desired objective. You'll be able to see not only how you match up with each specific asset class, but also how you are invested in three broad areas: stocks, bonds, and alternative investments.

Step 3: Plan your transactions. If you find that you are over or under your desired percentage in any given asset class, this step will help you plan trades to bring the allocation closer to your target. This area serves as a useful planning tool for working out exactly how much of each investment to buy or sell. At rebalancing time, this may involve several different trades, so it is nice to be able to keep their impacts and inter-actions clear. I recommend rebalancing your portfolio every one or two years (see "Buy Low, Sell High Through Annual Rebalancing," below).

Each of these steps corresponds to a tab in Chapter 3 Spreadsheets on the attached CD-ROM. To see how the calculations work, take a look at the sample worksheets for this tool (click the "List Assets," "Review Assets," and "Plan Transactions" tabs in Sample Worksheets). When you're ready to enter your data, open Chapter 3 Spreadsheets and click the appropriate tab.

Step 1: Categorize your assets

Here you'll organize your assets by category. Click the "List Assets" tab in Chapter 3 Spreadsheets to begin.

Review your records

Before you enter your data in the spreadsheet, you'll need to determine which mutual funds or other assets you own and the amount (dollar value) you own of each asset.

Gather Your Materials

- Your most recent brokerage statements or a detailed record of all your financial assets.
- Prospectuses for your mutual funds or a computer connected to the Internet to confirm the asset classes to which your current funds and securities belong.

To find out the particular asset class of your funds, go to the fund company's website or www.morningstar.com. On Morningstar, enter the fund's symbol in the box in the upper left-hand corner labeled "Quotes." Click on the small arrow to the right of that box and you'll be taken to the Morningstar information page for that fund. Scroll down to the Morningstar Style Grid, a nine-box grid which places your fund on a spectrum from small to large.

Asset Class Terminology

You might find some minor differences in the ways that different organizations refer to different asset classes. The guiding rule is that—just like the game of horseshoes—close is good enough. Still, it may help to review a few areas where discrepancies are common:

- **Foreign, International, and Global:** Typically, a "Foreign" fund invests its assets entirely outside the U.S. But "International" and "Global" funds are commonly invested throughout the world's markets, including in the U.S.

- **Small, Mid-Cap, and Large:** These labels refer to the size of the firms in which a particular equity fund is invested. Mid-Cap and large funds tend to perform similarly. Small-Cap funds tend to deliver returns that are less correlated with the other two types of funds, adding diversification to your holdings.

- **Value, Blend, and Growth:** Some funds are listed as being made up mostly of either "Value" or "Growth" stocks; those that aren't will either call themselves a "Blended" fund or say nothing on the subject. Rational Investing portfolios hold a larger proportion of value stocks than are found in the market overall, known as tilting the portfolio toward value stocks (stocks that are beaten down in price due to problems at the company). (To learn more, see *Work Less, Live More*, Chapter 3.)

- **Short-Term, Medium- or Intermediate-Term, and Long-Term:** Bond funds are usually described in these terms, which correspond to the duration or average maturity of the bonds held in the fund. The longer the average maturity, the more sensitive the fund's price will be to movements in interest rates. For example, if a fund has an average maturity of 15 years, small movements in interest rates will move the fund's value considerably, adding to the riskiness of holding that fund. Typically, bonds and bond funds that mature in less than three years are considered short-term, from three to seven years are considered medium-term or intermediate, and above seven years are considered long-term funds.

TIP

Make note of your fund management fees. When you're looking up asset classes, jot down your fund management fees, which you will need below. This fee information, also known as an "Expense Ratio," can be found on the fund summary information page at www.morningstar.com, the company's website, or at http://finance.yahoo.com.

Put your assets in the right categories

First, enter the date in cell C4.

Next, you'll list each of the funds or securities you own by asset class and put the dollar amount you own next to it.

As you look at the spreadsheet, you'll see that each asset class is listed on line 6. Scroll to the right to see all of them listed in columns A through AF. Enter the name of each asset you hold and the dollar amount you own (rounded to the nearest thousand) directly under the corresponding asset class. Put the fund name in the first column and the amount of your investment in the second column under each asset class. The spreadsheet will add up everything.

> **EXAMPLE:** If you have $25,200 worth of Fidelity Small Cap Independence Fund (FDSCX), which belongs in the U.S. Small asset class, enter the name of the fund (FDSCX) in column C and the amount you hold, rounded to the nearest thousand ($25,000), in column D.
>
> If you have $40,900 worth of Fidelity International Discovery Fund (FIGRX), which belongs in the International Large asset class, enter the name of the fund (FIGRX) in column E and the amount ($41,000) in column F.

If your fund is split between two or more asset classes, then apply this percentage split as you list your fund holdings. For example, if you own Vanguard Wellington Fund, a quick look at the prospectus or Vanguard's or Morningstar's website will tell you the fund invests 65% in U.S. Large Stocks and 35% in U.S. Medium Term Bonds (I typically ignore any short-term cash reserves the funds hold). Apply these percentages to the amount invested in that fund.

EXAMPLE: If you have $50,000 worth of Wellington Fund, divide it into two amounts: 65% goes into the U.S. Large Stocks asset class, and 35% goes into the U.S. Medium-Term Bonds asset class. Excel will calculate these amounts for you.

To calculate the 65% that belongs under U.S. Large Stocks, enter the following formula in the appropriate cell under column B: =.65*50000

Likewise, enter the corresponding formula in the appropriate cell under Medium-Term U.S. Bonds in column P: =.35*50000

The correct amounts of $32,500 for the U.S. Large Stocks and $17,500 for U.S. Medium-Term Bonds would then be included in their respective asset class totals.

See your Excel's built-in help function if you need more information about how to compute a formula in Excel.

Add your other assets

Next, include any unusual investments you own—for example, investment-grade gold coins or shares in private companies that you believe you may be able to sell in the future. You'll see these asset classes listed beginning in column W. Do your best to accurately estimate the price of any illiquid investments, such as investment real estate, venture capital, or private partnerships or equity stakes. Lean toward conservative valuations if you're in doubt.

List these assets in the best available category—metals, for instance, might go under commodities and any hedge funds that pursue esoteric hedging strategies can go under Market-Neutral Hedge Funds. If you invest in small, thinly traded public companies or private companies, either through a venture capital or private equity fund or through your own direct investments, they would be classified under Private Equity/ Venture Capital. Direct investments in oil & gas drilling properties would go under the Oil & Gas heading. (A list of asset classes and sample investments for each one is listed in Appendix A.)

When you think you have all your assets accounted for, check the total in cell AH29 to be sure this amount looks roughly equivalent to your total financial holdings. If your totals look off, then double-check your entries to look for any data entry errors. If the amount in cell AH29 does not match AH30, that's another indicator that you have made some sort of error in entering data, so review each total and subtotal carefully.

Step 2: Review your asset allocation

Click the "Review Assets" tab in the Chapter 3 Spreadsheets to begin.

Determine your allocation percentages

The spreadsheet comes loaded with the asset allocation percentages of the Rational Investing portfolio listed in column B. See if they feel comfortable for you. If you'd like to experiment with other asset allocations, you can enter different percentages in column C. For instance, if you are comfortable taking on more risk, have consulted a fee-only financial adviser and come up with a different plan, or you are many years from semi-retirement, you may wish to increase the percentage of stocks and reduce your proportion of bonds.

If you make changes in column C, be sure the total of all allocation percentages equals 100%. If you don't make any changes, the spreadsheet will calculate your target percentages based on the Rational Investing portfolio.

Review your over- and under-allocations

You can now easily see where your investments are over or under your target amounts in each asset class. Column D shows the target amount for each asset class, and column F shows the actual amount you currently have invested. The difference—in column G—is the amount that you are over or under your target allocation. A positive number in column G means you are over your target amount, and a negative number (in red) means you are under your target amount. For example, $3,000 in column G means that you are $3,000 over-invested in that particular asset class, and that you should reduce your holdings by $3,000 in order to bring it in line. (You can easily check this by comparing the target amount with the actual amount you hold.)

Step 2: Review Asset Allocation

Portfolio Total:	$ 875,000

Analysis of Category of Funds

Category	Rational Investing Portfolio %	Your target %	Target amount	Actual %	Actual amount	Misallocation amount
	TARGET amounts			**ACTUAL amounts**		
U.S. Large Stocks (USL)	12.0%	20.0%	175,000	19.0%	166,000	(9,000)
U.S. Small Stocks (USS)	8.5%	8.0%	70,000	17.1%	150,000	80,000
International Large Stocks (INTL)	5.0%	6.0%	52,500	3.4%	30,000	(22,500)
International Small Stocks (INT S)	10.0%	7.0%	61,250	6.7%	59,000	(2,250)
Emerging Market Stocks (EMG)	6.5%	6.0%	52,500	4.6%	40,000	(12,500)
Short-Term Bonds/Money Market (ST BD MM)	4.0%	4.0%	35,000	7.4%	65,000	30,000
Long-Term U.S. Government Treasury Bonds (US LT BD)	4.0%	5.0%	43,750	6.9%	60,000	16,250
U.S. Medium-Term Bonds (US MT BD)	10.0%	20.0%	175,000	17.1%	150,000	(25,000)
International Medium-Term Bonds (INT MT BD)	12.0%	11.0%	96,250	11.4%	100,000	3,750
GNMA Mortgage Bonds (GNMA)	5.0%	0.0%	-	0.0%	0	0
High-Yield Bonds (HY BD)	4.0%	0.0%	-	0.0%	0	0
Oil and Gas (OIL)	3.0%	0.0%	-	0.0%	0	0
Market-Neutral Hedge Funds (HEDGE MN)	2.0%	0.0%	-	0.0%	0	0
Commodities (COMM)	4.0%	3.0%	26,250	2.9%	25,000	(1,250)
Commercial Real Estate (REIT)	5.0%	10.0%	87,500	3.4%	30,000	(57,500)
Venture Capital / Private Equity (VC PE)	5.0%	0.0%	-	0.0%	0	0
Totals:	**100.0%**	**100.0%**	**875,000**	**100.0%**	**875,000**	**0**

A misallocation of $3,000 or anything less than 1% one way or the other is not worth worrying much over, but larger numbers will need your attention. Remember that this spreadsheet just captures a snapshot of your portfolio at this moment in time—your allocations will drift as markets go up and down over the course of the year. In a year or two you can rebalance your portfolio again. Studies have shown that rebalancing more frequently than once a year is actually counterproductive, unless one or more asset classes has become significantly out of balance.

Look at your broad category analysis

To see how your investments are allocated among the broad categories of stocks, bonds, and alternative investments (such as oil & gas, commodities, or private equity/venture capital), look at the broad category analysis in lines 25 through 30. As in the previous section, the amount that you are over or under your target allocation is in column G. Compare your actual percentages in column E to the results of your risk assessment questionnaire from the beginning of this chapter, to see if your holdings are consistent with the level of risk with which you are comfortable. For example if you said you would be comfortable holding about 50% stocks, but are actually only holding 20%, then you know you are shortchanging yourself now with your current investment mix.

This portion of the spreadsheet shows how closely your asset allocation comes to the target percentages of the Rational Investing portfolios (roughly 40% stocks, 40% bonds, and 20% alternative investments). If you are not close to the target amounts, then you may want to bring things in line by rebalancing your portfolio, as discussed below.

Step 3: Plan your transactions

Now, turn to the third tab on the spreadsheet, "Plan Transactions." It's time to plan how you will bring your current portfolio in line with your target percentages.

Deciding how and when to realign your portfolio is your personal decision. You should not make changes any faster than is comfortable for you—for instance, buying into an asset class that has had a long period of appreciation may feel uncomfortable or unwise. Most of these feelings are not supported by actual market performance, but we are nonetheless emotional creatures, and as long as we are moving closer to getting our portfolios balanced, we are doing well.

Don't feel the need to get everything done all at once. But do create a timetable for yourself—perhaps over a year or two—and push yourself to take a series of smaller steps toward getting the proper asset allocations in place. You may also want to consult your tax adviser before making any major portfolio shifts; sometimes reorganizing a portfolio generates taxable capital gains. (Read more about capital gains taxes in Chapter 5.)

When you're ready to select suitable investments for each asset class, see Appendix A for some suggestions. The list in the appendix is not exhaustive and you may have other funds you prefer. If you do, compare your preferred fund to the ones on Appendix A—you might discover a better performing or lower-fee fund there.

Make a Plan

Look at columns A through D of the spreadsheet, labeled "Summary of Imbalances." Here you will again see the amount by which you are over or under-invested in each asset class (this is the same information that's in the Asset Allocation tab in column G). A positive number in column D means you are over your target amount, and a negative number (in red) means you are under your target amount. You'll want to buy or sell investments in each asset class where you have a significant gap. I usually rebalance any asset class that is more than $2,000 to $3,000 over or under my target at the time of my annual or biannual rebalancing.

To start, pick an asset class where you are the most over-invested. Click on the "List Assets" tab and review the funds and securities you have in that asset class to choose the fund you will sell a portion of.

Now come back to the "Plan Transactions" tab and look at columns F through M, labeled "Planned Trades." This is where you'll enter the amount that you plan to sell. Enter this number in column F (under Trade #1) on the correct row for the asset class you're selling. Be sure to enter a negative number because you'll be reducing the amount of your investment in that asset class.

You will see that the trade shows up in red, representing a negative number. It is added to the total under "Effect of Trades." To the right is a column labeled "New Gap," which shows the difference between your target and actual amounts after you make the proposed trade. In other words, if you were to make the trade you just entered, it would reduce the imbalance in that asset class down to the amount now showing under "New Gap." If that number is small or zero, then you are done for that asset class once you make that trade. If you want to make multiple sales from different funds in that asset class to accomplish your total need for selling in that asset class, use the additional columns in the Planned Trades area.

Repeat this process for each asset class in which you are over-funded. For each trade you plan to make, enter the amount you plan to sell or buy one column to the right (enter the second trade in the "Trade #2" column, the third trade in the "Trade #3" column, and so on).

Next, do the same for the asset classes in which you are under-funded, except that instead of selling you'll buy more investments in those classes. You can either buy more of a fund that you already own in that class or invest in a new fund. It's your choice. (See Appendix A for a list of funds I recommend.) When you enter the amounts you intend to purchase, enter them as positive numbers.

Make notes in column M, indicating the fund you will be buying or selling and any other information that will help you when it's time to make the trades.

Organize your trades

Now that you've figured out what steps you'll take to bring your portfolio back into alignment, it is worth pausing to consider the whole process before making the trades. Ask yourself:

- How far away from my target allocations am I today?
- How far off will I be once I complete all the trades I have proposed for myself?
- Do I have good reasons for any remaining gaps?

You may have good reasons why you would rather not move to a complete alignment with your chosen asset allocation. As long as you know what they are, and why you are taking the steps in the order and at the speed you wish, then consider your asset allocation balanced and complete until you pick it up again. But if you don't complete the trades needed to rebalance your portfolio, and you're not sure why, it may be a symptom of something bigger—perhaps a secret wish to time market movements and come out ahead in the short term, or a reluctance to sell a fund that has made you money in the past. These are normal and understandable feelings, but they generally don't produce the best long-term investing performance. You may want to consult an adviser to help you through these sorts of impasses.

Target Asset Allocation

Step 3: Plan Transactions

Summary of Imbalances

Planned Trades

Category	Current $	Target $	Current gap	Trade #1	Trade #2
U.S. Large Stocks	$ 166,000	$ 175,000	$ (9,000)	$ 10,000	
U.S. Small Stocks	150,000	70,000	80,000	(75,000)	
International Large Stocks	30,000	52,500	(22,500)		
International Small Stocks	59,000	61,250	(2,250)		
Emerging Market Stocks	40,000	52,500	(12,500)		
Short-Term Bonds/Money Markets	65,000	35,000	30,000	(5,000)	
Long-Term U.S. Treasury Bonds	60,000	43,750	16,250		
U.S. Medium-Term Bonds	150,000	175,000	(25,000)	25,000	
International Medium-Term Bonds	100,000	96,250	3,750		
GNMA Mortgage Bonds	0	0	0		
High Yield Bonds	0	0	0		
Oil and Gas	0	0	0		
Market Neutral Hedge Funds	0	0	0		
Commodities	25,000	26,250	(1,250)		
Commercial Real Estate	30,000	87,500	(57,500)	60,000	
Venture Capital/Private Equity	0	0	0		
TOTALS:	**$875,000**	**$875,000**	**$ 0**		

Trade #3	Trade #4	Trade #5	Effect of Trades	New Gap	NOTES
			$ 10,000	$ 1,000	Sell some SP500 Index fund
			(75,000)	5,000	Execute sale of excess small cap holdings ASAP
			0	(22,500)	Make remaining purchases 12/07
			0	(2,250)	
			0	(12,500)	Add more next year
			(5,000)	25,000	Holding Tank Pending Other Transactions
			0	16,250	
			25,000	0	proceeds of small cap and SP500 Index sales
			0	3,750	Place Remaining Trades approx 10/07
			0	0	
			0	0	
			0	0	
			0	0	
			0	(1,250)	Place remaining trades approx 10/07
			60,000	2,500	Use REITS until private property deals close
			0	0	
			$ 15,000	$ 15,000	

The following worksheet will help you organize your trades. You can use it to keep track of which trades you'll make first, and when. You may need to take your cash flow into consideration when planning the trades—meaning you'll sell assets first, wait for the funds to arrive, and then purchase assets the following day. If you do it right, the net effect of the trades on your available cash will generally be very close to zero—you should be able to pay for your purchases with the proceeds from the sales.

Fund	Amount	Date I plan to make trade	Notes
1.			
2.			
3.			
4.			
5.			
6.			
7.			

Update your spreadsheet

After you make a trade, update your holdings on your spreadsheet. Click on the "List Assets" tab and remove or add assets (as described in Step 1, above) so that the spreadsheet corresponds to your new portfolio. The changes you make will be reflected on the "Review Assets" tab, and you'll be able to see how your trades have changed your allocations.

Buy Low, Sell High Through Periodic Rebalancing

I recommend that you review your asset allocation and rebalance your assets on a regular periodic basis, between one and two years.

Studies have shown that once an asset class starts to outperform its historical averages, it tends to stay on that trajectory for a few years. So the annual rebalancing may cut short a good thing because you'll be selling some of your winners while they are still going up. The opposite might also be true—you'll be buying more of a declining asset class as it goes down and you may be able to wait to buy it later for even less. But then again, you might not.

If you try to predict the market, you can find lots of reasons to do nothing or to try to time the market and jump in and out to increase your profits. People who try to time the market have learned—generally through bitter experience—that they cannot consistently predict the market. Vanguard founder John Bogle says that most investors far underperform the market, even if they are wise enough to invest in low-fee funds. The reason: Too much buying and selling, chasing performance, and jumping into hot new funds just as they peak. By staying invested in low-turnover or index funds and rebalancing consistently and periodically, investors can guarantee they will earn market returns. Though this may seem depressingly "average," it will put you far ahead of what average investors actually earn in the real world.

At any given time, some investments will be losers, others gainers. By following the Rational Investing approach, simply staying fully invested in a diverse set of investments, your actual performance will likely be far better over time than if you jump in and out of the market to catch each rising wave. Periodic rebalancing is a discipline to keep our baser instincts in check by making it as much like clockwork as possible. It's like having an annual checkup—just do it and don't think too much about it. This is the way to generate the best long-term investment returns, and to do pretty well in the short and medium term as well.

So make it a habit. On a regular annual or biannual basis, pull out this spreadsheet and repeat Steps 1, 2, and 3, above. You'll update the value of your holdings in each asset class, review your asset allocation, and plan and make trades to bring each asset class into alignment with your target percentages. Once you're completed these steps, you've rebalanced your portfolio.

Consider rebalancing between the months of February and October, whenever it suits your needs. I don't recommend rebalancing during November, December, or January because mutual funds tend to pay large taxable distributions in December, and if you rebalance late in the year you may have to pay tax on funds you have only recently purchased. Also, markets tend to shift around the new year when large institutions do their rebalancing—these shifts could temporarily create a more volatile market, as well as widen trading spreads (the difference between a securities' buying and selling prices, which is kept as profit by financial intermediaries).

Rebalancing More Frequently

Like a regular physical, periodic rebalancing helps you stay on track. There are times, however, when you might want to rebalance more often. For example, if there has been a remarkable run in a single asset class and its allocation in your portfolio has moved 50% or more above its intended proportion, then you may want to consider an unscheduled one-time rebalancing to sell some of that asset and buy something else that hasn't performed as well. Also, if your financial circumstances change and a large sum, 15% or more, is added to or taken out of the portfolio midyear, then it's also worth rebalancing.

This mechanical method of determining your trades is a powerful tool for ensuring that you sell a portion of your winners at their higher prices and buy more shares of lower priced assets. The simple rigors of this system help you consistently "buy low, sell high"—something that human nature, left to its own devices, often finds devilishly hard to accomplish. And you'll do all this in just one or two days each year, leaving plenty of time for other pursuits that genuinely interest you.

Are You Paying Too Much in Fees?

Another important aspect of managing your portfolio is using low-fee funds. Fortunately, in recent years, asset management fees have begun getting the attention they deserve, and some fees are starting to drop. (Fees in the average U.S. stock fund total 1.54%, though most investors pay less since they invest more heavily in low-fee funds.) Still, many investors continue to pay 1% or 2% of the value of their assets each year to brokerage firms and other advisers. This is a large amount of money—especially when you consider that it is paid yearly—and it can dramatically reduce your investment returns over time. In 20 years of paying 2% fees, you will have paid over 40% of your assets in fees.

In investing, the bromide "you get what you pay for" does not seem to apply. Investors who opt for low-cost passive or index-style funds (funds that tend to hold their stocks a long time, in contrast to high-cost active funds that buy and sell to try to beat the market averages) typically outpace their active investing counterparts by a wide margin over time.

For instance, compare a fund with a 0.3% fee to a fund that charges 1.3%. Assume you start with $50,000 in each fund and that the funds each grow at 8% per year on average. At the end of 25 years, the low-fee fund will have grown to $319,240, while the higher-fee fund will be worth $66,433 less, or $252,977. This amounts to a cumulative difference of 26%.

RESOURCE

The impact of higher fees. Vanguard has developed a helpful calculator for assessing the impact of higher fees over time. Visit their website to give it a try: www.vanguard.com/jumppage/library/ ?src=fieldguide&origin=spotlighton03.

The table below may surprise you. According to Morningstar mutual fund ranking screens taken in 2007, the funds listed in the table were the top performers in their respective categories—that is, they returned the highest returns among all of the funds in their asset classes.

A quick look at the fees demonstrates the wide range among these top-rated funds. For the top 15 performing U.S. Stock funds at that time, the fees varied by nearly a factor of ten, from low-fee Vanguard funds charging around 0.25% to the Wasatch Micro-Cap fund charging over 2%.

U.S. Bond funds showed a similar story, with fees among the top five performers ranging from 0.25% to 1.2%, nearly a five-fold increase. Global equity funds are generally more expensive to manage, but good performing funds can certainly be found at fees far below the 2% fees being charged by some of these funds.

Fees for Top Performing Mutual Funds

Top 15 U.S. Equity Funds: 10-Year Return	Expense Ratio
Wasatch Micro Cap	2.18 %
Bridgeway Ultra-Small Company	1.09
CGM Realty	0.92
Fidelity Select Brokerage & Investment	0.95
Royce Heritage Service	1.43
Calamos Growth A	1.2
Bridgeway Aggressive Investors	1.58
Morgan Stanley Inst US Real Estate A	0.89
BlackRock Global Resources Inv	1.34
Meridian Value	1.09
Hartford Capital Appreciation	1.26
Phoenix Real Estate Securities A	1.3
ING Van Kampen Real Estate	0.9
Vanguard Health Care	0.25
Vanguard Energy	0.28

Top 5 General Bond Funds: 10-Year Return	Expense Ratio
Loomis Sayles Investment Grade	0.55 %
Calvert Income A	1.2
Vanguard Long-Term Bond Index	0.18
Managers Bond	0.99
Vanguard Long-Term Investment-Grade	0.25

Top 5 Global Equity Funds: 10-Year Return	Expense Ratio
ING Russia A	2.13 %
Nicholas-Applegate Intl Growth Opp	1.38
Mutual European Z	1.04
Julius Baer International Equity A	1.31
ING International SmallCap A	1.74

Source: Morningstar.com 10/06

Because your fees are ultimately paid out of your available annual spending amount, their impact on your spending money can be quite large.

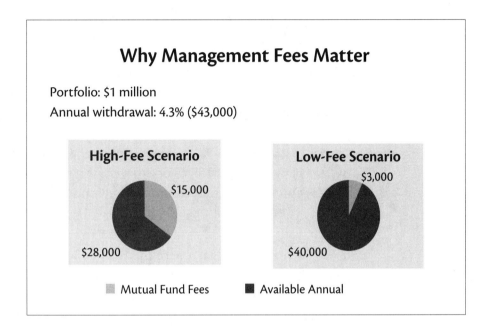

Why Management Fees Matter

Portfolio: $1 million
Annual withdrawal: 4.3% ($43,000)

High-Fee Scenario
$15,000
$28,000

Low-Fee Scenario
$3,000
$40,000

Mutual Fund Fees   Available Annual

Paying 1.5% in annual fund management expenses results in annual fees of $15,000 on a $1 million portfolio, or 34% of the investor's available annual spending of $43,000. By lowering fees to 0.3%, the annual fees are reduced to just $3,000 on the same portfolio, or about 7% of available annual spending. This leaves $40,000 available for spending, $12,000 more than the high-fee investor has to spend.

You can probably agree on the general wisdom of a low-fee, buy-and-hold approach, but do you actually know how much you pay in fees each year? Use the spreadsheet discussed below to calculate this number. It may help you identify areas where you are overpaying.

Step 1: List your assets

To begin, click the "Portfolio Fees" tab in Chapter 3 Spreadsheets. The form comes loaded with the fees, as of press time, for a number of the funds you might want to consider using to implement the Sandwich or Rational Investing portfolios.

Gather Your Materials

- You'll need your most recent brokerage statements, or a detailed record of all your financial assets. If you recently calculated your asset allocation as discussed above, your assets will be listed there.
- You'll also need prospectuses for your mutual funds or a computer connected to the Internet to figure out each fund's fees, also known as the "expense ratio." You can find the fees by looking at the fund company's website or by entering the fund's ticker symbol in the upper left-hand corner at www.morningstar.com or at http://finance.yahoo.com.

If you own an interest in any of the funds that are already listed on the spreadsheet, enter the amount you own in column C next to the fund's name and the spreadsheet will calculate the annual fee for you. If you don't own any of a particular fund, simply leave that line blank with zero value, or delete it. It won't affect later calculations.

For funds you own that are not already listed on the spreadsheet, enter the fund names and symbols in column B beginning on line 47. List the amount you own in column C.

If you own individual stocks or bonds, add the value of all of your individual stocks and bonds together and enter the total number below your other funds.

Step 2: Enter your fund fees

For any funds you own that are not already listed on the spreadsheet, you'll need to turn to the fund prospectus or online sources to find the fee (also known as the expense ratio) for each fund. Look for the total fees or expense ratio expressed as a percent, since that is what you are paying.

If the funds you own charge back-end or front-end loads (fees charged when you buy or sell the funds), be sure to include these fees on the spreadsheet. List them on a new line (below the funds). Calculate the annual fee amount by dividing the one-time charge by the number of years you expect to own the fund. (Generally, it is best to buy and hold no-load funds to avoid these one-time charges.)

> **EXAMPLE:** Mary pays $1,500 for a 5% front-end load on a $30,000 fund investment that she expects to hold for five years. She adds another line to the spreadsheet to list the load fee. The annual amount of the fee is $300 ($1,500 divided by five years). She also includes (on a separate line) the regular fund fee she pays every year.

The fee for your individual stocks and bonds should be zero, assuming you generally buy and hold these securities. If you pay an annual maintenance fee for your brokerage account, or if you trade individual stocks each year, estimate the commissions you paid in the last 12 months and enter that amount in cell E46.

Step 3: Evaluate your results

After completing steps one and two, you should have a complete picture of your total portfolio management fees. Look down the list of dollar amounts in column E and see if any jump out at you as being particularly high. Pay particular attention to any funds with fees over 1%, and decide whether you can switch to a similar but less expensive fund in the same asset class.

> **EXAMPLE:** Jordan has $20,000 invested in BREBX, an international small-growth company fund that charges an annual fee of 2.43%. After doing this exercise, he realizes that his total fee per year for owning that fund is $486, which he feels is high compared to his other investments. He switches to another fund in the same asset class with similar performance, VINEX, which charges an annual fee of 0.43%. Now, he pays only $86 per year in fees for the same amount of investment—a savings of $400 per year.

Also, look at line 3 to see the average percentage of your portfolio that you are paying in fees each year. An average fee of under 0.5% per year is reasonable for long-term investors, and some investors even get their average below 0.25% per year. But if your average expense is greater than 0.5% of your portfolio, your long-term investment performance may be compromised—you may be doing more to help your brokers and advisers fund their retirements than you are to fund your own. Consider switching to a lower fee fund.

> **EXAMPLE:** Paul and Jenny each invest $100,000 of IRA savings in different funds, each of which returns 8% per year before fees. Paul's fund has a 1.3% annual fee and Jenny's fund carries a 0.3% annual fee. If Jenny invested the amount she saved in fees, after 15 years her IRA would have an additional $41,934 simply as a result of the 1% lower annual fee.

Decreasing Risk

Interested in the theory underlying Rational Investing? Modern Portfolio Theory is the Nobel Prize-winning investing approach that provides the academic foundation for Rational Investing.

To begin to understand this theory, consider the following hypothetical situation.

Assume I could buy an asset that paid me a return on any day that had good weather. I put all my money into this investment, and watch my income from this portfolio rise and fall with the weather, creating a volatile stream of returns. Now assume that a new investment becomes available, which pays a return only on days that are not fair. We would call these two hypothetical assets "inversely correlated" because their performance moves in opposite directions.

If I purchased some of the second asset, I could in theory enjoy a nice steady income stream from this blended portfolio, receiving something every day, no matter the weather. Such a steady income stream might be particularly interesting to a retiree.

Though the real world is never as tidy as this hypothetical situation, the principle applies. If I can find inversely correlated or at least minimally correlated asset classes and blend them together in reasonable proportions, I can hope to have an overall portfolio with a reasonable return, but less risk—or variability—in returns. (This sort of variability is also known as "volatility" in a portfolio's returns.)

RESOURCE

The research behind Rational Investing. Rational Investing builds on the findings of top of academic finance researchers, proven over decades of testing and retesting.

- "Modern Portfolio Theory," by Harry Markowitz and Merton Miller, proves how investing across less-correlated asset classes can produce a portfolio with lower risk for a given return. To learn more, visit www.investopedia.com/articles/06/MPT.asp.

- "The Efficient Market Hypothesis," by Eugene Fama and Burton Malkiel, explains that although prices in the market may be inefficient—that is, too high or too low—they are mispriced randomly and there is no method to make use of this information to consistently beat the market. This suggests that you can do at least as well with index funds as you can with actively managed funds, while saving the higher fees that actively managed funds usually charge. You can read more at www.dfaus.com/library/articles/active_vs_passive.

- "The Three-Factor Model," by Eugene Fama and Kenneth French, explains that small and value stocks have consistently delivered superior returns. This supports the Rational Investing portfolio's tilt toward value stocks. You can learn more at www.dfaus.com/library/articles/explaining_stock_returns.

Looking at the table below, you'll see that Small International Equities are particularly inversely correlated with U.S. Medium-Term Bonds. We know this because the number at the intersection of these two asset classes (known as the correlation coefficient) is −0.48. This means that in years when U.S. Bonds declined, Small International Equities had a high probability of doing well.

The key is to find a blend of asset classes that historically has delivered relatively stable (nonvolatile) returns while still delivering reasonably high rates of return. Using sophisticated computer modeling and the longest available historical databases, I developed the Rational Investing portfolio in 2002 to meet these goals. I've refined the portfolio and continue to follow it today because it's ideally suited to long term semi-retirees. It has a respectable long-term average return of 10.2% before fees, and its value is quite stable (with a standard deviation of returns, the technical way of measuring volatility, below 7%, half that of the S&P 500.) These returns and volatility may deteriorate in the future, but they are the historical average returns for the portfolio between 1988 and 2006.

Correlation of Returns Between Pairs of Asset Classes

Fund Symbol	VC PE	ST BD MM	EMG	COMM	REIT	INT MT BD	INT L	OIL	HY BD	GNMA	US LT BD	US MT BND	USL	HEDGE MN	INT S	USS
VC PE	1.00															
ST BD MM	-0.25	1.00														
EMG	0.49	-0.15	1.00													
COMM	0.08	0.24	0.28	1.00												
REIT	0.23	-0.02		0.19	1.00											
INT MT BD	-0.17	-0.33	0.05	-0.20	-0.33	1.00										
INT L	0.61	-0.24	0.54	-0.03	0.02	0.00	1.00									
OIL	0.06	0.01	0.25	0.75		-0.11	0.00	1.00								
HY BND	0.53	-0.21	0.29	-0.15	0.01	0.31	0.36	-0.34	1.00							
GNMA	-0.10	0.51	-0.26	0.00	-0.01	0.17	-0.40	-0.36	0.27	1.00						
US LT BD	-0.01	0.09	-0.35	-0.20	-0.07	0.31	-0.14	-0.51	0.35	0.77	1.00					
US MT BND	-0.17	0.26	-0.32	-0.12	-0.13	0.34	-0.41	-0.42	0.28	0.92	0.90	1.00				
USL	0.59	0.17	0.25	-0.02	0.24	-0.12	0.68	-0.23	0.56	0.11	0.15	-0.01	1.00			
HEDGE MN	0.40	0.19	0.23	0.27	0.08	-0.26		-0.10	0.31	0.49	0.33	0.42	0.15	1.00		
INT S	0.47	-0.39	0.73	0.22	0.08	0.01	0.70	0.26	0.09	-0.50	-0.38	-0.48	0.24	0.01	1.00	
USS	1.00	-0.26	0.52	0.08	0.21	-0.15	0.63	0.05	0.54	-0.12	-0.02	-0.19	0.60	0.38	0.48	1.00

VC PE: Venture Capital/Private Equity
ST BD MM: Short-Term Bond/Money Market
EMG: Emerging Markets Stocks
COMM: Commodities
REIT: Commercial Real Estate
INT MT BD: Medium-Term International Bonds

INT L: International Large Stocks
OIL: Oil and Gas
HY BD: High-Yield Bonds
GNMA: GNMA Mortgage Bonds
US LT BD: Long-Term U.S. Treasuries

US MT BND: Medium-Term Bonds
USL: U.S. Large Stock
HEDGE MN: Market-Neutral Hedge Funds
INT S: International Small Stocks
USS: U.S. Small Stock

Financing Your Retirement

Most people who plan for early or semi-retirement expect to finance it through income from savings, often supplemented by income from part-time work. (Early pensions seem to be only available to an elite few these days.) That means it's crucial to know how much income your savings will produce over the long run. Will it be enough to support you, or will you need to keep working and saving a few more years or longer?

In this chapter, you'll:

- Learn about Safe Withdrawal Rates—the maximum rate at which you can dip into your portfolio each year.
- Learn how to adjust your withdrawals sensibly when markets go up or down.
- Investigate the financial side of part-time work options—how much can you reasonably expect to earn from the "semi-" part of your semi-retirement?
- Use a spreadsheet to create your own long-term model for your semi-retirement, letting you test a variety of different saving, spending, inflation, and market-return scenarios to see how they hold up.

Take a look at FIRECalc—a long-term retirement forecasting tool.

In Chapter 2, you projected what a single year's finances would look like if you left full-time work, to discover whether your savings could support you. But while earnings and spending in a single average year may be in balance, each year can bring changes, which can affect the results you'll get as the years unfold. This chapter will help you figure out how to project budgets and changes through the varied terrain of longer time horizons. After all, the longer the semi-retirement the better!

How Much Can You Withdraw?

Remember Aesop's fable about the goose that laid golden eggs? With patience and good fortune, your portfolio can do something equally remarkable: provide regular income to support you and your family.

But of course, the fable had a moral. Recall what the greedy and impatient woodcutter did to the goose: After a while, certain that the goose was holding out on him, the man killed it to get all the golden eggs inside, and of course, found nothing. Draw too impatiently from your portfolio, and it may just collapse and stop producing for you altogether. But stick to a safe level of withdrawal, and your portfolio will keep producing through thick and thin.

The Safe Withdrawal Method is a step-by-step process designed to let you maintain your portfolio's inflation-adjusted value over time while withdrawing a substantial amount of income each year. Specifically, you should be able to withdraw up to 4.5% (though I prefer the slightly more conservative 4.3%) from a diversified portfolio each year to use for living expenses.

Work Less, Live More contains the first published studies to specifically test how well the Safe Withdrawal Method addresses the portfolio withdrawal needs of long-term retirees—people who plan to draw on their financial savings for support for 40 or more years. The Safe Withdrawal Method is a significant improvement over the conventional advice traditionally given to older retirees, who may need to live from income for only 20 or 25 years, and who don't mind spending down principal as they enter their final years. Semi-retirees, especially younger ones, cannot afford to spend down their funds. Instead, they need a withdrawal system that will meet their needs, through thick and thin, over the very long run.

Retirement researcher Keith Marbach and I looked at 80 years of market returns (1926 to 2006) and other historical data to see how long-term semi-retirees could comfortably make their savings support them. We found that the Safe Withdrawal Method had a two-pronged benefit: not only would it afford semi-retirees a somewhat higher annual withdrawal rate, but it would also keep portfolio values intact. Portfolio values wouldn't gradually shrink to near zero, as they do using traditional retirement savings withdrawal methods; in fact, they were unlikely to decrease at all over the long term, even when counted in constant dollars to adjust for inflation.

This was a remarkable breakthrough for long-term retirees. It said, in effect, that we can use a sensible and easily followed withdrawal method over several decades, withdrawing at rates near 4% and still keep the value of our initial savings substantially intact, in real inflation-adjusted terms. Although there are no 100% guarantees about the future and market returns, the studies show that our current portfolio will still be there to support us, and to pay for unknown future contingencies, including rising health care or nursing home costs, or to bequeath in the end to a charity or to those we love. This allows much enhanced peace of mind to those embarking on the semi-retirement path. We have greatly reduced the risk of running out of funds in old age and can rest secure that we are not being foolish when we leave full-time work to live off of our investments well before traditional retirement age.

So what is the Safe Withdrawal Method for long-term semi-retirees, and how do you follow it?

Step 1: Create a diversified portfolio

It's very important to keep your investments widely diversified, both to get the returns you'll need and to reduce the amount of volatility in your portfolio. You'll need at least a 7.5% return from your investments in order to generate the amount of your withdrawal and still keep up with inflation, which averages about 3% a year. This average return is possible with a diversified portfolio of moderately risky assets, including stocks and commercial real estate. Try a portfolio of low-fee investments similar to the Rational Investing or Sandwich portfolios discussed in Chapter 3. You'll also need to rebalance your portfolio periodically every year or two; that's also explained in Chapter 3.

Step 2: Withdraw no more than 4.5% each year

To calculate the most you can safely withdraw in a particular year, multiply the value of your investment portfolio by your Safe Withdrawal Rate. But what's the right rate? Looking at how investments have performed over the last 30 to 40 years, here's how it shakes out:

- Withdrawing 3% a year has, historically, been bulletproof over short and long terms.
- At an annual withdrawal rate of 4.5%, you run some risk that your portfolio's value will diminish over the years.
- By 5% there is a marked deterioration in the real value of portfolios over the long term.
- At withdrawal levels above 6%, almost no portfolio can keep its value over time.

I prefer the middle ground: a substantial but safe rate of 4.3%. (Though if you don't need that much to support yourself, then by all means reduce it.) Using that rate, you're likely to experience some short-term declines in portfolio value during periods of weak markets, but over the long haul you should be okay.

Now let's go step-by-step through this process. Use the "Safe Withdrawal" tab in the Chapter 4 Spreadsheets to calculate your own safe withdrawal amount. Or follow along looking at the example below.

Safe Withdrawal Calculation

Description	Amount
Total savings	$1,039,500
Illiquid assets (for example, boat, second home)	20,000
Liquid tangible assets (for example, gold)	5,000
Home equity surplus	50,000
Total assets	1,114,500
Safe Withdrawal Rate	4.30%
Annual safe withdrawal amount	**47,924**

Enter Your Total Savings

Each year, you'll calculate the total value of your investments. I like to do this at the same time each year—usually around New Year's Day—

because it allows me to calculate my investment performance for the prior year and set my budget for the coming year.

To calculate your total savings, simply take your most recent brokerage and mutual fund statements (including your retirement accounts) and add them up. Or, if you have one, use a consolidated online report from your brokerage firm. In addition to these liquid investments, be sure to include investments in commercial real estate, private companies, and other income-earning investments you own, using your best estimate of the fair market price for them if they were to sell today. Insert the amount on line 4 in the spreadsheet.

Enter Your Illiquid Assets

Illiquid assets are anything of value, beyond personal effects you need for daily living, that you are prepared to sell to raise cash should you need to do so. It's important to be brutally honest here. Include only those items that you'd truly be willing to sell, and only to the extent that their total amounts to a small percentage (under 15%) of your total savings. Examples of these sorts of assets include collectibles, boats, planes, classic cars, motor homes, or high-end jewelry. Typically these assets were not bought as an investment and don't earn income, but they have value and can be included for the purposes of calculating your Safe Withdrawal Rate. Still, don't overdo it, since these assets are not really the same as cash until you sell them and get the money invested in income-generating investments.

You can value these illiquid assets by checking in classified ads or online marketplaces to see what comparable items have sold for. Enter this amount on line 5. If you wish to be conservative and don't expect to sell these types of items, enter zero on this line.

Enter Your Tangible Liquid Assets

If you have not already included these in your savings totals, this is the time to estimate their value and add them into the mix. Examples include assets for which dealers are making a ready market, such as collector-quality coins, gold coins or bars, or unmounted diamonds. Enter this amount on line 6.

Calculate Your Home Equity Surplus

After participating in many heated conversations on this topic with other semi-retirees, I believe that it is appropriate to acknowledge the value of your home equity as an asset. But since you have to live somewhere, including your entire home equity value would overstate the value of your assets, at least for the purposes of calculating a safe withdrawal amount.

I think a good compromise is to include just part of your home equity here. So first, deduct the amount remaining due on your mortgage from the current value of your home to get your total home equity. Then, from this amount, deduct the cost of a downsized replacement home. If you get a positive number, enter it on line 7. I call this amount your home equity surplus amount. If you wish to be conservative in your planning, enter zero on this line.

> **EXAMPLE:** Jane and Mario are prepared to leave their $800,000 home if they need to sell it to raise money for living expenses. They believe that a smaller but comfortable home would cost $450,000. Although they aren't planning to move, entering their surplus equity gives them a more accurate picture of their financial resources.
>
> | Current home value | | $ 800,000 |
> |---|---|---|
> | Less current amount due on mortgage | – | (300,000) |
> | Equals total home equity | = | 500,000 |
> | Less replacement home cost | – | (450,000) |
> | Home equity surplus | = | $ 50,000 |

Your Safe Withdrawal Rate

As mentioned above, I recommend you use a Safe Withdrawal Rate no higher than 4% to 4.5%. I personally use a 4.3% withdrawal rate and use it in several of the calculations in this workbook, including the sample worksheet, above. Remember that 4.5% is a maximum rate; lower rates, of course, are safer and more conservative. Leave whatever you don't need to spend in your savings to grow more. The spreadsheet is loaded with a default rate of 4.3% on line 9.

Your Safe Withdrawal Amount

The spreadsheet will calculate your safe withdrawal amount by multiplying your total assets on line 8 by the Safe Withdrawal Rate on line 9, and the result will appear on line 10. This amount goes into your annual budget as the amount you can withdraw and spend over the course of the year.

Step 3: Make sure to include all your spending

When making your annual budget be sure to include all of your expenses—not only your obvious annual spending items but also a few other expenses that can be easy to overlook, such as money management fees. (See Chapter 2 for more on tracking your expenses).

In addition, you'll need to set aside in each year's budget an amount for depreciation of your cars and recurring major home maintenance items. You may buy a car only every ten years, but you use up some of its value each year and need to account for that. If it helps you save, you can transfer funds into a separate account, earmarked for the purpose, each year and then use the money when the time comes to buy a new car or paint the house.

Step 4: Rebalance your portfolio regularly

Every year or two you'll need to bring your portfolio back into line with its target asset allocation through the process known as portfolio rebalancing (discussed in Chapter 3).

Step 5: In tough times, use the 95% Rule

As you well know if you've been an investor long enough to be thinking about retirement, the value of your investments doesn't always stay stable or go up. Careful readers will have noticed one crucial feature of the Safe Withdrawal Method: By taking a percentage of portfolio value each year for spending, you will have less to spend in any year after markets have declined. When this happens, you may find it difficult or even impossible to lower your spending in lockstep with the market decline. It would be quite painful to lower your spending by 20%, for instance, from one year to the next.

Fortunately, human nature helps us manage a bit here, because after suffering a loss, we may naturally want to rein in spending at least a little. Semi-retirees have an additional resource to draw on that traditional retirees don't have in such a situation: by keeping work skills at least on a back burner, they can generate additional income by doing some part-time work.

The 95% Rule can be a big help at times like this. This rule, based on extensive historical testing, provides you with a safe way to smooth out spending reductions during down markets, giving you additional spending cash exactly when you need it most. The rule states that you can withdraw up to 95% of the amount you withdrew the previous year, even if it exceeds your safe withdrawal amount. Taking 95% of last year's withdrawal smooths out your spending, even though your portfolio value is fluctuating down. This additional bit of spending does not need to be repaid later—markets tend to rebound, and you'll likely need to call on the 95% Rule for only one or two years at a time. This safety net gives you a chance to gradually adjust your lifestyle and spending and has only a negligible impact on your portfolio's medium-term ability to recover and keep ahead of inflation. Over the longer run, there's little adverse impact on your portfolio's ability to keep up with its original inflation-adjusted value.

The table below shows how the 95% Rule works. Column A shows the portfolio value at the beginning of the year. Column B shows a safe withdrawal amount of 4%, and column C shows the amount this semi-retiree would withdraw using the 95% Rule. Each year, our semi-retiree would compare the amounts in columns B and C and withdraw the larger of the two amounts. After a year of negative returns in the market (Year 3 in the table, showing a market growth of –7%), the 95% Rule kicks in.

			Using the 95% Rule			
Year	Initial portfolio	4% withdrawal	95% of previous year's withdrawal	Apply the 95% Rule?	Market growth	Ending balance (A-B or C) x (1+E)
1	$1,000,000	$40,000	n/a	n/a	9%	$1,046,400
2	1,046,400	41,856	$38,000	no	2%	1,024,635
3	1,024,635	40,985	39,763	no	–7%	914,794
4	914,794	36,592	38,936	yes	6%	928,409
5	928,409	37,136	36,989	no	14%	1,016,051

Look at Year 4 in the table. The 4% withdrawal amount in column B ($36,592) is below the 95% Rule amount in the "95% of previous year's withdrawal" column ($38,936). In this case, the semi-retiree can choose to withdraw the larger amount (the "95% of previous year's withdrawal") that year. Taking this extra amount one year will not require the retiree to pay back any money into the portfolio.

Note that in Year 5, this semi-retiree will calculate a withdrawal amount based on the initial portfolio for that year. In this case, the amount in the "4% withdrawal" column is marginally higher than that in the "95% of previous year's withdrawal" column, and that larger amount would be withdrawn in Year 5.

 RESOURCE

Learn the facts behind the figures. *Work Less, Live More* (Chapter 4) further discusses the data supporting the 95% Rule and shows only a minor impact on long-term portfolio success from adjusting spending this way.

It's a relief to know that you can dig deeper into savings after an occasional bad year in the market. Still, you're reducing spending by 5% compared to the previous year, and you'll find you either need to reduce discretionary spending or ramp up your income from part-time work to make ends meet.

Step 6: Keep up with inflation

By following the Safe Withdrawal Method—using a diversified portfolio, withdrawing a safe percentage of your portfolio each year, using the 95% Rule when needed, and rebalancing your portfolio annually—your portfolio value and your annual safe withdrawal amount will keep up with inflation, at least over the medium and longer term. A string of bad years in the market could, of course, reduce your portfolio value, but in each historical period I've analyzed, the inflation-adjusted initial value of portfolios using this method were restored and exceeded over 30- and 40-year time frames.

Keeping up with inflation is an essential component of any long-term retirement withdrawal plan—it means nothing to claim success merely because your portfolio has not been whittled away to zero value by the time you expire. At least until you are quite elderly, your portfolio must not only stay solvent and grow, but must in fact grow enough to keep up with inflation to support withdrawals over a retirement that may last 50 or more years. The Safe Withdrawal Method does exactly that, as evidenced by its success through all the market ups, downs, and staggers over the past 135 years.

The table below shows the approximate amounts you would receive if you withdrew a percentage of your portfolio each year.

How Much Can You Withdraw Each Year?								
Percent of portfolio withdrawn each year	**Total amount of portfolio**							
	100,000	250,000	500,000	750,000	1,000,000	1,500,000	2,000,000	2,500,000	3,000,000
2.00%	2,000	5,000	10,000	15,000	20,000	30,000	40,000	50,000	60,000
2.50%	2,500	6,250	12,500	18,750	25,000	37,500	50,000	62,500	75,000
3.00%	3,000	7,500	15,000	22,500	30,000	45,000	60,000	75,000	90,000
3.50%	3,500	8,750	17,500	26,250	35,000	52,500	70,000	87,500	105,000
4.00%	4,000	10,000	20,000	30,000	40,000	60,000	80,000	100,000	120,000
4.30%	4,300	10,750	21,500	32,250	43,000	64,500	86,000	107,500	129,000
4.50%	4,500	11,250	22,500	33,750	45,000	67,500	90,000	112,500	135,000
4.70%	4,700	11,750	23,500	35,250	47,000	70,500	94,000	117,500	141,000
5.00%	5,000	12,500	25,000	37,500	50,000	75,000	100,000	125,000	150,000

The white area of the table (4% to 4.5% of portfolio) is generally a safe withdrawal rate.

Supplementing Your Income With Part-Time Work

For plenty of people who want to retire early, the very notion of work may seem repugnant: Work is the bad guy, the one you're trying to get away from. Why would you want to go to all this effort to save, live frugally, plan, and sacrifice if you're still going to have to work? If your spreadsheets show that you need a bigger nest egg to safely retire, then why not just work a few more years until you have enough, rather than contemplate a semi-retirement that includes part-time work?

These are all valid points. The way you balance your finances, work, and life is a very personal decision, and there is no universal right way. But many retirees who leave their careers intent on never doing another day of work change their minds inside of a year or two. Once the stress is gone, the backlog of chores and projects whittled away, and a number of new hobbies embarked upon, you may find yourself open, even pining, for something concrete, creative, or intellectually challenging to sink your teeth into. The thought of a lifetime of errands and amusements might suddenly seem frighteningly vacant. You might feel that you want to do something that matters; something that places demands on you to come through for others.

At the same time, you may appreciate a little extra cash flowing in, either to compensate for market deterioration or to provide a few extras that won't fit into your budget. At this point, a variety of work options may appear, which can neatly solve these two problems: They'll keep you challenged, engaged, and sharp, and also earn you some extra cash to keep the budget in trim.

You'll need to be sure that any new work activity you undertake, whether paid or unpaid, does not pull you back into the sort of stressful or demeaning rat race from which you've only recently escaped. Work done during semi-retirement should feel different for you. If not, it may just start to seem like a huge step backward—more stress, lower pay, and less status. For that, you might just as well have stayed in your old career.

Work in semi-retirement doesn't have to be like that at all. When it's done right, you'll find that as you change your attitudes about your relationship with work, you become free to create a uniquely personal situation that feels quite different from the career work you left behind. This kind of work fits you like a glove—allowing you freedom, flexibility, self-respect, and a chance to grow and serve. And if you need extra income to close the gap in your budget, your work should be designed to provide that too.

> **EXAMPLE:** Frank is a lifelong sailor who dreams of leaving his investment banking career and launching into semi-retirement as a boat delivery skipper—delivering sailboats for their owners. He'll be paid $1,000 for a typical two- to three-day job. He can do ten or 15 trips a year (or a smaller number of longer trips, such as delivering a boat over five to ten days to or from the Caribbean). This will earn him $10,000 to $15,000 a year in just a month or so of work days (if a day of sailing can be considered work).

Frank is busy documenting his sailing experience to qualify for his Coast Guard captain's certificate and has put the word out that he's available to deliver boats if he can work it into his current vacation schedules. He is also building a roster of young sailors who crew with him for free or minimal pay. He enjoys the deliveries—the fact that they are paid does not diminish (in fact, it enhances) the enjoyment he has always felt on a boat on the water. He knows full-time delivery skippers can run themselves ragged doing scores of deliveries a year, but he figures by keeping it to ten to 15 trips a year he'll be sure not to burn out.

Here are some exercises to get you thinking and generating ideas about semi-retirement work options you'll be excited about. Taking small steps now to get these possibilities started should help you to move safely and confidently into a life beyond full-time career work.

Finding Work You'll Love

1. If you were free to choose your work, what are the one or two income-earning activities you would most like to do?

    Example: Ian is an avid hiker who would like to leave his management career and lead backpacking trips for teens.

    _____

    _____

    _____

2. What steps could you take today or this year to better position yourself to be able to earn your target level of income in semi-retirement from these favorite activities?

    Example: Ian plans to earn certifications in emergency medicine and youth counseling to improve his credentials. He will also begin networking to find organizations that might be looking for his services, and meet others doing similar work in other locales who might be willing to share some of their marketing secrets.

    _____

    _____

    _____

3. Could you begin earning this income now, in your spare time, as a way to increase savings while also ramping up your semi-retirement income stream?

    Example: Ian will volunteer to lead three scout and church youth groups on multiday backpacking trips during his vacation this summer. One of these trips will earn him a stipend. The experience and references are more valuable than the funds now, however, because he is still employed full-time in his management career. He is also making brochures for two paid trips scheduled for next summer, which he plans to start marketing in the fall.

    _____

    _____

    _____

4. List five ways you could earn $3,000 or more per year during semi-retirement, doing work that you would enjoy.

	Activity	Estimated net income per year	Steps to take to make this possible
Example	Lead youth backpacking trips	$3,750 to $5,000 (five trips per year at $750 to $1,000 per trip)	Develop experience and references, certifications, marketing materials, and contacts who can employ me.
	Children's photography	$2,400 to $3,000 (12 sessions per year at $200 per session)	Take photography classes, develop portfolio by taking pictures of friends' children, and volunteer to assist professional photographers to gain experience.
	1.		
	2.		
	3.		
	4.		
	5.		

You and your partner or spouse should each answer these four questions, and then talk about your ideas. Use a separate sheet to dig more deeply into the types of things you can do now to lay the groundwork for realizing this type of semi-retirement income in the years ahead.

How Much Could You Make Working Part-Time?

Remember that semi-retirement is supposed to leave you plenty of free time to enjoy yourself. How many hours per week or per year do you think you could work before it started to feel like too much?

The following exercise will help you calculate the amount of income you can expect to earn from your semi-retirement work. See whether the income you can comfortably earn comes close to covering your target or required income from work in semi-retirement. If you don't have an idea of this number already from the Savings, Income, and Expenses spreadsheet in Chapter 2 (line 19), you can get it from line 19 of the Long-Term Planning spreadsheet, which you will complete later in this chapter.

The following worksheet is also available on the CD-ROM—click the "Potential Revenue" tab in Chapter 4 Spreadsheets.

Potential Revenue From Part-Time Work

Hourly Work		Project-based Work	
Number of hours per week		Number of projects per year	
Number of weeks per year		Revenue per project	
Amount earned per hour		Expenses per project	
Gross annual income	0	Net project revenue	0
Less expenses		Less general annual expenses	
Net annual revenue	0	Net annual revenue	0

This worksheet gives you a quick way to estimate the income you can expect to receive from part-time work. If your work options are more complex—for example, you expect to start a company or you have many different types of small money-making ideas you want to pursue simultaneously, then you will probably want to make a more detailed estimate, perhaps by using this worksheet multiple times, once for each different type of project or activity.

You can calculate your expected income using either the hourly work column or the project-based work column. To calculate hourly work, enter the number of hours per week and the number of weeks per year you expect to work. Then enter your hourly rate. Multiply these three numbers together, subtract your expenses, and you'll have your expected net annual revenue.

> **EXAMPLE:** Laura is a semi-retiree who is good at math, so she decides to offer math tutoring to local high school students. She expects to work a total of six hours per week, 26 weeks per year, at a rate of $75 per hour. Her gross annual income will be $11,700. After she subtracts her expenses of $700 for books and supplies, she'll be left with a net annual revenue of $11,000.

Your semi-retirement work might come in the form of projects rather than hourly work. For example, you might want to start a party planning and catering service or write grants for nonprofit groups or deliver sailboats.

Calculating your income using the project-based work column is very similar. Enter the number of projects you expect to do each year, the typical revenues and costs, and the net profit from each. Subtract your general overhead expenses for running and advertising your business, and you'll have your net profit for the year.

RESOURCE

More about part-time work options. See *Work Less, Live More*, Chapter 6, for descriptions of how other people have found fulfilling part-time work in semi-retirement.

Looking Into the Future: How Will Your Savings Hold Up?

Now that you have a general idea of how much investment income you'll have available for living expenses after you leave full-time work, it's time to look more closely at how your financial situation is likely to play out.

The spreadsheets discussed next will let you plug in some variables that apply just to you. For example, maybe you're expecting your son or daughter to become self-supporting four years from now, reducing some of your ongoing food and other expenses. Or perhaps you are determined to begin a long-postponed remodeling project within the next few years. You can play with the numbers to see how these kinds of events will affect your finances as you follow a strategy of diversified investment and sensible withdrawals.

If you're concerned that you might not have enough income for a comfortable life during a long retirement, you may want to play some "what if" with the spreadsheets. Go ahead and put in some unhappy numbers—high inflation or low investment returns or unexpected expenses—and see what happens. You will probably end up feeling reassured about the reliability of this investing and spending strategy, and less likely to panic if times do get tough down the road.

Planning for the Long Term

In Chapter 2, you looked at balancing your spending and income in a single average year. But of course you want your semi-retirement investments to last for many years, so you need to plan across a multiple-year horizon. Investment earnings will rise and fall, inflation may tick up, and annual expenses may drop as children leave the nest or rise as you spend more on travel or medical bills.

The Long-Term Planning spreadsheet covers 20 years, which is generally long enough to establish patterns and clarify the issues you'll face over the long term. After using this spreadsheet, readers have told me they have a newfound appreciation for the importance of considering inflation first when evaluating portfolio returns, as well as a sense of confidence about how part-time work can fill the gaps caused by reduced withdrawals during periods of market downturn.

To see how the calculations work, click the "Long-Term Planning" tab in the Sample Worksheets on the attached CD-ROM. When you are ready to enter your information, open the Chapter 4 Spreadsheets and click the "Long-Term Planning" tab. Let's look at the spreadsheet in detail and see what it can show you.

Step 1: Enter your personal information

You need to enter this information only once (in column C, lines 4, 10, and 11) and the columns to the right will automatically fill in.

Line 4: Current Year. Enter the current year or the year in which you hope to retire on line 4.

Line 10: Current Age. Enter your current age on line 10. If you are still working, use the age at which you intend to retire or semi-retire. If you and your spouse or partner are doing this exercise together, you can be conservative and use the age of the younger of the two of you.

Line 11: Value of Your Financial Assets. Enter the value of your assets on line 11. If you already completed your safe withdrawal calculation earlier in this chapter, enter the amount of your total assets from line 8 of the Safe Withdrawal spreadsheet here. This is the value of your financial savings enhanced with a few additional items and is explained in "How Much Can You Withdraw?" above. If you don't have this worksheet completed, just use your best estimate of the total value of your investments (excluding your primary residence).

Step 2: Enter the four factors

The results you'll get from this spreadsheet depend on four factors:
- Expected rate of return
- Assumed inflation rate

- Your withdrawal rate, and
- Your annual spending in today's dollars.

These factors show up in lines 5, 6, 7, and 8, with a space to enter them for each of the 20 years covered by the spreadsheet. The spreadsheet comes loaded with default numbers for your convenience and, in the case of the external economic rates, to give you a sense of historical norms. If you think these preloaded values are either excessively conservative or generous, feel free to change them.

Line 5: Expected Rate of Return. The spreadsheet's default figures predict up and down annual market returns that produce an average rate of return of 8.66% per year, which is a bit below the historical returns for the Rational Investing or Sandwich portfolios. (See Chapter 3 for more information about these portfolios.) If your investments are aligned with either of these portfolios, then you can leave the numbers in the spreadsheet as is. If not, you can change the average return over the 20-year period to whatever you expect or would like to test. If you do this, you'll need to change the annual values themselves, because the value in cell B5 is calculated by a formula and is the average (the compound annual growth rate) of the values for each of the individual years.

For example, you might think that future market returns will be higher or lower than historical rates, or you may wonder what would happen if a string of several good or bad years were to come along. If you think you'll be earning higher returns, through either exceptional stock-picking or a run of terrific luck, then you could try putting in returns values for that would produce an average of, say, 11% or 13%. On the other hand, you might feel that the stock market has been riding high too long and is due for a fall. By putting in the kinds of annual market returns you feel would reflect that dismal scenario, you'll be able to see the hypothetical impact on your portfolio and retirement spending.

Line 6: Assumed Inflation Rate. The spreadsheet comes loaded with inflation rates on line 6 that fluctuate between 2% and 4% and average to 3%—the historical average over the last several decades. As with the rate of return, you can enter any annual inflation rate you want to test.

If you think our profligate economic ways will come home to roost and saddle us with higher inflation in the years ahead, try entering annual inflation rates that will change the average to 4% or 5% or even higher. Or if you feel we're headed for a recession, with rising unemployment and reduced economic activity keeping a lid on inflation, you might want to enter annual inflation figures that are lower, and that will produce an average of 2% or even 0% inflation, as we experienced for a time during the early part of this decade.

Line 7: Withdrawal Rate. Your withdrawal rate is loaded at 4.3%, a historically sensible level to balance long-run safety with today's spending needs. You can keep that rate or you can choose another that better meets your needs. If you feel you simply cannot survive on 4.3%, then crank up the numbers to 5% or even higher. These higher numbers combined with some extended downturns in the market will give you a clear understanding of how your portfolio value can be irreparably corroded by the triple onslaught of withdrawals, market declines, and inflation. If, on the other hand, you have a healthy portfolio and modest spending needs, you can see what the impact of a 2% or 3% withdrawal rate will be, and how your portfolio will continue to grow, even in inflation-adjusted terms, over the course of your retirement. This can give you strong reassurance about the safety of your plan.

Line 8: Annual Spending in Today's Dollars. If you intend to keep spending as much during your retirement years as you do now, enter your current spending, in today's dollars, in each year's column on line 8. (All the relevant calculations will be brought back into today's dollars to make it easy to compare, and they are clearly marked throughout the spreadsheet as figures in today's dollars.)

Many people, however, like to plan for changes in spending. For example, you might want to plan for increases in spending—such as travel expenses, health care insurance, or property taxes. Or you may anticipate that your expenses will go down—such as when kids become self-supporting or you move to a less expensive area.

You can use your expected Social Security benefits or pensions to lower your annual spending needs. If, for instance, you expect to continue spending $53,000 per year throughout retirement, but expect to receive the equivalent of $10,000 per year from Social Security starting at age 62, then simply enter your spending as $43,000 ($53,000 less your $10,000 Social Security benefit) starting in the appropriate year. Because Social Security benefits are also inflation-adjusted, you can put everything in today's dollars.

Line 9: One-Time Receipts and Expenses. If you anticipate any one-time expenses or downsizing, or you expect to receive any new income—for instance a non-inflation-adjusted pension—add these amounts under the appropriate year on line 9. Enter spending as a negative number (because it reduces your portfolio). And enter income, such as pension benefits and asset sales (like selling your boat) as a positive number (because it adds to your portfolio). Enter the amounts you expect to receive in future, as opposed to today's, dollars. For example, the sample spreadsheet shows that in the second year, 2009, our retiree expects to receive $50,000 in cash, say from the net equity from downsizing to a smaller home. This is entered on line 9 under 2009.

		Current Year		
	Average	2007	2008	2009
Expected rate of return	8.7%	6%	11%	5%
Assumed inflation rate	3.0%	3%	3%	4%
Your withdrawal rate	4.3%	4.30%	4.30%	4.30%
Your annual spending in today's dollars (includes fund mgt fees, amortization, and taxes on withdrawals)	$ 43,000	43,000	43,000	43,000
Asset Sales(+) or Purchases(−) (future dollars)	$ 2,500		50,000	
Your current age		54	55	56

Step 3: Interpret your results

Once you've entered all your data, it's time to interpret your results. Most people want to get a quick idea of how they're doing to see if there are any glaring problems or discrepancies. If your planned expenditures exceed your income, then the spreadsheet will show the gap that needs to be filled, one way or another, to ensure that you stay solvent.

You can see your gap on line 18 "Additional work/other income required." The numbers there show the gap between your safe withdrawal amount and the amount you plan to spend each year, and as such are the most direct measure of the viability of your plan. If the amounts on line 18 are negative, congratulations! You have no gap and should have more than enough funds for retirement.

If the amount is positive, however, that's how much money you'll need to earn from part-time work to make ends meet. If that is more than you'd like to earn during semi-retirement, then it's time to get creative about other ways to start closing the gap. For instance, you could:

- cut your annual spending
- sell some assets to generate cash, or
- delay semi-retirement a few more years and build a bigger nest egg.

Before you take any of these steps, however, take a careful look at the assumptions you've made in your model. Particular places to look are:

Assumed Rate of Return. Is it much below the historical average of 8% or 9%? If so, you might try bumping up various years' expected returns on line 5 until the number comes closer to this range. How did that affect your gap?

Inflation. Have you assumed greater inflation than 3% on average? If you were particularly pessimistic on inflation, try bringing the number back in line with the historical average and see if that improves your gap.

Withdrawal Rate. Were you especially conservative here? Though 4.3% may feel high to you, it has historically been a reasonable rate. If your level is below that, increasing it will have an immediate benefit on closing your gap.

See whether these steps have helped bring your line 18 into a more acceptable range. If so, you can take a breath of relief and start moving the numbers around again, playing "what if," and testing your various theories, hunches, opinions, and questions to gain a better appreciation for how the various parts of the model interact and how the future might unfold.

Next, we'll look at some other parts of the spreadsheet to gain a full appreciation for what it can tell you. Locate the double line between lines 14 and 15. The area above it deals with actual dollars earned each year—meaning dollars earned in the future's inflated currency. In contrast, the area below the double line deals with real dollars— meaning the numbers on those lines have been adjusted for inflation and are labeled as "today's dollars." This allows direct comparison with today.

For example, take a look at the sample worksheet data. The current value of the portfolio is $750,000 (shown in cell C11). In the year 2015 (shown in column K), the portfolio's value in future dollars is $920,277 (in cell K11) but it's worth only $780,409 when adjusted to today's dollars (in cell K15). Comparing these two numbers tells you whether the portfolio will be worth more or less in 2015 than it is today. In this case, it's worth more because in 2015 the $750,000 portfolio will be worth $780,409 in today's dollars. Though you may have more dollars in the future, only real inflation-adjusted dollars can tell you where you'll stand.

Lines 15 and 16: Portfolio Growth. When all the earning and spending is done how will the portfolio finally fare? Line 15 shows you, in today's dollars, how your portfolio has grown or shrunk. Positive numbers mean it has grown. Negative numbers mean your savings will be worth less than it is today—your spending, in conjunction with the inflation and market returns, will have actually reduced the value of the portfolio compared with today. This is not a sustainable practice over the long run. The Rational Investing and Safe Withdrawal methods outlined in this book are designed, during average conditions, to generate a slight (1% or so) real increase in portfolio value over time. This provides for a slightly higher standard of living each year and a sense of making financial progress, as opposed to living under the dark cloud in which each year leaves you a little worse off.

Look across line 15 for any large negative numbers. These represent the low points in your plan, the years during which you would have fallen furthest from your initial starting point. Do the numbers get steadily worse, or do they dip and then head back to positive territory? If the latter, you are seeing how a few bad years in the market returns can push portfolio values down, but also how a few good or even average years of returns will tend to bring things back again. Do you think you would be able to accept a low point like this? These models are useful for having a safe, early peek at the future, giving you time to adjust, both financially and psychologically, to what might be reality one day.

Line 16 shows you, in today's dollars, how your portfolio has grown or shrunk as a percentage. Looking this far into the future, you hope to see rates that are positive, perhaps between 1% and 2%, which show that you are at least keeping even and even making some measurable improvement in your inflation-adjusted financial condition over time, despite taking these annual withdrawals to support your living expenses.

If your numbers are negative, it may be because you have selected rates of return that are, on average, smaller than historical levels, or have selected spending levels that are higher than safe withdrawal levels. If you are pessimistic about market returns in the future, then you may need to adjust for this viewpoint with a higher degree of savings, a lower level of spending, or a combination of both.

Markets have certainly had long, difficult slogs, and we can expect that again at some point in our semi-retirements, but markets rebounded from the Great Depression, from wars, stagflation, and terrorism. People will still need things to eat, places to live, ways to move around, and all the equipment and services to make these things available to them. If something awful happens, we will all be in it together, whether or not we are semi-retired.

Planning for a Market Decline

What reactions did you have to the Long-Term Planning exercise? Were you surprised by any of the numbers that came out of it? Any fear about facing some of the portfolio degradation from rough market patches?

Here is a table that shows some of the market ups and downs from 1988 through 2006. It compares the Rational Investing portfolio to the S&P 500 and a portfolio that is made up of 60% S&P 500 and 40% short-term Treasury Bills. You will notice that the returns from the Rational Investing portfolio are more stable than the other two, a benefit that you may start to appreciate in your own experimenting with the Long-Term Planning spreadsheet. The more stable the returns, the less likely it is that you'll have the big negative years that can cause so much worry.

Look at the returns from 2000 through 2002, when the markets went down. If you were a semi-retiree with your funds invested in the S&P 500, you might have been very concerned about your portfolio during those years. Now we know that strong markets started up again in 2003, but how would you have felt toward the end of 2002 before the upturn began?

What if your first three years of semi-retirement were similar to those down years? Take time now to think about the issues you might face and come up with creative ways you could deal with them. Being psychologically prepared for tough times that might come down the road is half the battle. And having time on your side to prepare alternatives and strategies for dealing with future problems should address the rest.

Rational Investing Portfolio Asset Allocations, Historical Returns, Standard Deviation

Asset Classes	Portfolio Asset Allocation	Historical Return 1988-2004 **	Historical Standard Deviation**	Longest Historical Return++
U.S. Large Stocks	12.0%	13.00%	15.65%	11.70%
U.S. Small Stocks	8.5%	17.00%	18.73%	14.70%
International Large Stocks	5.0%	4.19%	16.25%	13.00%
International Small Stocks	10.0%	4.73%	17.97%	16.00%
Emerging Market Stocks	6.5%	9.61%	26.59%	14.00%
Short-Term Bonds/Money Market	4.0%	7.25%	2.59%	3.70%
Long-Term U.S. Treasuries	4.0%	9.44%	7.89%	5.40%
Medium-Term U.S. Bonds	10.0%	7.78%	4.44%	7.30%
Medium-Term International Bonds	12.0%	7.95%	7.50%	
GNMA Mortgage Bonds	5.0%	7.91%	3.92%	8.88%
High-Yield Bonds	4.0%	8.06%	7.96%	
Oil and Gas	3.0%	12.66%	15.25%	
Market-Neutral Hedge Funds	2.0%	11.19%	4.59%	
Commodities	4.0%	7.85%	22.02%	12.24%
Commercial Real Estate	5.0%	11.95%	14.23%	16.50%
Venture Capital/Private Equity	5.0%	14.17%	18.48%	11.87%
	100.0%			

** Source: Wilson International

++ Sources: DFA Matrix Book 2004, U.S. Equity Series 1928-present, Vanguard, Cambridge Associates Venture Index, Goldman Sachs Commodities Index

List five things you could do to help get through a period of sustained market declines:

	Steps you could take	What you can do now to prepare
Example	Look into home downsizing options	Evaluate smaller homes in your area
	Consider moving to Central America	Learn Spanish, read expatriate literature about Panama or Mexico
	1.	
	2.	
	3.	
	4.	
	5.	

Using FIRECalc for Long-Term Planning

Though the Long-Term Planning spreadsheet is a powerful model for seeing into the future, it doesn't predict your actual portfolio's performance based on historical data for the various asset classes you hold. For that level of sophistication, you'll need a different tool: FIRECalc.

FIRECalc is a great online tool (www.firecalc.com) that analyzes how your spending strategy would have held up historically. These results are more informative than using average returns each year or creating scenarios as in the Long-Term Planning spreadsheet because they reflect the actual patterns of historical returns in each of the various asset classes. To use FIRECalc, you'll enter the amount of your savings, how much you plan to spend each year, and how long you need your retirement to last, among other items. To gauge your strategy's likely success, the calculator looks at investment returns since 1871 and calculates how your strategy would have panned out historically.

FIRECalc has benefited from the input of a large number of users in the early retirement community. It is free (though donations are requested if you find the tool helpful) and its features do not exist, to my knowledge, in any commercial product. FIRECalc's author—a fellow semi-retiree, Bill Sholar—has programmed a tick box to select the *Work Less, Live More* 95% Rule. If you choose this option, then FIRECalc will use all of the facets of the Rational Investing method, including annual rebalancing, annual percentage-of-portfolio withdrawals, and the 95% Rule. It will define your success percentage against the benchmark of having your final portfolio value at least as big, in inflation-adjusted terms, as your beginning value for each historical period tested. FIRECalc also gives you the flexibility to reasonably simulate the performance of the Rational Investing portfolio.

When you go to the FIRECalc website, click on the "Advanced" tab and it will show you a series of five screens. I'll take you through an example using the data below.

Screen 1: How much will you spend?

On this screen, enter the annual spending amount ($43,000 in our example) and check the "Optional" box to select the 95% Rule. Enter "40" in the box that asks you for the number of years to test. If your portfolio survives intact (in inflation-adjusted terms) for 40 years, it will be a snap to continue supporting yourself for the remaining years of your life.

You can also enter your estimated Social Security benefit and other changes in withdrawals on this page if desired. For this example I did not, because I wanted to test a pure 4.3% withdrawal rate throughout the period.

Screen 2: How much do you have?

Enter the current value of the retirement portfolio as $1,000,000. On this screen, you can also enter any one-time lump sum changes you expect in the portfolio value.

Advanced FIRECalc

Advanced FIRECalc lets you select numerous options and schedule numerous changes in your retirement plan. Visit each of the tabs below to see the choices and enter your information. To make it easier to experiment with various settings, you can submit your entries from any tab. Results open in a separate window.

(If you prefer the format of questions in the previous version of FIRECalc, use the classic version.)

How much will you spend?	How much do you have?	How is it invested?	Options

Annual Spending: How much do you need (or want) to live on each year? FIRECalc will take this amount from your portfolio at the start of each year, unless your spending needs are changed by modifications you enter below.

By default, future withdrawals are adjusted for inflation, so your spending power is unchanged during the term of your retirement (except for adjustments you enter below).   `43000`

☑ **Optional:** You can base withdrawals on your portfolio value each year, rather than using an inflation-adjusted amount. This is the "95% Rule" from *Work Less, Live More*. Minimum withdrawal will be `95` percent of the previous year's withdrawal. [Description]

When will the plan end? (You can enter either the calendar year or the number of years from now.)   `40`

Scheduled modifications to spending/withdrawals from portfolio

Social Security: If you want FIRECalc to automatically reduce the withdrawals from your portfolio once your Social Security starts (or your retirement year, whichever is later), to keep your income constant, then supply your estimates here.

Your Social Security: `0` starting in   `2020`

Spouse's Social Security: `0` starting in   `2022`

If you expect a pension in the future, and want to decrease your withdrawals when it starts, enter the information here. You can also use this section to enter, for example, a decrease in your withdrawals once your mortgage is paid off, or a future increase in your withdrawals to cover increased spending. The change will begin in the year you indicate (or your retirement year, whichever is later).

◉ **Increase** ○ **Decrease** your withdrawals by   `0` starting in   `2010` Inflation adj? ☑

◉ **Increase** ○ **Decrease** your withdrawals by   `0` starting in   `2012` Inflation adj? ☑

◉ **Increase** ○ **Decrease** your withdrawals by   `0` starting in   `2016` Inflation adj? ☑

☐ Use Bernicke "Reality Retirement Plan" (phased decreases in spending after age 55). Current age: `48` [Description]

Current value of your retirement portfolio: `1000000`
One-time changes to your portfolio such as proceeds of a home sale, etc.
(Enter in today's dollars; the actual amount will be adjusted for inflation.)
◉ **Add** ○ **Subtract** a lump sum to/from your portfolio `0` What year `2010`
◉ **Add** ○ **Subtract** a lump sum to/from your portfolio `0` What year `2020`
◉ **Add** ○ **Subtract** a lump sum to/from your portfolio `0` What year `2025`

Screen 3: How is it invested?

Enter the fund management fee (expense ratio), in this case 0.0%, because in our example the fund management fees are already included in the spending budget you created in Chapter 2. FIRECalc gives you the opportunity to subtract these fees from your market returns, but doing so again would be double-counting.

Click the second button and enter an asset class mix totaling 50% stocks and 50% bonds. This will give you a close approximation of the result you'd achieve with the Rational Investing portfolio. FIRECalc cannot exactly duplicate the result of the Rational Investing portfolio because ultralong data series of alternative investments such as REITs (Real Estate Investment Trusts) and commodities are not available, and FIRECalc does not yet have international equities data. But the result will still give you good idea of performance.

How much are you paying in investing fees (expense ratio)? (Typically 0.18 to 2)   `0`%

FIRECalc's calculations should be based on a portfolio invested in...

○ Total market, split between equities and fixed income. Include performance since `1871` (must be after 1870 and early enough to show a full cycle and preferably many cycles).

Fixed Income [?]: ⊖ Commercial Paper, ⊙ Long Interest Rate, ⊖ 30 Year Treasury, or ⊖ 5 Year Treasury.

Percentage of your portfolio that is in equities `75`%

◉ A mixed portfolio consisting of the following assets (based on performance since 1927):

(You may enter actual dollar amounts in each class, or relative amounts. Whatever you enter will be converted to a percentage of the total, and performance will be calculated on each asset proportionally.)

US Micro Cap `10`	US Small `10`	US Small Value `10`	S&P 500 `10`
US Large Value `10`	US LT Treasury `15`	LT Corporate Bond `30`	1 Month Treasury `5`

○ A portfolio with consistent annual market growth of `10` %, fixed income returns of `4.0` %, and an inflation rate of `3.0` %.

○ A portfolio with variable ("monte carlo") performance, with a mean total portfolio return of `10` % and variability (standard deviation) of `10` %. Assume an inflation rate of `3.0` %.

Screen 4: Options

Enter the year you will retire (2007, in our example) and choose your inflation rate (3% in our example, which is the default rate). Note that when you have selected the 95% Rule option, the "Terminal Value" option is disabled. This is another FIRECalc feature you may want to explore that lets you set a floor under which you would not wish your portfolio value to slip.

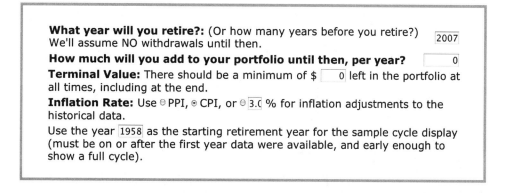

What year will you retire?: (Or how many years before you retire?) We'll assume NO withdrawals until then.   `2007`

How much will you add to your portfolio until then, per year?   `0`

Terminal Value: There should be a minimum of $ `0` left in the portfolio at all times, including at the end.

Inflation Rate: Use ⊖ PPI, ⊙ CPI, or ⊖ `3.0` % for inflation adjustments to the historical data.

Use the year `1958` as the starting retirement year for the sample cycle display (must be on or after the first year data were available, and early enough to show a full cycle).

Screen 5: Results

Click "Submit" at the bottom of the results page, and the results will pop up in a separate browser window.

In our example, the results indicate a 100% success rate, meaning the portfolio stays at or above its inflation-adjusted million-dollar initial portfolio value over 40 years. The graphs show that during the Great Depression, the inflation-adjusted ending value of the withdrawals was about the same as its starting value, in other words $43,000. But in all other cycles, historically the retiree could have withdrawn a much higher inflation-adjusted amount by the end of the period than the initial $43,000. Ending portfolio values after 40 years ranged from somewhat greater than the initial $1 million to over $3.5 million. The average was $2.1 million, meaning that on average, semi-retirees following this conservative, safe method would have doubled the real value of their portfolios and spending over the 40 years.

FIRECalc Results Based on Historical Performance of Selected Assets

Your plan is to spend $43,000 a year, or 4.30% of your starting portfolio. Following the "95% Rule," from *Work Less, Live More*, each subsequent annual withdrawal will be the greater of 95% of your previous year's withdrawal, or 4.3% of your *current* portfolio, with no adjustment for inflation (unlike the normal FIRECalc behavior, which uses your *starting* portfolio, and makes adjustments for inflation). Although the calculations are based on unadjusted withdrawals, the charted withdrawals are shown using 2007 dollars.

FIRECalc looked at the 39 possible 40 year periods in the available data, starting with a portfolio of $1,000,000 and taking out $43,000 the first year of your retirement, and the same 4.3% of the *current* portfolio (or 95% of the previous year's withdrawal) annually thereafter.

The key result: a 100.0% Success Rate

In the 95% Rule from *Work Less, Live More*, success means the portfolio was as big (after adjustment for inflation) at the end of the 40 years as it was when you started. FIRECalc found that 0 cycles failed, for a success rate of 100.0%.

Would you be eating cat food after following the 95% Rule? Here are the annual withdrawals for the last year of the 40 year cycle for each of the 39 cycles, shown in 2007 dollars.

And here is how your portfolio would have ended up in each of the 39 cycles. The range was $1,000,000 to $3,367,958, with an average of $1,758,320. (Note: values are in terms of the dollars as of the beginning of the retirement period for each cycle.)

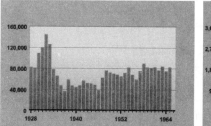

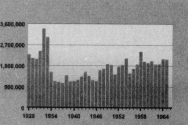

(All values are in inflation-adjusted dollars, except as indicated.)

RESOURCE

Try an even more detailed tool. You may also want to look at the ESPlanner tool (www.esplanner.com), which creates extensive reports and tables on suggested spending over the course of your lifetime from detailed salary, budget, and spending information you enter. It's not for the faint of heart—it includes a 100-page user manual. It does not test your portfolio against actual historical market returns, but rather uses "Monte Carlo" simulations—that is, those generating thousands of plausible scenarios to test.

Now that you've got a good picture of a financially sound semi-retirement, we can turn now to a surprisingly pleasant aspect of semi-retirement planning: understanding the new low-tax world you'll find yourself in once you stop earning the bulk of your income from a salary. ●

Don't Worry About Taxes

For semi-retirees, taxes generally bring good news. As hard as it may be to believe, you may find your tax bill in semi-retirement is lower than you'd anticipated. The reason is fairly simple: You've been taxed on your savings once already. When you're living modestly on a blend of interest, dividends, part-time work income, capital gains, and the sale of appreciated assets, you'll likely find yourself in a lower tax bracket, with much of your income sheltered by numerous exemptions, credits, and deductions built into the tax code. Building good tax estimates into your planning will often help you see that you are closer than you thought to having enough funds to leave full-time work for good.

Still, it takes planning to achieve the maximum benefit. In this chapter you will find:

- resources and tips to help reduce your taxes in semi-retirement
- worksheets to help you estimate your taxes online, and
- easily overlooked tax strategies for small landlords and the self-employed.

SEE AN EXPERT

Remember to consult your tax adviser. Taxes are a complicated subject, and this book is not a substitute for professional advice. Even if you file your own taxes, I encourage you to speak with a tax adviser at times of major financial decisions to understand your unique tax picture.

How the Tax Code Helps Retirees

Though it is impossible to explain the complex United States tax code in a few short paragraphs (or long ones, for that matter), it is possible to abstract a few commonly overlooked but prominent features of the code—its underlying logic—to show how the tax code helps semi-retirees. The benefits you'll likely receive were not intended for semi-retirees, but were perhaps designed to give a boost to other important groups, notably traditional elderly retirees, struggling entrepreneurs, wealthy investors, and the working poor.

Four Principles That Help Semi-Retirees

Here are the four primary principles underlying the federal tax code that help semi-retirees the most.

Income Is Taxed Most When It's Earned as Salary

The tax rates applied to qualified dividends and capital gains are lower than those on ordinary income—sometimes much lower. (Tax rates on qualified dividends and capital gains can be as low as 5%, while those on regular income, interest, or nonqualified capital gains run as high as 35%.) So when you earn investment income from these favored investment sources, you pay lower taxes than you would if you earned the same amount as a salary. This provision supports elderly retirees, who may count on dividends to supplement their pensions, and it helps semi-retirees who receive income from qualified dividends and capital gains. Interest income from bonds, CDs, and savings accounts is taxed the same as salary income; however, you can shelter those interest-bearing investments in IRAs or other tax-advantaged savings accounts. Pension and annuity income—common among retirees but less of a factor among semi-retirees—is not tax-favored; it is taxed as ordinary income.

Lower Income Means a Lower Tax Bracket

As you know, our federal tax code is a progressive one, meaning it taxes people at higher rates as they make more income. For those living at or near national medians (about $53,000 for a family with two adults) or even for those spending in the $100,000 per year range, federal taxes can still remain quite modest through a combination of exemptions, deductions, and low tax rates. For most semi-retirees earning under $100,000 per year, your federal marginal tax rate will be 10% or 15%, and you can expect to pay an overall average tax of 3% to 5% of your spending. (See "A Tale of Three Families," below, for an example of a semi-retiree family spending $100,000 a year and paying no federal tax.)

While it may come as a shock to those who have been working and paying federal taxes for many years, a 2007 study found that 40% of U.S. citizens who file tax returns pay no federal income tax. As a semi-retiree, you may well become one of this group.

Self-Employment Brings Tax Benefits

The tax code has always allowed businesses to deduct expenses from revenues and be taxed only on the remaining profit. For self-employed semi-retirees, this means you have the ability to offset numerous expenses needed for your business (such as office expenses, information, tools, and materials) and even for yourself and your family (such as health insurance premiums) against the income you earn. By deducting your expenses, you reduce the amount of income that is taxed. After you've deducted all of your expenses, the remaining income will be subject to income tax, including a double helping of Social Security/Medicare tax (known as self-employment tax) and regular income tax. If your business has losses, however, the big benefit is that you can use these losses to offset other personal income you have that year.

Capital Gains Aren't Taxed Until You Sell Assets

Capital gain is profit that results when an asset becomes more valuable than its purchase price—that is, the asset appreciates. When you sell the asset, you "realize" the capital gain, and you will owe taxes on that gain. But until you sell the asset, any appreciation or increase in value is not taxed; the gain is said to be "unrealized." This means that the asset or capital can keep growing and compounding—tax-deferred—without being diminished each year by taxes on those gains. This helps you increase your portfolio while paying taxes only on a small fraction of that growth—you'll only pay capital gains taxes on those occasions when you need to sell an appreciated asset to supplement income.

People in the 10% and 15% tax brackets pay reduced tax on capital gains and qualified dividends (only 5% in 2007; in 2008 through 2010 there will be no tax on this income for people in this tax bracket), while those with higher income pay long-term capital gains tax rates of 15%.

Benefits and Deductions You Can Use

Some benefits and deductions that are available to any taxpayer are particularly helpful to semi-retirees. Taken together, they can shelter a large portion of your earnings from tax and help lower your taxes on the rest of your income.

Personal Exemptions

Your personal exemption is the amount of income that's excluded from your taxable income. It reduces your taxable income by $3,400 (in 2007) for every person in your family, including dependent children. People who earn full-time salaries often cannot use the full amount of this and other deductions because many deductions phase out as income rises. But semi-retirees can usually take advantage of these deductions because of their lower income levels.

Child Tax Credit

The child tax credit is a credit based on the number of qualifying dependent children in the family. If you have dependent children, you can deduct $1,000 per child, directly off of any tax you owe. This credit phases out as your income rises, but lower-earning semi-retirees can usually take full advantage of this credit.

Roth Conversions

You can convert your existing IRA or 401(k) plan to a Roth IRA only if you meet certain requirements, one of which is that your adjusted (household or individual) gross income is $100,000 or less in the year of conversion. Many semi-retirees, who generally have modest incomes, can convert their existing IRAs or 401(k) accounts to Roth IRAs. By doing so, they pay taxes now but then allow the balance to grow and be distributed tax-free over their lifetime and perhaps even over the lifetimes of their children.

Some wonder whether it is a good idea to convert to Roth IRAs. In general, if you have the funds to make a conversion without dipping into the IRA itself to pay the tax, and can do so while remaining in the 10% or 15% federal tax bracket, converting is probably a good idea.

My personal love for the Roth IRA is born of an inclination, shared by many early semi-retirees, to "take my medicine early" in order to reap possible benefits later. In the case of IRAs, the potentially punitive tax brackets I could be pushed into by needing to take large mandatory distributions in my years after age 70 make me continue to nibble away at the conversions each year, using up any remaining 15% tax bracket amounts available.

In addition, the idea of handing over the Roth to my heirs and having it grow tax-free and be distributed over their lifetimes is very appealing. In effect, we could be getting as much as 100 years of tax-free compounding and distribution on these funds—an exceptional opportunity.

Sales Tax

Because semi-retirees typically pay relatively low state income tax yet continue to consume at average levels, the sales tax you pay each year may well exceed any state income taxes you pay. You now have the option of deducting, on your federal tax return, your actual sales tax paid rather than deducting the state income tax you paid. Deduct the larger of the two.

Property Taxes, Charities, and Mortgage Interest

All taxpayers can deduct property taxes, donations to tax-exempt charities, and mortgage interest. The total of these deductions can lower taxable income and move you into a lower tax bracket—meaning that each additional dollar of income might be taxed at 10% to 15% instead of the 25% to 35% or more that is typical among well-paid workers.

IRA and 401(k) Plans (Roth or Traditional)

You must have work income (from a part-time job or self-employment) to contribute to these tax-advantaged savings accounts. Contributions to traditional IRA or 401(k) accounts are deductible, and their earnings are tax-deferred. Roth contributions are not deductible, but neither are their distributions taxable. Semi-retirees often try to earn enough income in their business or part-time employment to be able to make the maximum annual contribution to these plans.

A good guideline for deciding which plan to contribute to in semi-retirement is as follows: if your marginal tax rate (tax bracket) is 15% or below, then contribute to the Roth IRA or Roth 401(k). If your marginal tax rate is above 15%, then contribute to the traditional IRA or 401(k) and plan to convert these funds to Roth status later at more favorable tax rates in years when your income is lower.

In 2008, Roth IRA contribution limits increased to $5,000 per individual ($6,000 for people over 50). In addition, in 2010, the $100,000 income restriction for eligibility to convert to Roth IRAs is scheduled to expire.

Kiddie Tax

Now, children up to age 18 (instead of age 14) must pay taxes on their investment (unearned) income at the parents' tax rate, above a $1,700 threshold. While not everyone's children have sufficient financial assets for this to matter, semi-retirees who do may have an unexpected break from this newly souped-up tax. The average taxpaying parents' marginal tax rate is likely to be 25% or more, which is well above the tax rate their teenaged children might otherwise pay on their investment earnings. Semi-retired parents, on the other hand, will probably have marginal tax rates of between 10% and 15%, which brings the tax bite on their kids' investment income down to more favorable levels.

Tax Facts Semi-Retirees Need to Know

Use this table to get a general idea of tax numbers that may apply to you—for example, to find your tax bracket, capital gains rates, or the amount of the standard deduction. The numbers are updated yearly on my website, so go to www.workless-livemore.com for the most up-to-date information.

Marginal Tax Brackets (2007)

Rate	Single	Married or Qualified Widow(er)	Head of Household
10%	Up to $7,825	Up to $15,650	Up to $11,200
15%	From $7,825 to $31,850	From $15,650 to $63,700	From $11,200 to $42,650
25%	From $31,850 to $77,100	From $63,700 to $128,500	From $42,650 to $110,100
28%	From $77,100 to $160,850	From $128,500 to $195,850	From $110,100 to $178,350
33%	From $160,850 to $349,700	From $195,850 to $349,700	From $17,350 to $349,700
35%	$349,700 and above	$349,700 and above	$349,700 and above

Qualified Dividends and Capital Gains Tax Rates

Years	Rate	For income levels between:		
		Single	Married	Head of Household
2007	5%	0 and $31,850	0 and $63,700	0 and $42,650
2008-2010	0%	0 and $31,850	0 and $63,700	0 and $42,650
2007-2010	15%	above $31,850	above $63,700	above $42,650

Maximum Contribution to Tax-Advantaged Savings Accounts

	Under 50	50 and Older
Roth IRA	$ 4,000	$ 5,000
Roth 401(k)	15,500	20,500
Traditional IRA	4,000	5,000
Traditional 401(k)	15,500	20,500
Coverdell	2,000	2,000
SIMPLE IRA	10,500	10,500

Health Savings Accounts (2007)				
	Under 55		55 and Older	
	Single	Married	Single	Married
	$2,850	$5,650	$3,650	$6,450

Personal Income Tax Deductions and Exemptions (2007)			
Rate	Single	Married or Qualified Widow(er)	Head of Household
Standard Deductions	$ 5,350	$ 10,700	$ 7,850
Personal Exemption	3,400	3,400	3,400

Other Provisions
Gift Tax Exclusion: $12,000
Sales tax deductible in lieu of state income tax paid: 2006 and 2007

A Tale of Three Families

To get a quick feel for the new tax environment you'll be in during semi-retirement—and to see how much a semi-retired family might earn without paying federal tax—it's worth comparing three families' tax situations:

- Bill and Mary, who run their own business and have investment income
- Ralph and Alice, full-time salary earners, and
- Jasper and Mei, who live on investment earnings.

Each family has two kids and could live on the same street. Their income and assets, however, are quite different. Both Bill and Mary and Ralph and Alice bring in about the median U.S. household income, or $53,000. Bill and Mary have significant savings, which they use for living expenses. Ralph and Alice save just 0.3% of their income per year—the national savings rate—and don't have significant savings.

Jasper and Mei bring in, solely from investments, about $82,500—significantly more than the other two families. In addition, because they sell (and realize capital gains on) a modest amount of appreciated assets they end up being able to spend $100,000 per year, nearly twice the other's spending.

The first two couples spend about the same amount each year. Jasper and Mei spend nearly twice as much as the other two families—but pay the least amount of federal tax.

Three Families Tax Comparison						
	Income	Deductions	Federal tax	Payroll and self-employment tax	Total tax	Tax as a percentage of income
Bill and Mary	$53,000	$10,300	$0	$1,554	$1,554	2.93%
Ralph and Alice	$53,000	$14,051	$1,044	$3,211	$4,255	8.03%
Jasper and Mei	$82,500	$28,062	$2	$0	$2	0.00%

As you can see, Ralph and Alice pay nearly three times as much federal and payroll taxes as Bill and Mary do. Jasper and Mei pay almost no taxes at all.

Most people contemplating semi-retirement can't believe they could actually be in a situation where they no longer pay significant income taxes. The first three pages of each of these families' tax returns are reproduced below. Let's look more closely at them for some of the key lessons.

Taxes Are Low at the National Median Income

Our first two families have incomes at the national median of $53,000 per year. Neither family pays a large amount of tax, thanks to our progressive income tax code. But Ralph and Alice do pay more in nonprogressive Social Security and Medicare taxes, bringing their total taxes to nearly three times that of Bill and Mary, for roughly the same disposable income and lifestyle. Their Social Security and Medicare payroll taxes are not listed in their federal tax return, but are directly deducted by their employer and listed in the table above.

In other words, even salary earners Ralph and Alice don't pay much federal income tax at these moderate income levels—they mostly pay federal payroll taxes. Therefore, by keeping your income in this median range during semi-retirement, even if your income derives mostly from annuities or pensions (which are taxed as ordinary income), your federal taxes should remain very manageable.

Self-Employment Income Is Taxed

If you are self-employed, eventually your business will need to distribute salary income and pay self-employment taxes, along with the employer and employee shares of Social Security and Medicare taxes. In the case of Bill and Mary, these are the only taxes they pay (see bubble A on Bill and Mary's return, below). If they earned the same amount of income only from investments, they would pay no federal taxes at all. Nonetheless, they have created a profitable small business; earning income from it and then paying taxes on it is still better than earning no income at all. More importantly, their business income allows them to semi-retire at this national median income with a smaller portfolio now, instead of needing to build up their savings to the point where they could live solely off investment income.

Form 1040

Department of the Treasury—Internal Revenue Service

U.S. Individual Income Tax Return 2006 (99) IRS Use Only—Do not write or staple in this space.

For the year Jan. 1-Dec. 31, 2006, or other tax year beginning , ending — OMB No. 1545-0074

Label
(See instructions on page 16.) Use the IRS label. Otherwise, please print or type.

Your first name: **Ralph** M.I. Last name: **Example** Suffix
Your social security number: 111-11-1111

If a joint return, spouse's first name: **Alice** M.I. Last name: **Example** Suffix
Spouse's social security number: 222-22-2222

Home address (number and street). If you have a P.O. box, see page 16. **122 Evergreen Ave** Apt. no.

▲ You **must** enter your SSN(s) above. ▲

City, town or post office, state, and ZIP code. If you have a foreign address, see page 16. **Rye NY 10580**

Checking a box below will not change your tax or refund.

Presidential Election Campaign ▶ Check here if you, or your spouse if filing jointly, want $3 to go to this fund (see page 16) ▶ ☐ You ☐ Spouse

Filing Status

Check only one box.

1 ☐ Single
2 ☒ Married filing jointly (even if only one had income)
3 ☐ Married filing separately. Enter spouse's SSN above and full name here. ▶

4 ☐ Head of household (with qualifying person). (See page 17.) If the qualifying person is a child but not your dependent, enter this child's name here. ▶
5 ☐ Qualifying widow(er) with dependent child (see page 17)

Exemptions

6a ☒ Yourself. If someone can claim you as a dependent, **do not** check box 6a . . . .
b ☒ Spouse . . . .

c Dependents:

(1) First name	Last name	(2) Dependent's social security number	(3) Dependent's relationship to you	(4) ✓ if qualifying child for child tax credit (see page 19)
Boy	Example	333-33-3333	Son	☒
Girl	Example	444-44-4444	Daughter	☒
				☐
				☐

If more than four dependents, see page 19.

d Total number of exemptions claimed . . . .

Boxes checked on 6a and 6b: **2**
No. of children on 6c who:
• lived with you: **2**
• did not live with you due to divorce or separation (see page 20): **0**
Dependents on 6c not entered above: **0**
Add numbers on lines above ▶ **4**

Income

Attach Form(s) W-2 here. Also attach Forms W-2G and 1099-R if tax was withheld.

If you did not get a W-2, see page 23.

Enclose, but do not attach, any payment. Also, please use Form 1040-V.

7 Wages, salaries, tips, etc. Attach Form(s) W-2 . . . . | 7 | 53,000
8a **Taxable** interest. Attach Schedule B if required . . . . | 8a |
b Tax-exempt interest. **Do not** include on line 8a . . . | 8b |
9a Ordinary dividends. Attach Schedule B if required . . . . | 9a |
b Qualified dividends (see page 23) . . . . | 9b |
10 Taxable refunds, credits, or offsets of state and local income taxes (see page 24) | 10 |
11 Alimony received . . . . | 11 |
12 Business income or (loss). Attach Schedule C or C-EZ . . . . . . | 12 |
13 Capital gain or (loss). Attach Schedule D if required. If not required, check here ▶ ☐ | 13 |
14 Other gains or (losses). Attach Form 4797 . . . . | 14 |
15a IRA distributions . . . . . . | 15a | b Taxable amount (see page 25) | 15b |
16a Pensions and annuities . . . | 16a | b Taxable amount (see page 26) | 16b |
17 Rental real estate, royalties, partnerships, S corporations, trusts, etc. Attach Schedule E . . . . | 17 |
18 Farm income or (loss). Attach Schedule F . . . . | 18 |
19 Unemployment compensation . . . . | 19 |
20a Social security benefits . . . . . | 20a | b Taxable amount (see page 27) | 20b | 0
21 Other income. List type and amount (see page 29) . . . . | 21 |
22 Add the amounts in the far right column for lines 7 through 21. This is your total income ▶ | 22 | 53,000

Adjusted Gross Income

23 Archer MSA deduction. Attach Form 8853 . . . . | 23 |
24 Certain business expenses of reservists, performing artists, and fee-basis government officials. Attach Form 2106 or 2106-EZ . . . | 24 |
25 Health savings account deduction. Attach Form 8889 . . . . . . | 25 |
26 Moving expenses. Attach Form 3903 . . . . . . | 26 |
27 One-half of self-employment tax. Attach Schedule SE . . . . . | 27 |
28 Self-employed SEP, SIMPLE, and qualified plans . . . . | 28 |
29 Self-employed health insurance deduction (see page 29) . . . . | 29 |
30 Penalty on early withdrawal of savings . . . . . | 30 |
31a Alimony paid b Recipient's SSN ▶ | 31a |
32 IRA deduction (see page 31) . . . . | 32 |
33 Student loan interest deduction (see page 33) . . . . . | 33 |
34 Jury duty pay you gave to your employer . . . . | 34 |
35 Domestic production activities deduction. Attach Form 8903 . . . . | 35 |
36 Add lines 23 through 31a and 32 through 35 . . . . | 36 |
37 Subtract line 36 from line 22. This is your **adjusted gross income** . . . . . . ▶ | 37 | 53,000

For Disclosure, Privacy Act, and Paperwork Reduction Act Notice, see page 80.
(HTA)

Form **1040** (2006)

Form 1040 (2006)   Ralph and Alice Example   111-11-1111   Page **2**

Tax and Credits	38	Amount from line 37 (adjusted gross income).	38	53,000
	39a	Check if: ☐ **You** were born before January 2, 1942, ☐ Blind. ☐ **Spouse** was born before January 2, 1942, ☐ Blind. Total boxes checked ▶ 39a		
Standard Deduction for—	b	If your spouse itemizes on a separate return or you were a dual-status alien, see page 34 and check here . . ▶ 39b ☐		
• People who checked any box on line 39a or 39b **or** who can be claimed as a dependent, see page 34.	40	**Itemized deductions** (from Schedule A) **or** your **standard deduction** (see left margin)	40	14,051
	41	Subtract line 40 from line 38	41	38,949
	42	If line 38 is over $112,875, or you provided housing to a person displaced by Hurricane Katrina, see page 36. Otherwise, multiply $3,300 by the total number of exemptions claimed on line 6d	42	13,200
	43	**Taxable income.** Subtract line 42 from line 41. If line 42 is more than line 41, enter -0-	43	25,749
• All others:	44	**Tax** (see page 36). Check if any tax is from: **a** ☐ Form(s) 8814 **b** ☐ Form 4972	44	3,104
Single or Married filing separately, $5,150	45	**Alternative minimum tax** (see page 39). Attach Form 6251	45	
	46	Add lines 44 and 45 . . . . ▶	46	3,104
Married filing jointly or Qualifying widow(er), $10,300	47	Foreign tax credit. Attach Form 1116 if required	47	
	48	Credit for child and dependent care expenses. Attach Form 2441	48	
	49	Credit for the elderly or the disabled. Attach Schedule R	49	
Head of household, $7,550	50	Education credits. Attach Form 8863	50	
	51	Retirement savings contributions credit. Attach Form 8880	51	
	52	Residential energy credits. Attach Form 5695	52	
	53	Child tax credit (see page 42). Attach Form 8901 if required	53	2,000
	54	Credits from: **a** ☐ Form 8396 **b** ☐ Form 8839 **c** ☐ Form 8859	54	
	55	Other credits: **a** ☐ Form 3800 **b** ☐ Form 8801 **c** ☐ Form	55	
	56	Add lines 47 through 55. These are your **total credits**	56	2,000
	57	Subtract line 56 from line 46. If line 56 is more than line 46, enter -0- . . . . ▶	57	1,104
Other Taxes	58	Self-employment tax. Attach Schedule SE	58	
	59	Social security and Medicare tax on tip income not reported to employer. Attach Form 4137	59	
	60	Additional tax on IRAs, other qualified retirement plans, etc. Attach Form 5329 if required	60	
	61	Advance earned income credit payments from Form(s) W-2, box 9	61	
	62	Household employment taxes. Attach Schedule H	62	
	63	Add lines 57 through 62. This is your **total tax** . . . . ▶	63	1,104
Payments	64	Federal income tax withheld from Forms W-2 and 1099	64	
	65	2006 estimated tax payments and amount applied from 2005 return	65	
If you have a qualifying child, attach Schedule EIC.	66a	**Earned income credit (EIC)**	66a	
	b	Nontaxable combat pay election . . . . . ▶	66b	
	67	Excess social security and tier 1 RRTA tax withheld (see page 60)	67	
	68	Additional child tax credit. Attach Form 8812	68	
	69	Amount paid with request for extension to file (see page 60)	69	
	70	Payments from: **a** ☐ Form 2439 **b** ☐ Form 4136 **c** ☐ Form 8885	70	
	71	Credit for federal telephone excise tax paid. Attach Form 8913 if required	71	60
	72	Add lines 64, 65, 66a, and 67 through 71. These are your total payments . . . . ▶	72	60
Refund	73	If line 72 is more than line 63, subtract line 63 from line 72. This is the amount you **overpaid**	73	
	74a	Amount of line 73 you want refunded to you. If Form 8888 is attached, check here . . . ▶ ☐	74a	
Direct deposit? See page 61 and fill in 74b, 74c, and 74d, or Form 8888.	b	Routing number [ ] ▶ **c** Type: ☐ Checking ☐ Savings		
	d	Account number [ ]		
	75	Amount of line 73 you want **applied to your 2007 estimated tax** . . . ▶	75	
Amount You Owe	76	**Amount you owe.** Subtract line 72 from line 63. For details on how to pay, see page 62 . . . . . ▶	76	1,044
	77	Estimated tax penalty (see page 62)	77	
Third Party Designee		Do you want to allow another person to discuss this return with the IRS (see page 63)? ☐ **Yes.** Complete the following. ☐ **No**		
		Designee's name ▶ Phone no. ▶ Personal identification number (PIN) ▶		
Sign Here		Under penalties of perjury, I declare that I have examined this return and accompanying schedules and statements, and to the best of my knowledge and belief, they are true, correct, and complete. Declaration of preparer (other than taxpayer) is based on all information of which preparer has any knowledge.		
Joint return? See page 17. Keep a copy for your records.		Your signature Date Your occupation Daytime phone number		
		Spouse's signature. If a joint return, **both** must sign. Date Spouse's occupation		
Paid Preparer's Use Only		Preparer's signature Date Check if self-employed ☐ Preparer's SSN or PTIN		
		Firm's name (or yours if self-employed), address, and ZIP code EIN Phone no. State ZIP code		

Form **1040** (2006)

SCHEDULE A (Form 1040) Department of the Treasury Internal Revenue Service (99)	Schedule A—Itemized Deductions ► Attach to Form 1040. ► See Instructions for Schedule A (Form 1040).	OMB No. 1545-0074 2006 Attachment Sequence No. 07

Name(s) shown on Form 1040: Ralph and Alice Example

Your social security number: 111-11-1111

Medical and Dental Expenses

Caution. Do not include expenses reimbursed or paid by others.

1	Medical and dental expenses (see page A-1)	1	
2	Enter amount from Form 1040, line 38 . . [2] 53,000		
3	Multiply line 2 by 7.5% (.075)	3	3,975
4	Subtract line 3 from line 1. If line 3 is more than line 1, enter -0-	4	0

Taxes You Paid
(See page A-3.)

5	State and local income taxes	5	1,051
6	Real estate taxes (see page A-3)	6	3,000
7	Personal property taxes	7	
8	Other taxes. List type and amount ► _____	8	
9	Add lines 5 through 8	9	4,051

Interest You Paid
(See page A-3.)

Note. Personal interest is not deductible.

10	Home mortgage interest and points reported to you on Form 1098	10	8,000
11	Home mortgage interest not reported to you on Form 1098. If paid to the person from whom you bought the home, see page A-3 and show that person's name, identifying no., and address ►		
	Name _____		
	Address _____		
	TIN _____	11	
12	Points not reported to you on Form 1098. See page A-4 for special rules	12	
13	Investment interest. Attach Form 4952 if required. (See page A-4.)	13	
14	Add lines 10 through 13	14	8,000

Gifts to Charity
If you made a gift and got a benefit for it, see page A-4.

15	Gifts by cash or check. If you made any gift of $250 or more, see page A-5	15	2,000
16	Other than by cash or check. If any gift of $250 or more, see page A-5. You **must** attach Form 8283 if over $500	16	
17	Carryover from prior year	17	
18	Add lines 15 through 17	18	2,000

Casualty and Theft Losses

19	Casualty or theft loss(es). Attach Form 4684. (See page A-6.)	19	

Job Expenses and Certain Miscellaneous Deductions
(See page A-6.)

20	Unreimbursed employee expenses—job travel, union dues, job education, etc. Attach Form 2106 or 2106-EZ if required. (See page A-6.) ► _____	20	
21	Tax preparation fees	21	
22	Other expenses—investment, safe deposit box, etc. List type and amount ► _____	22	
23	Add lines 20 through 22	23	0
24	Enter amount from Form 1040, line 38 . . [24] 53,000		
25	Multiply line 24 by 2% (.02)	25	1,060
26	Subtract line 25 from line 23. If line 25 is more than line 23, enter -0-	26	0

Other Miscellaneous Deductions

27	Other—from list on page A-7. List type and amount ► _____	27	

Total Itemized Deductions

28	Is Form 1040, line 38, over $150,500 (over $75,250 if married filing separately)? [X] **No.** Your deduction is not limited. Add the amounts in the far right column for lines 4 through 27. Also, enter this amount on Form 1040, line 40. }► [ ] **Yes.** Your deduction may be limited. See page A-7 for the amount to enter.	28	14,051
29	If you elect to itemize deductions even though they are less than your standard deduction, check here ► [ ]		

For Paperwork Reduction Act Notice, see Form 1040 instructions.
(HTA)

Schedule A (Form 1040) 2006

Taxes Are Lowest on Investment Income

Jasper and Mei's tax return is the most interesting because it shows how far a semi-retiree family can go before paying federal income tax. In this case, the couple does not pay self-employment tax because they don't own a business. They have a large portfolio of $2.5 million and live entirely off a blend of income from it (see bubble B on Jasper and Mei's tax return, below). Their income consists of:

- $35,000 of taxable interest
- $20,000 of qualified dividends, and
- $27,500 of realized taxable capital gains.

This gives them $82,500 in income. Last year, they also sold appreciated assets worth $45,000, $27,500 of which are the capital gains listed above and the remaining $17,500 of which is additional income, bringing their total spending funds for the year to $100,000.

Overall, Jasper and Mei aren't depleting their capital, even though they sold some assets. Their 401(k)s and IRAs, which are worth $500,000 (20% of Jasper and Mei's savings), would have easily generated interest income of $17,500. Jasper and Mei are simply drawing from the portfolio in a tax-wise manner, and they could expect to do the same thing every year hereafter.

Even though their home mortgage is paid off, they have fairly large deductions totaling $28,062 (see bubble C on their tax return, below). They are able to deduct a portion of their health insurance, their property tax (which is high at $16,000 per year, but that amount is fairly equivalent to what other people would pay for their mortgage interest and a more modest property tax), and charitable donations of $8,000.

When Jasper and Mei's income and deductions are combined (see bubble D on their tax return, below), the tax is very modest. Personal exemptions and the favorable tax treatment of capital gains and qualified dividends mean that their tax is just $2,062, which is about 2% of their annual spending of $100,000. The child tax credit of $1,000 per child brings this down to $62, which was further reduced in 2006 by a one-time $60 credit for phone excise tax.

| Form **1040** | Department of the Treasury—Internal Revenue Service
U.S. Individual Income Tax Return 2006 | (99) | IRS Use Only—Do not write or staple in this space. |

For the year Jan. 1-Dec. 31, 2006, or other tax year beginning , ending — OMB No. 1545-0074

Label (See instructions on page 16.) Use the IRS label. Otherwise, please print or type.

Your first name: Bill — M.I. — Last name: Example — Suffix
Your social security number: 111-11-1111

If a joint return, spouse's first name: Mary — M.I. — Last name: Example — Suffix
Spouse's social security number: 222-22-2222

Home address (number and street). If you have a P.O. box, see page 16.: 349 Evergreen Ave — Apt. no.

You **must** enter your SSN(s) above. ▲

City, town or post office, state, and ZIP code.: Rye NY 10580

Presidential Election Campaign ► Check here if you, or your spouse if filing jointly, want $3 to go to this fund (see page 16) ► ☐ You ☐ Spouse

Checking a box below will not change your tax or refund.

Filing Status — Check only one box.
1 ☐ Single
2 ☒ Married filing jointly (even if only one had income)
3 ☐ Married filing separately. Enter spouse's SSN above and full name here.
4 ☐ Head of household (with qualifying person). (See page 17.) If the qualifying person is a child but not your dependent, enter this child's name here.
5 ☐ Qualifying widow(er) with dependent child (see page 17)

Exemptions
6a ☒ Yourself. If someone can claim you as a dependent, **do not** check box 6a
b ☒ Spouse
c Dependents:

(1) First name / Last name	(2) Dependent's social security number	(3) Dependent's relationship to you	(4) ✓ if qualifying child for child tax credit (see page 19)
Boy Example	333-33-3333	Son	☒
Girl Example	444-44-4444	Daughter	☒

Boxes checked on 6a and 6b: 2
No. of children on 6c who: • lived with you: 2 • did not live with you due to divorce or separation (see page 20): 0 Dependents on 6c not entered above: 0
Add numbers on lines above ► 4

d Total number of exemptions claimed

Income
7 Wages, salaries, tips, etc. Attach Form(s) W-2 — 7
8a Taxable interest. Attach Schedule B if required — 8a 15,000
b Tax-exempt interest. Do not include on line 8a — 8b
9a Ordinary dividends. Attach Schedule B if required — 9a 10,000
b Qualified dividends (see page 23) — 9b 10,000
10 Taxable refunds, credits, or offsets of state and local income taxes (see page 24) — 10
11 Alimony received — 11
12 Business income or (loss). Attach Schedule C or C-EZ — 12 11,000
13 Capital gain or (loss). Attach Schedule D if required. If not required, check here ► ☐ — 13 17,000
14 Other gains or (losses). Attach Form 4797 — 14
15a IRA distributions — 15a — b Taxable amount (see page 25) — 15b
16a Pensions and annuities — 16a — b Taxable amount (see page 26) — 16b
17 Rental real estate, royalties, partnerships, S corporations, trusts, etc. Attach Schedule E — 17
18 Farm income or (loss). Attach Schedule F — 18
19 Unemployment compensation — 19
20a Social security benefits — 20a — b Taxable amount (see page 27) — 20b 0
21 Other income. List type and amount (see page 29) — 21
22 Add the amounts in the far right column for lines 7 through 21. This is your total income ► — 22 53,000

Adjusted Gross Income
23 Archer MSA deduction. Attach Form 8853 — 23
24 Certain business expenses of reservists, performing artists, and fee-basis government officials. Attach Form 2106 or 2106-EZ — 24
25 Health savings account deduction. Attach Form 8889 — 25
26 Moving expenses. Attach Form 3903 — 26
27 One-half of self-employment tax. Attach Schedule SE — 27 777
28 Self-employed SEP, SIMPLE, and qualified plans — 28
29 Self-employed health insurance deduction (see page 29) — 29 8,000
30 Penalty on early withdrawal of savings — 30
31a Alimony paid b Recipient's SSN ► — 31a
32 IRA deduction (see page 31) — 32
33 Student loan interest deduction (see page 33) — 33
34 Jury duty pay you gave to your employer — 34
35 Domestic production activities deduction. Attach Form 8903 — 35
36 Add lines 23 through 31a and 32 through 35 — 36 8,777
37 Subtract line 36 from line 22. This is your **adjusted gross income** ► — 37 44,223

For Disclosure, Privacy Act, and Paperwork Reduction Act Notice, see page 80. (HTA) — Form **1040** (2006)

Form 1040 (2006)		Bill and Mary Example		111-11-1111				Page **2**
Tax	38	Amount from line 37 (adjusted gross income).				38		44,223
and	39a	Check if: You were born before January 2, 1942, ☐ Blind. Total boxes						
Credits		Spouse was born before January 2, 1942, ☐ Blind. checked ▶ 39a						
Standard Deduction for—	b	If your spouse itemizes on a separate return or you were a dual-status alien, see page 34 and check here ▶ 39b ☐						
• People who checked any box on line 39a or 39b or who can be claimed as a dependent, see page 34.	40	**Itemized deductions** (from Schedule A) or your **standard deduction** (see left margin)				40		10,300
	41	Subtract line 40 from line 38				41		33,923
	42	If line 38 is over $112,875, or you provided housing to a person displaced by Hurricane Katrina, see page 36. Otherwise, multiply $3,300 by the total number of exemptions claimed on line 6d				42		13,200
	43	**Taxable income.** Subtract line 42 from line 41. If line 42 is more than line 41, enter -0-				43		20,723
• All others:	44	**Tax** (see page 36). Check if any tax is from: **a** ☐ Form(s) 8814 **b** ☐ Form 4972				44		1,036
Single or Married filing separately, $5,150	45	**Alternative minimum tax** (see page 39). Attach Form 6251				45		
	46	Add lines 44 and 45				46		1,036
	47	Foreign tax credit. Attach Form 1116 if required		47				
Married filing jointly or Qualifying widow(er), $10,300	48	Credit for child and dependent care expenses. Attach Form 2441		48				
	49	Credit for the elderly or the disabled. Attach Schedule R		49				
	50	Education credits. Attach Form 8863		50				
	51	Retirement savings contributions credit. Attach Form 8880		51				
Head of household, $7,550	52	Residential energy credits. Attach Form 5695		52				
	53	Child tax credit (see page 42). Attach Form 8901 if required		53	1,036			
	54	Credits from: **a** ☐ Form 8396 **b** ☐ Form 8839 **c** ☐ Form 8859		54				
	55	Other credits: **a** ☐ Form 3800 **b** ☐ Form 8801 **c** ☐ Form ___		55				
	56	Add lines 47 through 55. These are your **total credits**				56		1,036
	57	Subtract line 56 from line 46. If line 56 is more than line 46, enter -0- ▶				57		0
Other Taxes	58	Self-employment tax. Attach Schedule SE				58		1,554
	59	Social security and Medicare tax on tip income not reported to employer. Attach Form 4137				59		
	60	Additional tax on IRAs, other qualified retirement plans, etc. Attach Form 5329 if required				60		
	61	Advance earned income credit payments from Form(s) W-2, box 9				61		
	62	Household employment taxes. Attach Schedule H				62		
	63	Add lines 57 through 62. This is your **total tax** ▶				63		1,554
Payments	64	Federal income tax withheld from Forms W-2 and 1099		64				
	65	2006 estimated tax payments and amount applied from 2005 return		65				
If you have a qualifying child, attach Schedule EIC.	66a	**Earned income credit (EIC)**		66a				
	b	Nontaxable combat pay election ▶ 66b						
	67	Excess social security and tier 1 RRTA tax withheld (see page 60)		67				
	68	Additional child tax credit. Attach Form 8812		68				
	69	Amount paid with request for extension to file (see page 60)		69				
	70	Payments from: **a** ☐ Form 2439 **b** ☐ Form 4136 **c** ☐ Form 8885		70				
	71	Credit for federal telephone excise tax paid. Attach Form 8913 if required		71	60			
	72	Add lines 64, 65, 66a, and 67 through 71. These are your total payments ▶				72		60
Refund	73	If line 72 is more than line 63, subtract line 63 from line 72. This is the amount you **overpaid**				73		
Direct deposit? See page 61 and fill in 74b, 74c, and 74d, or Form 8888.	74a	Amount of line 73 you want refunded to you. If Form 8888 is attached, check here. ▶ ☐				74a		
	▶ b	Routing number _____ ▶ c Type: ☐ Checking ☐ Savings						
	▶ d	Account number _____						
	75	Amount of line 73 you want **applied to your 2007 estimated tax** ▶		75				
Amount You Owe	76	**Amount you owe.** Subtract line 72 from line 63. For details on how to pay, see page 62 ▶				76		1,494
	77	Estimated tax penalty (see page 62)		77				

A (margin marker beside Other Taxes section, lines 58–63)

Third Party Designee	Do you want to allow another person to discuss this return with the IRS (see page 63)? ☐ **Yes.** Complete the following. ☐ **No**
	Designee's name ▶ _____ Phone no. ▶ _____ Personal identification number (PIN) ▶ _____

Sign Here

Under penalties of perjury, I declare that I have examined this return and accompanying schedules and statements, and to the best of my knowledge and belief, they are true, correct, and complete. Declaration of preparer (other than taxpayer) is based on all information of which preparer has any knowledge.

Joint return? See page 17. Keep a copy for your records.

Your signature	Date	Your occupation	Daytime phone number
Spouse's signature. If a joint return, **both** must sign.	Date	Spouse's occupation	

Paid Preparer's Use Only

Preparer's signature ▶	Date	Check if self-employed ☐	Preparer's SSN or PTIN
Firm's name (or yours if self-employed), address, and ZIP code ▶		EIN _____ Phone no. _____	
		State _____ ZIP code _____	

Form **1040** (2006)

SCHEDULE A
(Form 1040)

Department of the Treasury
Internal Revenue Service (99)

Schedule A—Itemized Deductions

OMB No. 1545-0074

2006

Attachment
Sequence No. **07**

▶ **Attach to Form 1040.**   ▶ **See Instructions for Schedule A (Form 1040).**

Name(s) shown on Form 1040
Bill and Mary Example

Your social security number
111-11-1111

Medical and Dental Expenses		Caution. Do not include expenses reimbursed or paid by others.			
	1	Medical and dental expenses (see page A-1)	1		
	2	Enter amount from Form 1040, line 38 . . 2	44,223		
	3	Multiply line 2 by 7.5% (.075)	3	3,317	
	4	Subtract line 3 from line 1. If line 3 is more than line 1, enter -0-		4	0
Taxes You Paid (See page A-3.)	5	State and local income taxes	5	850	
	6	Real estate taxes (see page A-3)	6	3,000	
	7	Personal property taxes	7		
	8	Other taxes. List type and amount ▶ ___	8		
	9	Add lines 5 through 8		9	3,850
Interest You Paid (See page A-3.)	10	Home mortgage interest and points reported to you on Form 1098	10		
	11	Home mortgage interest not reported to you on Form 1098. If paid to the person from whom you bought the home, see page A-3 and show that person's name, identifying no., and address ▶			
Note. Personal interest is not deductible.	Name ___ Address ___ TIN ___		11		
	12	Points not reported to you on Form 1098. See page A-4 for special rules	12		
	13	Investment interest. Attach Form 4952 if required. (See page A-4.)	13		
	14	Add lines 10 through 13		14	0
Gifts to Charity If you made a gift and got a benefit for it, see page A-4.	15	Gifts by cash or check. If you made any gift of $250 or more, see page A-5	15	2,000	
	16	Other than by cash or check. If any gift of $250 or more, see page A-5. You **must** attach Form 8283 if over $500	16		
	17	Carryover from prior year	17		
	18	Add lines 15 through 17		18	2,000
Casualty and Theft Losses	19	Casualty or theft loss(es). Attach Form 4684. (See page A-6.)		19	
Job Expenses and Certain Miscellaneous Deductions (See page A-6.)	20	Unreimbursed employee expenses—job travel, union dues, job education, etc. Attach Form 2106 or 2106-EZ if required. (See page A-6.) ▶ ___	20		
	21	Tax preparation fees	21		
	22	Other expenses—investment, safe deposit box, etc. List type and amount ▶ ___	22		
	23	Add lines 20 through 22	23	0	
	24	Enter amount from Form 1040, line 38 . . 24	44,223		
	25	Multiply line 24 by 2% (.02)	25	884	
	26	Subtract line 25 from line 23. If line 25 is more than line 23, enter -0-		26	0
Other Miscellaneous Deductions	27	Other—from list on page A-7. List type and amount ▶ ___		27	
Total Itemized Deductions	28	Is Form 1040, line 38, over $150,500 (over $75,250 if married filing separately)?			
		X **No.** Your deduction is not limited. Add the amounts in the far right column for lines 4 through 27. Also, enter this amount on Form 1040, line 40. } ▶		28	5,850
		☐ **Yes.** Your deduction may be limited. See page A-7 for the amount to enter.			
	29	If you elect to itemize deductions even though they are less than your standard deduction, check here ▶ ☐			

For Paperwork Reduction Act Notice, see Form 1040 instructions.
(HTA)

Schedule A (Form 1040) 2006

Taxes Are Highest on Salary Earners

If Jasper and Mei had earned $100,000 from salaries (rather than from their portfolio) and had the same exemptions and deductions, they would have paid $14,624 in combined federal income and payroll taxes. Also, a salaried couple earning this amount may be subject to the Alternative Minimum Tax (AMT)—a second tax that gets added to your normal tax if you have too many deductions or exemptions for the amount of income you earned. In our example, AMT does not apply to Jasper and Mei.

RESOURCE

More about AMT. If you think you might owe AMT, you can use the AMT Assistant at www.irs.gov to calculate your taxes. Enter "AMT Assistant" into the search field to get the version for the year you need.

A clear and helpful resource that can help you better understand AMT can be found at: www.fairmark.com/amt/amt-101.htm.

The Tax Benefits of Starting Your Own Business

One thing that sometimes comes as a surprise to those who have spent their lives working for others is that a small business can offer its owners a number of important tax advantages. This is true whether or not the company is profitable, though some of the best benefits apply only to profitable companies. And the satisfactions, flexibility, and control of self-employment can be a perfect match for the newly independent and evolving semi-retiree.

When setting up a new semi-retirement business, start with the simplest form—a sole proprietorship. Once you know what the likely trajectory and needs of the business will be, you can investigate other business forms and decide whether you want to switch to a more complex form, such as an LLC or corporation.

Of course, earning income through self-employment will generate some income taxes, and probably self-employment tax too. But the

Form **1040**

Department of the Treasury—Internal Revenue Service

U.S. Individual Income Tax Return 20**06** (99) IRS Use Only—Do not write or staple in this space.

For the year Jan. 1–Dec. 31, 2006, or other tax year beginning , ending OMB No. 1545-0074

Label
(See instructions on page 16.)
Use the IRS label.
Otherwise, please print or type.

Your first name M.I. Last name Suffix	Your social security number
Jasper Example	111-11-1111
If a joint return, spouse's first name M.I. Last name Suffix	Spouse's social security number
Mei Example	222-22-2222
Home address (number and street). If you have a P.O. box, see page 16. Apt. no.	▲ You **must** enter your SSN(s) above. ▲
189 Evergreen Ave	
City, town or post office, state, and ZIP code. If you have a foreign address, see page 16.	Checking a box below will not change your tax or refund.
Rye NY 10580	

Presidential Election Campaign ▶ Check here if you, or your spouse if filing jointly, want $3 to go to this fund (see page 16) ▶ ☐ You ☐ Spouse

Filing Status
Check only one box.

1 ☐ Single
2 ☒ Married filing jointly (even if only one had income)
3 ☐ Married filing separately. Enter spouse's SSN above and full name here. ▶
4 ☐ Head of household (with qualifying person). (See page 17.) If the qualifying person is a child but not your dependent, enter this child's name here. ▶
5 ☐ Qualifying widow(er) with dependent child (see page 17)

Exemptions

6a ☒ **Yourself.** If someone can claim you as a dependent, **do not** check box 6a
b ☒ **Spouse**

c Dependents:

(1) First name Last name	(2) Dependent's social security number	(3) Dependent's relationship to you	(4) ✓ if qualifying child for child tax credit (see page 19)
Boy Example	333-33-3333	Son	☒
Girl Example	444-44-4444	Daughter	☒
			☐
			☐

If more than four dependents, see page 19.

Boxes checked on 6a and 6b	2
No. of children on 6c who: • lived with you	2
• did not live with you due to divorce or separation (see page 20)	0
Dependents on 6c not entered above	0
Add numbers on lines above ▶	4

d Total number of exemptions claimed

Income

Attach Form(s) W-2 here. Also attach Forms W-2G and 1099-R if tax was withheld.

If you did not get a W-2, see page 23.

Enclose, but do not attach, any payment. Also, please use Form 1040-V.

7	Wages, salaries, tips, etc. Attach Form(s) W-2	7	
8a	Taxable interest. Attach Schedule B if required	8a	35,000
b	Tax-exempt interest. **Do not** include on line 8a	8b	
9a	Ordinary dividends. Attach Schedule B if required	9a	20,000
b	Qualified dividends (see page 23)	9b 20,000	
10	Taxable refunds, credits, or offsets of state and local income taxes (see page 24)	10	
11	Alimony received	11	
12	Business income or (loss). Attach Schedule C or C-EZ	12	
13	Capital gain or (loss). Attach Schedule D if required. If not required, check here ▶ ☐	13	27,500
14	Other gains or (losses). Attach Form 4797	14	
15a	IRA distributions 15a b Taxable amount (see page 25)	15b	
16a	Pensions and annuities 16a b Taxable amount (see page 26)	16b	
17	Rental real estate, royalties, partnerships, S corporations, trusts, etc. Attach Schedule E	17	
18	Farm income or (loss). Attach Schedule F	18	
19	Unemployment compensation	19	
20a	Social security benefits 20a b Taxable amount (see page 27)	20b	0
21	Other income. List type and amount (see page 29)	21	
22	Add the amounts in the far right column for lines 7 through 21. This is your total income ▶	22	82,500

Adjusted Gross Income

23	Archer MSA deduction. Attach Form 8853	23	
24	Certain business expenses of reservists, performing artists, and fee-basis government officials. Attach Form 2106 or 2106-EZ	24	
25	Health savings account deduction. Attach Form 8889	25	
26	Moving expenses. Attach Form 3903	26	
27	One-half of self-employment tax. Attach Schedule SE	27	
28	Self-employed SEP, SIMPLE, and qualified plans	28	
29	Self-employed health insurance deduction (see page 29)	29	
30	Penalty on early withdrawal of savings	30	
31a	Alimony paid b Recipient's SSN ▶	31a	
32	IRA deduction (see page 31)	32	
33	Student loan interest deduction (see page 33)	33	
34	Jury duty pay you gave to your employer	34	
35	Domestic production activities deduction. Attach Form 8903	35	
36	Add lines 23 through 31a and 32 through 35	36	
37	Subtract line 36 from line 22. This is your **adjusted gross income** ▶	37	82,500

For Disclosure, Privacy Act, and Paperwork Reduction Act Notice, see page 80.
(HTA)

Form **1040** (2006)

Form 1040 (2006)   Jasper and Mei Example   111-11-1111   Page **2**

Tax and Credits	38	Amount from line 37 (adjusted gross income).	38	82,500
	39a	Check if: ☐ **You** were born before January 2, 1942, ☐ Blind. ☐ **Spouse** was born before January 2, 1942, ☐ Blind. Total boxes checked ▶ 39a		
Standard Deduction for—	b	If your spouse itemizes on a separate return or you were a dual-status alien, see page 34 and check here . . ▶ 39b ☐		
● People who checked any box on line 39a or 39b or who can be claimed as a dependent, see page 34.	40	**Itemized deductions** (from Schedule A) **or** your **standard deduction** (see left margin)	40	28,062
	41	Subtract line 40 from line 38	41	54,438
	42	If line 38 is over $112,875, or you provided housing to a person displaced by Hurricane Katrina, see page 36. Otherwise, multiply $3,300 by the total number of exemptions claimed on line 6d	42	13,200
	43	**Taxable income.** Subtract line 42 from line 41. If line 42 is more than line 41, enter -0-	43	41,238
● All others:	44	**Tax** (see page 36). Check if any tax is from: **a** ☐ Form(s) 8814 **b** ☐ Form 4972	44	2,062
Single or Married filing separately, $5,150	45	**Alternative minimum tax** (see page 39). Attach Form 6251	45	
	46	Add lines 44 and 45 ▶	46	2,062
Married filing jointly or Qualifying widow(er), $10,300	47	Foreign tax credit. Attach Form 1116 if required 47		
	48	Credit for child and dependent care expenses. Attach Form 2441 48		
	49	Credit for the elderly or the disabled. Attach Schedule R 49		
Head of household, $7,550	50	Education credits. Attach Form 8863 50		
	51	Retirement savings contributions credit. Attach Form 8880 51		
	52	Residential energy credits. Attach Form 5695 52		
	53	Child tax credit (see page 42). Attach Form 8901 if required 53 2,000		
	54	Credits from: **a** ☐ Form 8396 **b** ☐ Form 8839 **c** ☐ Form 8859 54		
	55	Other credits: **a** ☐ Form 3800 **b** ☐ Form 8801 **c** ☐ Form _____ 55		
	56	Add lines 47 through 55. These are your **total credits**	56	2,000
	57	Subtract line 56 from line 46. If line 56 is more than line 46, enter -0- ▶	57	62
Other Taxes	58	Self-employment tax. Attach Schedule SE	58	
	59	Social security and Medicare tax on tip income not reported to employer. Attach Form 4137	59	
	60	Additional tax on IRAs, other qualified retirement plans, etc. Attach Form 5329 if required	60	
	61	Advance earned income credit payments from Form(s) W-2, box 9	61	
	62	Household employment taxes. Attach Schedule H	62	
	63	Add lines 57 through 62. This is your **total tax** ▶	63	62
Payments	64	Federal income tax withheld from Forms W-2 and 1099 64		
	65	2006 estimated tax payments and amount applied from 2005 return 65		
If you have a qualifying child, attach Schedule EIC.	66a	**Earned income credit (EIC)** 66a		
	b	Nontaxable combat pay election . . . . . ▶ 66b		
	67	Excess social security and tier 1 RRTA tax withheld (see page 60) 67		
	68	Additional child tax credit. Attach Form 8812 68		
	69	Amount paid with request for extension to file (see page 60) 69		
	70	Payments from: **a** ☐ Form 2439 **b** ☐ Form 4136 **c** ☐ Form 8885 70		
	71	Credit for federal telephone excise tax paid. Attach Form 8913 if required 71 60		
	72	Add lines 64, 65, 66a, and 67 through 71. These are your total payments ▶	72	60
Refund	73	If line 72 is more than line 63, subtract line 63 from line 72. This is the amount you **overpaid**	73	
	74a	Amount of line 73 you want refunded to you. If Form 8888 is attached, check here . . . ▶ ☐	74a	
Direct deposit? See page 61 and fill in 74b, 74c, and 74d, or Form 8888.	▶ b	Routing number _____ ▶ **c** Type: ☐ Checking ☐ Savings		
	▶ d	Account number _____		
	75	Amount of line 73 you want **applied to your 2007 estimated tax** . . ▶ 75		
Amount You Owe	76	**Amount you owe.** Subtract line 72 from line 63. For details on how to pay, see page 62 . . . ▶	76	2
	77	Estimated tax penalty (see page 62) 77		
Third Party Designee		Do you want to allow another person to discuss this return with the IRS (see page 63)? ☐ **Yes.** Complete the following. ☐ **No**		
		Designee's name ▶ Phone no. ▶ Personal identification number (PIN) ▶		
Sign Here Joint return? See page 17. Keep a copy for your records.		Under penalties of perjury, I declare that I have examined this return and accompanying schedules and statements, and to the best of my knowledge and belief, they are true, correct, and complete. Declaration of preparer (other than taxpayer) is based on all information of which preparer has any knowledge.		
		Your signature Date Your occupation Daytime phone number		
		Spouse's signature. If a joint return, **both** must sign. Date Spouse's occupation		
Paid Preparer's Use Only		Preparer's signature ▶ Date Check if self-employed ☐ Preparer's SSN or PTIN		
		Firm's name (or yours if self-employed), address, and ZIP code ▶ EIN Phone no. State ZIP code		

Form **1040** (2006)

SCHEDULE A (Form 1040)	Schedule A—Itemized Deductions	OMB No. 1545-0074

Department of the Treasury
Internal Revenue Service (99)

▶ Attach to Form 1040. ▶ See Instructions for Schedule A (Form 1040).

2006
Attachment
Sequence No. 07

Name(s) shown on Form 1040: Jasper and Mei Example
Your social security number: 111-11-1111

D

Medical and Dental Expenses

Caution. Do not include expenses reimbursed or paid by others.

1 Medical and dental expenses (see page A-1) — 1 | 8,000
2 Enter amount from Form 1040, line 38 — 2 | 82,500
3 Multiply line 2 by 7.5% (.075) — 3 | 6,188
4 Subtract line 3 from line 1. If line 3 is more than line 1, enter -0- — 4 | 1,812

Taxes You Paid (See page A-3.)

5 State and local income taxes — 5 | 2,250
6 Real estate taxes (see page A-3) — 6 | 16,000
7 Personal property taxes — 7
8 Other taxes. List type and amount ▶ — 8
9 Add lines 5 through 8 — 9 | 18,250

Interest You Paid (See page A-3.)

Note. Personal interest is not deductible.

10 Home mortgage interest and points reported to you on Form 1098 — 10
11 Home mortgage interest not reported to you on Form 1098. If paid to the person from whom you bought the home, see page A-3 and show that person's name, identifying no., and address ▶
Name / Address / TIN — 11
12 Points not reported to you on Form 1098. See page A-4 for special rules — 12
13 Investment interest. Attach Form 4952 if required. (See page A-4.) — 13
14 Add lines 10 through 13 — 14 | 0

Gifts to Charity

If you made a gift and got a benefit for it, see page A-4.

15 Gifts by cash or check. If you made any gift of $250 or more, see page A-5 — 15 | 8,000
16 Other than by cash or check. If any gift of $250 or more, see page A-5. You **must** attach Form 8283 if over $500 — 16
17 Carryover from prior year — 17
18 Add lines 15 through 17 — 18 | 8,000

Casualty and Theft Losses

19 Casualty or theft loss(es). Attach Form 4684. (See page A-6.) — 19

Job Expenses and Certain Miscellaneous Deductions (See page A-6.)

20 Unreimbursed employee expenses—job travel, union dues, job education, etc. Attach Form 2106 or 2106-EZ if required. (See page A-6.) ▶ — 20
21 Tax preparation fees — 21
22 Other expenses—investment, safe deposit box, etc. List type and amount ▶ — 22
23 Add lines 20 through 22 — 23 | 0
24 Enter amount from Form 1040, line 38 — 24 | 82,500
25 Multiply line 24 by 2% (.02) — 25 | 1,650
26 Subtract line 25 from line 23. If line 25 is more than line 23, enter -0- — 26 | 0

Other Miscellaneous Deductions

27 Other—from list on page A-7. List type and amount ▶ — 27

Total Itemized Deductions

28 Is Form 1040, line 38, over $150,500 (over $75,250 if married filing separately)?
[X] No. Your deduction is not limited. Add the amounts in the far right column for lines 4 through 27. Also, enter this amount on Form 1040, line 40. — 28 | 28,062
[ ] Yes. Your deduction may be limited. See page A-7 for the amount to enter.
29 If you elect to itemize deductions even though they are less than your standard deduction, check here ▶ [ ]

For Paperwork Reduction Act Notice, see Form 1040 instructions. (HTA)

Schedule A (Form 1040) 2006

tax bite is modest and will still leave you ahead financially. In any case, don't let the tax cart lead the horse. Pursue your interests while working to make them profitable, and know that tax benefits will be available in the end. People who start a business primarily for the tax benefits often end up worse off, and risk an audit.

If your business does lose money, though, you can use those business losses to offset other income. And all businesses, whether or not they are profitable, can deduct many of the following expenses:

- Home office expenses, including a prorata share of the home's depreciation.
- Business-related entertainment expenses (semideductible).
- Business travel and automobile expenses (fully deductible).
- Expenses related to keeping up with your business and markets (such as newspaper and magazine subscriptions, basic cable TV for home office, and other telecom and media).
- Profitable sole proprietorships and partnerships (and LLCs structured for tax purposes this way) can often deduct health care insurance premiums up to the limit of profits.
- Corporations (including S corporations and LLCs structured for tax purposes as a corporation) can often deduct health insurance premiums even if the firm is not profitable.

RESOURCE

For more information about small business tax matters:

- Read *Deduct It! Lower Your Small Business Taxes* and *Home Business Tax Deductions: Keep What You Earn*, by Stephen Fishman (Nolo).
- Learn about choosing a legal format for your new business in *LLC or Corporation? How to Choose the Right Form for Your Business*, by Anthony Mancuso (Nolo).
- Visit www.401khelpcenter.com for a good collection of links for small businesses considering starting a 401(k) plan.
- For a complete discussion about the deductibility of health insurance premiums for the self-employed, see Chapter 5 of *Work Less, Live More* (2nd Edition).

Small business owners may contribute to a personal Roth or traditional IRA, as long as the income has been paid to the owners in the form of salary, which means they will also have paid self-employment tax. The company might also be able to sponsor a traditional or Roth 401(k), or SEP IRA, which can provide a significant tax advantage for owners, with much larger contributions possible than with regular personal IRAs.

Even a sole proprietorship, one-person LLC, or partnership, can contribute to a Roth 401(k), which allows contributions from earned income up to $15,000 per year, and an extra $5,000 per year if the contributor is over 50 years old. Transferring this kind of wealth into a Roth 401(k), for instance, and putting it beyond the reach of taxation throughout your lifetime and that of your designated beneficiary is an important tax benefit. Any small business owner who expects annual profits of more than $5,000 to $10,000 should seriously consider contributing to one of these plans.

Investing in real estate offers numerous tax benefits, and has long been a favorite semi-retirement investment and avocation. I asked fellow Nolo author Stephen Fishman for a top ten list of tax tips for residential real estate investors. Read more in *Every Landlord's Tax Deduction Guide*, by Stephen Fishman (Nolo).

 RESOURCE

More information about being a landlord. Read *Every Landlord's Legal Guide*, by Marcia Stewart, Ralph Warner, and Janet Portman (Nolo), and *Every Landlord's Guide to Finding Great Tenants*, by Janet Portman (Nolo). You can also find many pages of useful tips covering all facets of small-scale real estate investing at www.nolo.com in the property and money section, under Landlords and Property Management and under Real Estate.

Top Ten Tax Deductions for Landlords

1. **Interest.** The largest tax deduction for many landlords is for interest, which can include interest paid on a mortgage for the property and credit card interest for goods or services used in the rental business.

2. **Depreciation.** Landlords can deduct the purchase price of a property and any improvements over a period of time—generally 27½ years for residential real estate.

3. **Repairs.** Each year, landlords can deduct the full amount that they spend on repairs and maintenance on rental property, such as repainting, fixing gutters or floors, fixing leaks and broken windows, or plastering.

4. **Local travel.** Landlords can deduct the cost of local travel for property-related matters, such as traveling to their property, to the hardware store, or to meet a tenant. Specific Internal Revenue Service (IRS) rules determine whether travel is calculated using the standard mileage rate (48.5 cents per mile in 2007) or by tracking actual expenses.

5. **Long distance travel.** Long distance or overnight travel can be deducted as part of a landlord's activities, but should be properly documented—it gets extra scrutiny by the IRS.

6. **Home office expenses.** Certain home office expenses are deductible.

7. **Salaries.** The salaries and fees that landlords pay to employees and independent contractors for work done to a rental building are fully deductible.

8. **Casualty losses.** A portion of a building's value is deductible if the building is damaged or property stolen.

9. **Insurance.** Landlords can deduct insurance premiums paid to insure a rental building.

10. **Professional services.** Fees landlords pay for legal and professional services related to the property are also deductible.

Also, real estate taxes are fully deductible, profits from real estate investments can be taken out free of self-employment taxes, and numerous techniques exist for buying and selling appreciated investment real estate while deferring capital gains taxes.

Minimizing Your Capital Gains Tax

Mutual funds distribute taxable capital gains to holders each year in fairly unpredictable amounts, usually in December. These have nothing to do with whether you sell the fund; they are distributions that accrue and you must pay tax on them even if you never sell a share.

After several years of strong markets, funds may distribute 4% to 6% or more annually in taxable gains. Certain funds—commodities funds, for example—tend to make even larger annual distributions of taxable gain. During years of poor market performance these gains can slow down, but don't always do so. Most funds had plenty of capital losses to offset their gains during 2000 to 2005, but by 2006 investors were getting hammered with uncharacteristically large distributions.

Tax-wise investors need to plan carefully to get the right funds and asset allocations without subjecting themselves to high taxable distributions. The right funds can earn the same market returns while offsetting gains or holding them untaxed and deferred within the funds themselves. Investors who follow the Rational Investing method outlined in Chapter 3 do the same thing in their own portfolios— postponing paying taxes on gains perhaps indefinitely.

Plan and invest carefully, and you may be able to keep capital gains distributions from your stock mutual fund holdings to about 0.5% of the total portfolio value.

> ! CAUTION
>
> **Rebalancing your portfolio can increase your capital gains tax.** When you rebalance your portfolio you may generate income that will be taxed at the capital gains rate. This may drive your capital gains liability higher. Don't feel too bad if this happens to you: It is an unavoidable consequence of buying low and selling high, a useful investment discipline enforced by the rebalancing process. Nonetheless you might consider biannual rebalancing as a way to reduce these taxes. Studies show that overall portfolio performance has been about the same with annual or biannual rebalancing.

Here are four proven methods for deferring paying capital gains taxes.

Buy and Hold Low-Turnover Funds

Index funds and a handful of specifically managed low-turnover funds generally hold their assets for a long time, which reduces capital gains distributions and trading costs. Other funds that help keep capital gains taxes down set restrictions on active trading or charge fees for short-term investors. As a long-term investor who rebalances regularly, these restrictions will help you, not hurt you. Fund managers who pursue active trading strategies can eat their investors alive with trading costs, spreads, and large capital gains distributions while on average delivering submarket results. Investors always hope the returns from actively traded funds will compensate for these additional costs, of course, but on average they don't.

Buy Tax-Advantaged Mutual Funds

These funds, often index funds, take reducing capital gains taxes one step further. Their managers employ a number of techniques to offset gains and losses, reduce trading and turnover, and preserve the bulk of any gains deferred and untaxed within the fund. You can identify them by their names, which include TM or Tax Managed, often as an alternative to a non-tax-managed fund sold by the same firm. They generally carry some restrictions to discourage active traders from investing in the fund, which helps preserve returns and tax advantages for the long-term holders of the fund. Buy these funds from a reputable company whenever they are available in an asset class you are seeking. (You can read more about asset classes in Chapter 3.)

Buy Individual Securities or Small Managed Accounts

Individual securities—stocks or bonds—need never be sold (or in the case of bonds, can be held to maturity), which reduces capital gains taxes. These funds may, however, make it harder to rebalance your portfolio because you may need to sell small amounts of shares at higher expense. You might not even be able to sell a small amount of a bond holding if the denomination is large. You also need to be sure that you maintain diversity in your portfolio, which can be harder to accomplish with individual securities. Managed accounts—effectively your own personal mutual fund created and managed by your brokerage firm—are designed to solve some of these problems, but may carry a large fee that can outweigh their benefits.

Buy Index Exchange-Traded Funds (ETFs)

Exchange-traded funds, a type of mutual fund that trades throughout the day on stock exchanges, offer improvements over buying individual stocks or bonds (by spreading risk and providing liquidity) and over mutual funds. That's because Index ETFs are designed to do little or no selling within their pools, which eliminates the taxable distribution of capital gains generated by that trading. However, dividends paid by individual securities are still passed through to ETF holders. Index ETFs' distribution patterns are similar to those of a tax-managed fund, but are better than those of an average index fund.

As with any fund, be sure to watch the annual fees, and be aware that trading ETFs generates a brokerage commission that can add to costs. Avoid any ETFs that give their managers free rein to buy and sell securities within the fund and that do not track an index. These ETFs can give you all the disadvantages of an actively traded mutual fund with virtually no reporting transparency into what exactly you are buying, what the fees and expenses of the fund are, and what strategy your manager is supposed to be following.

RESOURCE

Want to learn more? See *Work Less, Live More* (Chapter 5) for more information on taxes and how they apply to semi-retirees. You'll find information on converting to Roth IRAs, setting up a Roth IRA for children, and five strategies for legally lowering taxes in semi-retirement.

Estimating Your Federal Income Tax

Calculating your expected tax can be useful at many junctures. For a start, it lets you see that your taxes in semi-retirement will probably be far less than what you pay now. And you can use those numbers in your budgeting and planning. Here are a few more ways in which an idea of your likely tax bill can help your planning:

- When you are rebalancing your portfolio, you may need to sell additional securities to pay your taxes, so having a good idea of the amount of taxes you'll owe on the transaction is helpful.

- You may be evaluating alternative investments—for instance, trying to decide whether to purchase taxable or tax-free municipal bonds. Being able to assess the likely tax consequences of each approach will help you decide which is the better course of action.

- When you convert traditional IRA funds to Roth IRAs, you'll need to plan carefully to know how much you can convert each year, and the transaction must be completed by your financial institution before the end of the year. That means you won't have time to collect all the data from your brokerage statements, which get issued in the new year, but will need to work with best estimates instead.

- Finally, as you become more interested in taxes and financial planning and conversant with your own tax situation, you'll be able to investigate different courses of action in your financial affairs. A simple and timely estimate of the tax consequences of a decision can help you make decisions that help reduce your taxes. That will save you money and headaches for many years to come.

Using the 1040 Tax Calculator

I recommend that you calculate your tax online, using the excellent 1040 tax calculator at http://turbotax.intuit.com/tax_help/tax_calculators/tax_estimator.jhtml.

A simple alternative calculator, which will let you quickly enter data and test scenarios (but does not calculate AMT), can be found at www.bloomberg.com/invest/calculators/tax1040.html.

Though this free software won't generate tax forms for filing your taxes or keep your data from one year to the next, it will give you a very close estimate of the amount of tax you can expect to pay based on your income, deductions, and other financial data.

The worksheets below will help you assemble the data you'll need to enter into one of the calculators. It is a good idea to record the data, possibly in the worksheet tabs in the Chapter 5 spreadsheets, to make it easy to reenter it whenever you want to use the calculator again.

RESOURCE

Tax preparation software. If you want a full-featured software service for keeping your tax records, calculating state and federal taxes, printing out forms, and even filing your electronic forms with your state and the IRS, a good option is *TurboTax* from Quicken (www.turbotax.intuit.com).

Also, taxpayers with taxable income below a certain amount ($52,000 for tax year 2006) can get free access to tax preparation software for calculating and filing federal and some state income taxes through the IRS FreeFile program. Go to www.irs.gov/efile and click FreeFile to get started.

Your Income

This worksheet will help you gather all of the information related to your income. To begin, click the "Income" tab in Chapter 5 Spreadsheets or use the worksheet below.

If you know the scenario you'd like to test, or if you have the information from your brokerage statements or last year's taxes, then you can enter the information directly into the calculator, but note that the online calculators will not save your data for future visits.

Here are some of the items you will include on your income worksheet:

Wages, salaries, and tips from your part-time employment, (though not from your own self-employment).

Taxable and tax-exempt interest from CDs, taxable bonds, and bank accounts.

Ordinary dividends, including any dividends and payments from bond funds, commodities funds, and real estate investment trusts (REITs) (these are sometimes referred to as nonqualified dividends). Also, see the discussion of qualified dividends, below, to ensure you enter the correct number here.

Qualified dividends are generally reported as a subset of total ordinary dividend income in most brokerage statements and year-end 1099 forms and are listed on Line 1b of Form 1099. This means that your reported total ordinary dividend income (shown on line 1a on your 1099 form) will contain the sum of both qualified and non-qualified dividends. You'll need to subtract to get the correct numbers (both of the recommended calculators require the data to be entered this way). The formula is:

$$\text{Total Ordinary Dividends} - \text{Qualified Dividends} = \text{Nonqualified Dividends}$$

Business income or loss is your net income from any unincorporated business, including any sole proprietorship, LLC, or partnership that is reported to the IRS on Schedule C.

Short- and long-term capital gain or loss. Take the net of your realized gains and losses for the year and enter them here. Many financial providers will give you online summaries of this information, which makes life much easier. This information is also available in your 1099, line 2a, if you are doing these estimates early in the year after receiving this information.

Pension and annuity distributions. Be sure to enter any Social Security benefits on their own line because they are taxed differently from other pension income.

Income from Schedule E is where you enter your net income from incorporated and limited partnerships, rental real estate, S corporations, trusts, or royalties.

What If You Don't Know Your Income In Semi-Retirement

Even if you don't know what your various income amounts might be in semi-retirement, you can still make reasonable estimates. Start with income you expect to receive from semi-retirement work. Then use the amount of your expected savings to generate approximate amounts for interest, qualified and other dividends, and other types of income you can expect.

If you are using the Rational Investing portfolio, with 10% to 25% of your investments in tax-advantaged retirement accounts, you can expect to receive about 3% of your total portfolio in combined taxable interest dividends Additional money for your living expenses (if you don't generate it from real estate rentals or work) will generally have to come from the sale of appreciated assets—meaning you'll sell off a portion of your portfolio for living expenses. You will typically do this during your portfolio rebalancing (discussed in Chapter 4), which means that the income you receive from the sales is also likely to be taxable, albeit at long-term capital gains rates. Total portfolio earnings and distributions from all sources can probably be capped at 5% of your portfolio.

> **EXAMPLE:** Julia anticipates that she'll need an additional $10,000 for her living expenses next year, so she sells $10,000 worth of stock. Because she paid $4,000 for that stock when she originally bought it, she'll owe taxes only on the $6,000 gain.
>
> | | |
> |---|---|
> | Sales price | $ 10,000 |
> | Less basis | 4,000 |
> | Taxable capital gain | $ 6,000 |

You are not spending portfolio principal when you sell some appreciated assets to fund living expenses, because other parts of your portfolio continue to earn interest.

Your Income

Source of Income	Amount
Wages, salaries, and tips	
Taxable interest	
Tax-exempt interest	
Ordinary dividends	
Qualified dividends	
Taxable refunds or credits of state and local income taxes	
Alimony received	
Business income or loss	
Short-term capital gain or loss	
Long-term capital gain or loss	
Other gains or losses	
Taxable IRA distributions	
Taxable pension and annuity distributions	
Income from Schedule E	
Farm income or loss	
Unemployment compensation	
Taxable Social Security benefits	
Other income	
Total	**$ -**

Reprinted with permission of KJE Computer Solutions, LLC

Your Adjustments

The second worksheet will help you gather information related to what the IRS calls your adjustments—those items that shelter your income. To begin, click the "Adjustments" tab in Chapter 5 Spreadsheets or use the worksheet below.

Use the definitions below or on the calculator itself for any items you are not certain of. You might also look at your last year's tax return or consult tax guides or professionals if you are unsure whether and how an adjustment will affect you.

Adjustments that a semi-retiree might commonly encounter include:

Health Savings Account (HSA) deduction. Enter the amount you have contributed to your HSA, if you have a high-deductible health insurance plan of this type. You can now contribute the maximum amount ($2,850 per year for singles, $5,650 for couples and families, and an additional $800 for those over 55), regardless of the exact size of your HSA-compatible policy's deductible.

Self-employment tax. If you own a profitable business and you've paid self-employment tax this year, then you will have been paying the equivalent of both an employer's and an employee's contribution (your self-employment tax is the Social Security and Medicare tax you pay on the profits from self-employment). As a result, you can deduct the employer's portion, equal to one-half of the total self-employment tax you've paid. The calculator will do this for you.

Self-employed health insurance. If you are self-employed and your sole proprietorship or partnership is profitable, you can also have your business purchase health insurance and deduct the premium here. Note that if you purchase the policy personally, it may not be fully deductible under new IRS rules. This is an example of how keeping a separate checking account for your business, possibly including the phrase "DBA (doing business as) company name" can help things run more smoothly for you.

IRA deduction. If you have a profitable business or other earned income, you can contribute up to a maximum of $5,000 for tax year 2008 to a traditional IRA and deduct that contribution here.

Self-employed SEP, SIMPLE, 401(k)s and similar retirement plans. If your business has set up such a plan, you would enter any contributions you have made during the year.

Your Adjustments

Type of Adjustment	Amount
Certain business expenses (see Form 2106)	
Health Savings Account (HSA) deduction	
Moving expenses	
One-half of self-employment tax	
Contributions to self-employed SEP, SIMPLE, and 401(k) or similar plans	
Self-employed health insurance deduction	
Penalty on early withdrawal of savings	
Alimony paid	
Tax-deductible contribution to IRA	
Student loan interest deduction	
Jury duty pay you have made to your employer	
Other	
Total:	**$ -**

Reprinted with permission of KJE Computer Solutions, LLC

Your Itemized Deductions

This worksheet will help you gather information needed to calculate your itemized deductions. To begin, click the "Deductions" tab in Chapter 5 Spreadsheets or use the worksheet below.

Typical deductions that semi-retirees are eligible for include:

Taxes you paid. These include local property taxes for homeowners, and the greater of either sales taxes you paid or state income taxes paid. Go to www.irs.gov to see the standard sales tax deduction for someone with your income. If you think your actual spending is higher, use your records of your spending to support a claim for higher amounts of sales tax paid during the year.

Mortgage interest paid. This can be quite a large deduction if you hold a mortgage on your home.

Charitable donations. Remember to carefully document your charitable contributions to qualified organizations.

Tax preparation fees. If you use an accountant or buy a book or software to help prepare your personal tax return you can deduct the fee. Checks written to financial advisers are also deductible here.

Your Deductions

Type of Deduction	Amount
Medical and dental expenses	
Taxes you paid	
Mortgage interest you paid	
Investment interest you paid	
Gifts to charity	
Casualty and theft losses	
Job expenses	
Investment expenses and tax preparation fees	
Other	
Total	-

Reprinted with permission of KJE Computer Solutions, LLC

Your Tax Credits

Finally, the Tax Credits worksheet will help you gather the data needed to complete your tax estimate. To begin, click the "Tax Credits" tab in Chapter 5 Spreadsheets or use the worksheet below.

Tax credits come directly off your tax bill. A tax deduction of $1,000 reduces your taxable income by $1,000—meaning someone in the 15% tax bracket saves $150 in taxes. A tax credit, however, directly reduces your final tax bill by the amount of the credit. So a $1,000 tax credit reduces your taxes by $1,000.

Semi-retirees might be eligible for some of the following credits:

Foreign tax credit. If your mutual funds hold international stocks or bonds, the funds will supply you, generally in February of each year, with a statement of foreign taxes paid.

Child and dependent credit. You may get a credit for payments for child care, but the credit is subject to certain limitations and phaseouts as income rises.

Child tax credit. All parents of dependent children are entitled to this credit ($1,000 for each child). You do not need to enter it into the calculator; it will be automatically computed from the information you enter about your dependents.

Residential and hybrid vehicle credit. If you bought an eligible hybrid car or made alternative energy improvements to your home, claim your credit here. Consult the sellers of these products and services for details of the tax credit.

Your Tax Credits

Type of Tax Credit	Amount
Foreign tax credit	
Child and dependent care credit	
Credit for the elderly or disabled	
Education credits	
Retirement savings contributions credit	
Residential energy and hybrid vehicle tax credit	
Child tax credit	
Child tax credit received previously	
Credits from Forms 8839 (Adoption), 8839 and 8859	
Other credits including credit for prior year AMT (Form 8801)	
Total:	-

Reprinted with permission of KJE Computer Solutions, LLC

Calculating Your Tax

After you've gathered all of your information using the four worksheets above, go to http://turbotax.intuit.com/tax_help/tax_calculators/ tax_estimator.jhtml and enter your data into the calculator. In addition to areas for income, deductions, credits and adjustments, you will be prompted to fill in other basic family information and other items triggered by your specific tax situation, which will give you an accurate picture of your tax liability. Click the "?" character to the right of any item for a pop-up window explaining the item.

RESOURCE

- www.fairmark.com: An authoritative insider's site for all things tax-related: tax changes, financial details, detailed scenarios and explanations, law, and background information on tax issues. Used by accountants, but clear enough for non-professionals.
- www.Money.cnn.com/pf/taxes: This professional site has plenty to offer on personal finance topics. The link will take you directly to the tax subsection, which has a good breaking news page.
- www.Marketwatch.com (from Dow Jones): Click the personal finance tab to view general or tax-specific articles. This is a high-quality site with strong reporting and deep content. And like Money.com, it's highly readable. This site also contains some good small business content.
- www.smallbusinessreview.com: A high-quality free site with topics of interest to small business owners.
- www.entrepreneur.com/tax: Contains useful articles about tax issues facing small business.
- www.irs.gov: From the people who make it all possible. A good place to download forms and find calculators and up-to-date information on tax law changes.

Enjoying Your Retirement

Scaling back from full-time work, especially while you're still in your 40s or 50s, is an incredible opportunity. If offers you the time and resources to invest in doing things you feel are important and worthwhile, instead of constantly working on someone else's agenda. It lets you set about solving some of the great questions of human existence: how to be happy and maybe help some of those around you to be happier, too.

Yet it may not be easy to take advantage of this opportunity. You'll change routines and may miss the camaraderie or intellectual stimulation that work gave you. You may feel less financially secure or feel guilt, boredom, or loss of status. These are all normal experiences for anyone who transitions from an active work-based life to a less structured lifestyle. Resources have been developed to help you make that transition, and this chapter will point you to several.

Many traditional retirees who retire at age 65 or older simply move along onto life's next stage. They may have been quite happy with their work lives and aren't particularly looking for something different or more fulfilling.

People who want to semi-retire, however, usually have different feelings and motivations. Some leave their careers early because of discouragement or frustration; others seek a deeper and more fulfilling engagement in life. The path to semi-retirement involves change: rethinking the way life has been and reorganizing it around new activities, schedules, and even values. This chapter will help get you started down the path of self-discovery. You'll look more deeply into your motivation to semi-retire and connect to your core purpose. If you're open to changing—even reinventing your life—you'll find exercises here that can help you figure out where you stand and where you might want to go.

In this chapter you'll:

- learn about some common troubles that affect many semi-retirees
- use strategic planning techniques to help decide how to better focus on your interests and values, and

- create a visual map of the current state of your life, plotting your happiness and satisfaction along nine dimensions—from your financial well-being to how much fun you have in your life, to how happy you are with your health.

The worksheets and exercises in this chapter are designed to help you start creating a fulfilling retirement—one that's built on your unique situation and needs. Investing some time in these worksheets can help you sift through your choices. You'll emerge with more clarity about what's important to you—and the steps you can take to ensure that more of your time gets spent on the right things.

RESOURCE

Semi-Retirement foibles. You may have days when you wonder whether semi-retirement is such a good idea after all. Sometimes you just need a good laugh and a reminder that others have walked this road and survived to joke about it.

- You'll always find kindred spirits to discuss your concerns with at www.early-retirement.org/forums, where all things early and semi-retirement get discussed 24/7.
- *How to Retire Happy, Wild, and Free: Retirement Wisdom That You Won't Get from Your Financial Advisor,* by Ernie Zelinski, will help you find fun and motivation in retirement. It's sure to get you laughing.

Semi-Retirement: What to Expect

Don't be surprised if you have some trouble adjusting to your more leisurely lifestyle. Based on my own experiences and those of the many semi-retirees I've met in the course of living this path and writing about it, I think it's likely that you'll pass through several stages on the road to creating your life in semi-retirement.

Stage 1. The first few months: school's out!

The first few months of semi-retirement are often marked by emotional highs and lows. Along with a euphoric sense of freedom, you start to do some of the things you always promised yourself you'd do as soon as you got the chance. But when you find they are done within a few weeks, you may start to wonder what can possibly come next and begin planning new projects or making a lot of long lists. Here are a few other things you might catch yourself doing in those first months of semi-retirement:

- Launch into a flurry of redecorating or furniture rearranging in some part of your house.
- Begin major excavations in the yard or start building a new deck.
- Surf the Internet to your heart's content, digging into the minutiae of Costa Rican real estate markets, analyzing all the various cell phones and plans, or visiting chat rooms to discuss your favorite hobbies with the other four people in the world who share your interest.
- Catalogue your music or photo collections.
- Make a list of friends you always wanted to have lunch with during your work years, but couldn't find the time, then work methodically through it as if it were your old job.
- Sign up for several adult education classes.
- Panic the first time you realize that you haven't made any income that week, and that after years of saving you're going to have to withdraw some money.
- Have a relaxed midday meal while everyone else is at work— and experience a giddy sense of playing hooky.
- Offer "helpful" advice to your partner or spouse on more efficient ways to conduct daily activities.

Stage 2.   One to five years: adjusting to your new world

The second stage is spent grappling with the bigger changes happening in your life. You may wonder who the scruffy-looking person looking back at you in the mirror is, or wonder how your ever used to dress for work and make it into an office on time every day. You start to explore the potential of your semi-retirement, but you aren't immune to some semi-retirement time-sinks, either. With plenty of free time you realize you can really get clear now about how best to spend your frequent flier miles and where to find the best deals in duct tape or anti-static dryer sheets. You may also:

- Research a survivalist colony in the mountains out west where people are known to live on $40 per month.
- Panic as you see your portfolio value drop, or find yourself starting to overspend your safe withdrawal amount—and then console yourself by scouring the house for loose coins and packing them into rolls to change at the bank.
- Go a few days forgetting to shower or get dressed.
- Start collecting zero-percent credit card offers, and juggling the balances for fun and profit.
- Begin saving and using coupons, perhaps for the first time in your life.
- Start taking regular afternoon naps.
- Discover the joys of $5 red wines and $3 white wines.
- Stay out of local stores during the day for fear someone will think you're unemployed.

Stage 3. Five years and beyond: sustaining a new equilibrium

After a few years of early or semi-retirement, along with the newfound financial prudence and frugality, you likely will have begun discovering some entirely new interests that start to take a substantial amount of your time. During this stage, you might also:

- Discover the joys of camping in national parks for a month or more.
- Have old friends or your physician remark on how much healthier or happier—maybe even younger—you look.
- Get caught in a rush-hour traffic jam and realize that you used to do this every day.
- Notice with calm detachment your peers becoming more financially successful, steaming along in suits, cutting deals, and typing into their BlackBerries.
- Realize that you haven't hurried anywhere in a really long time.

- Make new friends whom you never would have met back in your fast-lane years.
- Find that you've become uncompromising on getting a full night's sleep.

Get Yourself Some Energy

Without a solid store of personal and physical energy, it's nearly impossible to get through the day without feeling tired and crabby let alone embark on any meaningful undertaking in life. Generating sufficient energy means you can say "yes" to a spouse or child instead of ignoring them or wishing they would go away, so relationships can move forward and thrive. Having enough energy to care about fixing something rather than just slapping a band-aid on it or hoping the issue will resolve itself means that you stay on top of your physical environment and have confidence that you can resolve issues that may arise in your work, relationships, or daily life. You feel good because you're accomplishing things you care about, and your good feelings keep you healthy and give you more energy.

Diet, exercise, friendships, activities, physical environment, financial condition, overall health, attitude, and spiritual practices all play a role in creating and sustaining your energy level. By making it a habit to do things that restore and enhance your energy, you will be better equipped to follow the steps to financial independence and semi-retirement outlined in this book—and have plenty of energy left over to share.

Making Your Retirement Count

You've worked and planned a long time for semi-retirement. Now that you've finally arrived you'll want to take plenty of time to relax and start knocking off a lot of to-do list items around the house. These activities are understandable and important, and should rightly take up the first months—or even year or two—of your early retirement.

But once that period passes, you'll need more to keep you fulfilled. This is when, if you haven't already, you can start to spend your newfound time in ways that could lead you closer to an avocation, a purpose, or a long-dormant calling.

Psychologist Abraham Maslow, borrowing from Kurt Goldstein, described the fruits of this quest as self-actualization—the highest state of human evolution in his "hierarchy of needs." You've probably heard the term before, but what does it really mean? Maslow explained it this way: "A musician must make music, an artist must paint, a poet must write, if he is to be ultimately happy. What a man can be, he must be. This need we may call self-actualization .... This tendency might be phrased as the desire to become ... everything that one is capable of becoming."

Self-actualization—becoming all that we were meant to be—has a rightness about it that can also be experienced as being in a "flow." When you're in the flow, events happen naturally and almost effortlessly. Resources become available to help you, strength is found, and great feats of physical or mental achievement might even occur. Or maybe nothing quite so dramatic happens—you're in the park with your family or friends, the sun is shining, the dogs are playing, and you're just experiencing a magical feeling of camaraderie and well-being. Most of us have had these kinds of experiences—our best work and happiest moments can seem to be frozen in time. They may have lasted hours or even days, but the sense of total absorption in the moment erased time. This is the feeling of self-actualization. These experiences are available to anyone, but you as a semi-retiree have built-in advantages when it comes to finding ways to exist more frequently in this state: freedom and time.

Now that you're removed from the structures of full-time work, you have the flexibility to explore new sides of yourself outside the glaring lights of community opinion or expectations. If you want to explore your new feelings through poetry, now you can curl up with a book in a sunny window and browse or scribble. If you know you get a buzz of clarity and flow from taking hour-long walks every day, you have the freedom and time to make them happen. As a semi-retiree you have the precious gift of time to explore, discover, and develop that sense of flow.

The exercises below may help you uncover where you are being tugged, where your flow or self-actualization may be found, maybe even hidden in plain sight. The more you can work with your feelings in this area, the more confident you'll become about what you want to change, and why. This helps build the basis for action and the steps that follow, sustaining you as you begin living your life in a new way, on purpose.

Strategic Planning for Your Life

Business schools thrive by teaching MBA students and executives how to strip a company's many complexities down to a few essentials and emerge with a handful of golden insights about which initiatives to invest in, which to walk away from, and how to articulate a compelling mission for the years ahead. Get it right, and the organization thrives and evolves to a bright future. Ignore planning, and it seems to simply muddle along in a tragicomic shuffle—sticking one foot out, then shooting at it, sticking the other foot out, tripping over the first, and taking the gun out again to take aim.

Strategic planning can be valuable for individuals, too. It helps you look at your own life and decide what's important and why. Once you have a plan or goal for how you want to live your life, then bold ideas can take root, and actions will follow with just a little nudging. The following exercises are adaptations of the sorts of processes corporations go through as they aim for long-term success, and the same principles can apply to you personally. Start by answering the following questions, either here or using the Strategic Planning worksheet on the attached CD-ROM.

Strategic Planning for Your Life

1. What do I value?

Start with your values as the truest guide to your feelings and source of your purpose. You will probably have many things you value, and some of them may appear to have little to do with semi-retirement. Write them down anyway, and patterns may start to emerge. Try not to get stuck just with the big ideas—virtue, honesty, integrity, and the like—important as they may be. Go further, for instance, by visualizing a situation that would make you feel good, where all the parts line up as somehow special and even extraordinary. Then tease apart the different pieces there to see why it felt so right, and each of these will be another facet of your values.

Here is a simple example to help "tease" your values out of an image or fantasy you are particularly drawn to. Imagine that you summon up an image of your perfect home. You can see it now—a small cottage sitting in a lush garden—and you experience the peace and sense of homecoming you can imagine feeling there. As you examine this fantasy, you start to realize that the garden is appealing not only for its beauty, but also for the satisfaction you get from the gardening itself; you enjoy planning, planting, nurturing, and pruning plants, and creating a peaceful environment for meditation for yourself and others. Some of your values become apparent—a desire to be outdoors, a need for sanctuary, the willingness to work to create it, and an interest in sharing it.

Next you examine the home itself. It's not large, but it is well constructed, a natural part of the landscape, and made of traditional materials. You realize that you value something being right-sized rather than large and that a few carefully chosen possessions are okay for you, rather than having lots of material stuff. Because you know that this home is not going to be low-maintenance—that it will be a place you live in and care for, as opposed to a place you lock and leave—you understand that having a comfortable home matters more to you than the freedom to wander. And the preponderance of natural materials suggests you may value traditional aesthetics over modern technology and efficiency.

Of course, going through this exercise may lead you to understand that while you enjoy looking at or dreaming about a traditional cottage in a garden, you actually don't want to do the work involved in owning one, and that you actually value the freedom and simplicity of a less-aesthetic but higher-tech and trouble-free existence. Either way, the exercise helps you get closer to what you value so that you can start to make choices about how to spend your time in the next stage of your life.

_____

_____

_____

_____

_____

_____

2. **What do I aspire to?**

    Here, let your answers flow quickly. Write down the first few things that come to you. What do you want, either in the short term or in the future? Both are instructive because our short-term aspirations can be small steps that lead us to our longer-term aspirations. What would make you feel like a success?

    _____

    _____

    _____

    _____

    _____

    _____

3. **Are my aspirations consistent with my values?**

    Here's your chance to do a little analysis by comparing your values to your aspirations. If you find a meaningful mismatch, it will be interesting to dig more deeply into the reasons. Are there any values or aspirations you feel vaguely embarrassed by or that you might be starting to outgrow?

    _____

    _____

    _____

    _____

    _____

    _____

4. **What do I actually spend my time doing?**

Look at your most recent to-do lists and calendar or date book to get an idea of how you spend your time. Look beyond these lists, too. Are you taking steps on any long-term projects? What is really filling up your time that doesn't appear on your lists?

_____

_____

_____

_____

5. **Am I doing things that no longer feel right?**

Look at your response to the previous question and compare your aspirations to how you actually spend your time. People may aspire to such things as wisdom or living a healthful, peaceful existence, but their actions can be leading them to completely different ends. As John Lennon said, "Life is what happens to you while you're making other plans." Make a list of the bigger things you're doing that don't feel right or don't match anything you feel is particularly important.

_____

_____

_____

_____

6. **How can I spend more time doing what I care about?**

What activities or behaviors that no longer feel right (from the previous question) can you drop from your life to make room for more important things?

_____

_____

_____

Now, it's time for some tactical planning. Ask yourself what exactly you would need to do to disengage from or minimize some of the things filling up your days and spend more time doing what you care about. What do you need to do to close the gap between what you want to do and what you're actually doing? Write down three concrete steps and commitments now that will get you moving in the right direction.

Example 1: Jim wants to spend more time in nature. He decides to start working in a community garden and joins a local hiking club.

Example 2: Lauren wants more free time to spend with family. She feels that an extra half-hour each day would make a big difference in her family life. She decides to eliminate a committee involvement that she's outgrown and to leave work a little earlier each day.

1. _____

2. _____

3. _____

Which of the three items you wrote above are open to you now based on your skills, location, contacts, or knowledge? If none are available, or the only available options seem too difficult, keep thinking of more options. Frame them in positive terms by focusing on what you can do as opposed to what you can't do. Imagine the benefits of the change, as if it had already happened, as a way of convincing yourself that giving up something else might well be worth the sacrifice in order to make the shift. Be creative and open-minded about ways to stir up your current commitments, and think of small steps that are more easily achievable and would move you toward your goal.

_____

_____

_____

_____

_____

As in all good strategic planning processes, you'll want to digest the information for a while. In one week, come back to what you wrote here and see how you feel about it. If possible, share your process and findings with a trusted friend or your partner or spouse. Make some exploratory steps toward change. Then go back through the process again. With luck your answers and the actions that flow from them will become more complete and effective each go-round and you'll find yourself creating opportunities and making choices that will increasingly align your actions and values. This will bring more richness and satisfaction to your life.

RESOURCE

The Spirit of Retirement: Creating a Life of Meaning and Personal Growth, by James Autry, is about finding happiness and purpose in retirement, including lots of exercises and encouragement to reflect.

Retire Smart, Retire Happy: Finding Your True Path in Life, by Nancy K. Schlossberg.

How to Enjoy Your Retirement (3rd Edition) Activities from A to Z, by Tricia Wagner and Barbara Day. If you simply can't think of what to do with your newfound free time, then check out this book—guaranteed to help you get off the couch or away from the computer and into something more fun.

Finally, see the resources section at the end of Chapter 1 for links to three services that offer online planning tools and strategies to navigate the transition to semi-retirement.

Exploring the Nine Dimensions of Your Life: The Wheel

Let's turn to an exercise that will give you a snapshot of your life right now: an overall picture across nine principal spokes of a wheel (or dimensions) of your life. If the ancient Greek aphorism "Know thyself" has lasted this long, there must be something to it; this exercise can help you get there. You might even try answering the questions twice— once as you are today, and once as you were either at a certain point in the past or as you would hope to be in the future. Comparing your answers in this way can make the snapshots more instructive by giving you a clear sense of where you are changing or might need to change.

The nine dimensions (discussed below) are:

- avocation
- community/service
- relationships
- spirit
- health
- fun
- achievement
- material
- financial

Each dimension covers a major area of your life. The descriptions are designed to get you thinking and writing about your feelings and experiences. After you read each description, you'll be asked a series of questions. Write your answers, draw a picture, or jot down anything that comes up when you think about the questions (you may think of a movie or an old friend, for example). Give yourself plenty of room to explore the questions in idiosyncratic or creative ways. You can also use The Wheel worksheet on the attached CD-ROM to record your answers.

After you answer the questions, you'll choose a number on a scale of one to ten to represent how fulfilled or happy you are with this area of your life. At the end of this exercise, you'll plot these numbers on a wheel to visually depict how satisfied you are with your life right now.

The more time you spend on this exercise—taking time to probe, write, and reflect on the questions for each dimension—the more you'll learn. Keeping and re-reading your thoughts on each spoke can help you identify your values, unanswered aspirations, resentments, or frustrations as well as help you find a quiet sense of what is working. These insights are the coin of the realm during any life transition, particularly one such as semi-retirement where you have plenty of latitude to make changes and to create a more satisfying life.

Exploring the Nine Dimensions of Your Life: The Wheel

Spoke 1. Avocation

Your avocation is work you care about; constructive, creative work you would do even if you didn't get paid (something more than just sitting on the couch watching football games or going to amusement parks). But avocation isn't always quite so lofty—after all, you may need income from this work to support yourself in semi-retirement. When you're following your avocation, though, you feel lots of support, the work flows easily, and you may get kudos from others as they realize how naturally and effectively you are able to do this work. Your avocation won't always be set in stone or tied to one activity. As your life evolves, your understanding of your avocation may change.

1. How do you feel or react when you think about your avocation? How would you describe your avocation, or ideal work?

    Example: I feel panic and resentment when I think about my avocation because I don't know what my avocation is. It feels like I'm stuck doing work that I don't think is important but that earns me a living. I feel envious of people who love their work. I wish I'd had better career counseling or more courage to follow my heart when I was in college, instead of pursuing "practical" jobs. If I didn't have to worry about money, though, I guess I've always been intrigued by camping and backpacking. I guess if I were able to go backpacking several times a year that would come as close to a perfect life as I could imagine.

    _____

    _____

    _____

    _____

    _____

    _____

    _____

    _____

    _____

    _____

    _____

2. **What would you like to be doing in the area of avocation that you're not currently doing?**

   Example: Well, I guess I'd like to figure out what my avocation really is … and to think more about backpacking as an avocation. There might be other ideas, though. I'm confused and would like more clarity in this area.

   _____

   _____

   _____

   _____

   _____

   _____

   _____

3. **What are two personal goals related to your avocation?**

   Example: Figure out what it is or what they are, and then start taking steps to work it into a semi-retirement income stream without ruining the fun that drew me to it in the first place.

   _____

   _____

   _____

   _____

   _____

   _____

4. **What five concrete things can you do to move forward in this area? (Don't worry if your ideas don't seem directly connected to your goals—just write down whatever comes to you.)**

   Example: 1. Meet some people who backpack for a living. 2. Take a really long hiking trip this summer and stay out on the trail for at least three weeks. 3. Explore other possible avocation areas, especially something related to camping and the outdoors. 4. Meet other people who share my interests. 5. Subscribe to backpacking magazines and maybe write an article for one.

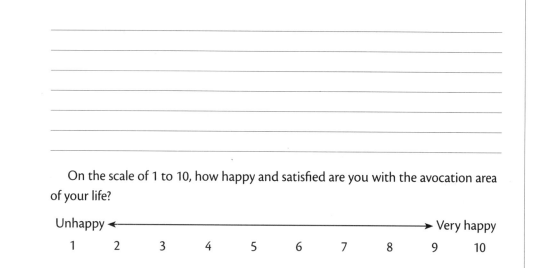

On the scale of 1 to 10, how happy and satisfied are you with the avocation area of your life?

Unhappy ⟵——————————————————————⟶ Very happy

1   2   3   4   5   6   7   8   9   10

Spoke 2. Community and Service

We are all part of many types of communities, whether professional, local, interest-based, or even online. Our communities help us realize that we are not alone, and they are very important to our long-term happiness. Though we may change friends and communities in semi-retirement, turning into a modern-day hermit is all too easy—don't let it happen.

One good way to support our communities is by helping other members, whether they're in acute need or just people in your neighborhood who need a little something. Charitable contributions can also be a form of service. Or service can simply stem from your stage in life—for example, as you become an elder in society, others may turn to you for support and wisdom. Ideally, service forms a type of bond where all parties grow and benefit.

RESOURCE

Community involvement and volunteering supports good physical and mental health among retirees and others. You can read more on the U.S. government's volunteering site www.getinvolved.gov.

1. What communities do you belong to? How do you feel or react when you think about community and service?

   _____

   _____

   _____

   _____

   _____

2. What would you like to be doing in this area of your life that you're not currently doing?

   _____

   _____

   _____

   _____

   _____

3. What are two personal goals in the area of community and service?

   _____

   _____

   _____

4. What five concrete things can you do to move forward in the area of community and service? (Don't worry if your ideas don't seem directly connected to your goals—just write down whatever comes to you.)

   _____

   _____

   _____

   _____

   On the scale of 1 to 10, how happy and satisfied are you with your involvements in community and your ability to be of service to others around you?

   Unhappy ◄——————————————————► Very happy

     1   2   3   4   5   6   7   8   9   10

Spoke 3. Relationships

Relationships are about being present with and available to others—your loving partner, children, friends (old and new), or family. Wherever we are, we can improve our relationships by helping others to build genuine trust in us, learning to trust others, being vulnerable, and mastering our fears of closeness with others. We can develop a healthy attitude of forgiveness and kindness. It's no secret that a strong web of relationships helps people live long and happy lives in retirement.

1. How do you feel about the relationships in your life?

    _____

    _____

    _____

    _____

    _____

    _____

    _____

    _____

2. What would you like to be doing in the area of relationships that you're not currently doing?

    _____

    _____

    _____

    _____

    _____

    _____

    _____

3. What are two personal goals related to relationships?

    _____

    _____

    _____

    _____

4. What five concrete things can you do to move forward in the area of relationships? (Don't worry if your ideas don't seem directly connected to your goals—just write down whatever comes to you.)

_____

_____

_____

_____

_____

_____

_____

On the scale of 1 to 10, how happy and satisfied are you with the depth and quality of the relationships in your life?

Unhappy ⟵—————————————⟶ Very happy

  1   2   3   4   5   6   7   8   9   10

Spoke 4. Spirit

Do you have a lively internal life? It may help to follow spiritual practices, enjoy religious involvement if you're drawn that way, or simply to develop the habit of introspection and thoughtfulness. Through these practices, we can learn to master our anger and baser instincts, carry love in our hearts as a habit, and over time develop something that humans have traditionally recognized as wisdom. Practices related to this spoke can help us move past old hurts and reactive thinking and gain inner clarity and kindness.

1. How do you feel about spiritual matters? What sort of spiritual practice or activities are important to you, if any?

_____

_____

_____

_____

_____

_____

2. What would you like to be doing in the area of spirit and spiritual matters that you're not currently doing?

_____

_____

_____

_____

_____

3. What two things would you like to change about your spiritual life or your involvement in spiritual matters?

_____

_____

_____

_____

4. What five tangible steps could you take to make the spiritual dimension of your life more meaningful? (Don't worry if your ideas don't seem directly connected to your goals—just write down whatever comes to you.)

_____

_____

_____

_____

_____

On the scale of 1 to 10, how happy and fulfilled are you in matters relating to the spiritual dimension in your life?

Unhappy ←——————————————————————→ Very happy

| 1 | 2 | 3 | 4 | 5 | 6 | 7 | 8 | 9 | 10 |

Spoke 5. Health

No surprises here. Staying healthy means attending to diet and exercise, getting appropriate medical care and preventive check-ups, and exercising prudence in your daily activities. You needn't become an organic-shopping ironman vegan—your idea of fun may be a day of hiking followed by a big spread of gourmet food. Just listen to your body, know the risks, and make sensible choices.

1. How do you feel about matters of health, fitness, or weight?

   _____

   _____

   _____

   _____

   _____

2. What would you like to be doing in the health and fitness area of your life that you're not currently doing?

   _____

   _____

   _____

   _____

   _____

3. What are two personal goals in the area of health and fitness?

   _____

   _____

   _____

4. What five concrete things can you do to move forward in the area of your physical vigor and health? (Don't worry if your ideas don't seem directly connected to your goals—just write down whatever comes to you.)

   _____

   _____

   _____

   _____

   On the scale of 1 to 10, how happy and satisfied are you with your health and physical condition?

   Unhappy ←————————————————————→ Very happy

   1   2   3   4   5   6   7   8   9   10

Spoke 6. Fun

Fun can be unstructured, unsought, unscheduled serendipity. Or it can be the result of careful planning and great expense. Fun needn't be explained or justified (as long as it doesn't involve hurting others)—if you love to do it, that is enough. Fun is our birthright, as essential to our full human experience as air and water. Retirees who forget about fun are setting themselves up for a pretty long and miserable trudge through their remaining decades. Along with the fun you plan, don't forget to do things that are just spontaneous, too. Sometimes you need to invest a fair amount of time and effort learning something for the real fun to pay off—learning a musical instrument, for example.

1. What feelings or reactions do you have to the whole notion of having more fun?

_____

_____

_____

_____

_____

2. What are some things you could be doing to have more fun?

_____

_____

_____

_____

_____

3. List two personal goals in this area.

_____

_____

_____

_____

4. List five concrete things that you would like to do for fun—perhaps something you've always wanted to do but haven't tried yet. (Don't worry if your ideas don't seem directly connected to your goals—just write down whatever comes to you.)

_____

_____

_____

_____

_____

On the scale of 1 to 10, how much fun do you have?

Not much fun ◄—————————————————► Lots of fun!

    1   2   3   4   5   6   7   8   9   10

Spoke 7. Achievement

Here, think about your personal sense of accomplishment or mastery in the areas you've chosen as priorities in your life. That may mean achieving a high level of specialized skill or knowledge, gaining respect or status in the community, or achieving a measure of control over your schedule and the daily ebb and flow of your life. It may also mean raising a family of well-adjusted people who are able to go into the world and engage it successfully. Your yardstick for achievement or success is uniquely yours.

1. What feelings or reactions do you have to achieving and success?

    _____

    _____

    _____

    _____

    _____

2. What would you like to be doing in this area of your life that you're not currently doing?

    _____

    _____

    _____

    _____

    _____

3. What are two personal goals that, if you accomplished them, would help you feel that you had achieved something important?

    _____

    _____

    _____

4. What five concrete things can you do move closer to feeling successful in your own eyes? (Don't worry if your ideas don't seem directly connected to your goals—just write down whatever comes to you.)

    _____

    _____

    _____

    _____

    _____

On the scale of one to 10, how successful and accomplished do you feel you are?

Not very successful ⟵——————————————⟶ Very successful

| 1 | 2 | 3 | 4 | 5 | 6 | 7 | 8 | 9 | 10 |

Spoke 8. Material

Everyone needs enough of the right sorts of things to feel comfortable and fulfilled. This is the material dimension—living in a pleasing physical environment in the place you are drawn to, having a home that supports your state of mind, keeping it uncluttered (if you want to), or having the stuff you need to do the things you want to do. It is related to having enough money (Spoke 9), but represents something more tangible—relating to the physical place you inhabit and your sense of peace and belonging in that place. Money alone won't buy this.

1. How do you feel or react to your physical surroundings?

    _____

    _____

    _____

    _____

2. What would you like to do in the area of your physical possessions and material surroundings that is different from what you are doing now?

_____

_____

_____

_____

3. List two personal goals in the material dimension of your life.

_____

_____

_____

4. What five concrete things can you do to move forward in the material dimension of your life? (Don't worry if your ideas don't seem directly connected to your goals— just write down whatever comes to you.)

_____

_____

_____

_____

_____

_____

On the scale of 1 to 10, how happy and satisfied are you with the material landscape of your life?

Unhappy ←————————————————————→ Very happy

  1   2   3   4   5   6   7   8   9   10

Spoke 9. Finances

You want to create enough financial resources in your life to live comfortably within your means. If you are semi-retired, you'll need to save and invest wisely and earn some income, which together will cover your expenses. Here, think about organizing your financial life so that you will be able to afford the things you need or want, and that you are not going to be living with regrets or undue financial uncertainty as you focus less on earning money during semi-retirement.

1. How do you feel about your financial security, wealth, and investing?

   _____

   _____

   _____

   _____

   _____

2. What would you like to be doing in the financial area of your life that you're not currently doing?

   _____

   _____

   _____

   _____

   _____

3. List two personal financial goals.

   _____

   _____

   _____

   _____

4. What five concrete things can you do to move forward in the financial dimension of your life? (Don't worry if your ideas don't seem directly connected to your goals—just write down whatever comes to you.)

   _____

   _____

   _____

   _____

   On the scale of 1 to 10, how happy and satisfied are you with the financial side of your life?

   Unhappy ⟵————————————————⟶ Very happy

   | 1 | 2 | 3 | 4 | 5 | 6 | 7 | 8 | 9 | 10 |

Completing the Picture

Now that you've come this far, the easiest and most fun part of this exercise is ahead of you: Creating a visual representation of your life. To do this, you'll plot the numbers you circled (for each spoke of the wheel) on the graph below, marking the appropriate point on each axis radiating out from the center of the wheel. Do this for each of the nine spokes, and then connect the dots to form a wheel.

What does your wheel look like? Everyone's wheel is lopsided—some are so lopsided that they would never turn, while others would give us a somewhat bumpy ride but at least move us along. Round wheels are a worthwhile goal, but a lopsided wheel is okay too. Only you can decide what is right for you. Your wheel shows how these different parts of your life are working for you now. What dimensions would you like to develop more fully?

Balancing Your Wheel

If you find one or more spokes are out of balance on your wheel, try this four-step process to help you move closer to where you'd like to be:

Accept where you are now. You may have decided how you feel about a particular spoke in haste or upon long deliberation. Either way, take another look at that dimension of your life and see whether the level of satisfaction you circled still feels accurate. Focus on how this area of your life measures up to what's important to you, and don't worry about how you think you measure up to someone else's ideas or cultural expectations. For example, if you're more than a few pounds over the ideal weight prescribed in insurance company charts but you feel robust and healthy, use a number for the health spoke that reflects how you personally feel about your health and vitality. When you feel you have an honest answer, accept it willingly, without shame or reservation. You'll find it easier to make lasting changes in your life once you have an honest, unvarnished understanding of where you stand today.

Think about how you got here. What experiences are shaping your feelings? What have you done or not done to try to make progress in this area in the past? Was there a time when you were more satisfied with this dimension of your life? What was different then? What is blocking you and what is helping you to move forward in this area?

Resolve to make some changes. Write down your commitment to yourself to make progress in this area. It's important to write it down because you'll need a strong resolve to overcome inertia or other blocks that have kept you from making changes in this area of your life. Resolve boosts the priority for an item and brings it to the front of your mind. If you have trouble making a commitment to yourself, it could be because you are not ready to grow and change in this area. If you are truly dissatisfied with this dimension of your life, think about why you haven't been able to change. Give yourself daily reminders that you really want to change.

Monitor your progress. Take concrete steps toward your goal. Take actions, make commitments, join, volunteer, explore, find a place where you can be welcome and effective, and get involved. Then observe your progress. Over the next weeks or months, watch closely to see what is working and what is not working. Continue to bring creativity and fresh ideas to the process and let go of things that aren't working without remorse or reproach. Try new approaches that seem like improvements.

How the Wheel Exercise Helped Me

I did a variation of the wheel exercise in the late 1990s that convinced me I needed to make a drastic change in my life. On the surface, things seemed to be fine. I was succeeding in the business world and holding my family relationships together, but much about my life was stale and flat.

In 1999, my wheel looked like this:

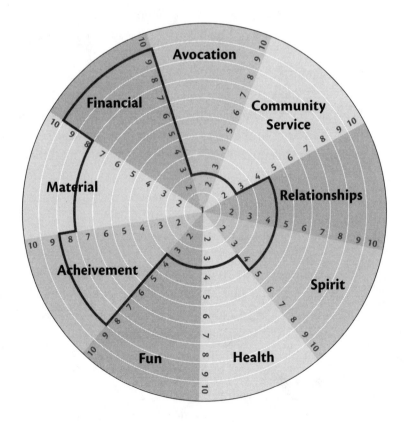

After doing the wheel exercise, it became clear to me that I had been shortchanging everything in my life to stay on top of the achievement, material, and financial dimensions of life. I was working more than 70 hours a week and what little time or energy I had left went to making sure that my kids and wife didn't forget what I looked like. I would also occasionally stumble into the gym or church to keep those sides of my life from flickering out entirely. I had friends at work, of course, but rarely had time to see anyone else. Something had to change.

Now, seven years into semi-retirement, I've been able to take back the time I used to devote to work and spend it on some of the long-neglected areas of my life. Today, I can honestly say that all my dimensions score at least a six. I have been fortunate to discover two avocations—writing and sculpting—and am happy to be able to pursue them both. I can commit time to helping others and being active and effective in my community. I see my children more and have numerous new friendships, though there is always room for more. I have a nearly daily practice of exercise and prayer, and have plenty of time for travel, fun, and hobbies—though I could always use more of those too! I have achieved most of the things that I have ever wanted (though I'm always setting my sights on new vistas) and feel financially secure in semi-retirement. I'm a much happier, relaxed, and fulfilled person today than I was ten years ago.

It is not an accident. The path of semi-retirement is rich with possibilities for you to remake your life, too, to better match your goals and dreams. With time to invest in the areas of life that are important to you, and the resources and peace of mind to provide a secure place from which to reflect and grow, there is no end to what you can accomplish.

You can recreate your life, in whatever way you wish. You can have energy, health, financial resources, and time. In semi-retirement, you can be buoyed by meaningful relationships that you have the time to nourish and keep strong, and you can have the freedom to decide what comes next for you. It is an ideal confluence of conditions in which to grow. It may take some hard work to create it, but once your semi-retirement lifestyle is in place, you'll have an ideal launch pad for the next half of your life.

Good luck to you in your semi-retirement!

In Peace,

Bob Clyatt

bob@workless-livemore.com

Asset Classes and Funds for the Rational Investing Portfolio

Funds for the Rational Investing Portfolio

Equities			
Asset Class	%	Funds (* Denotes index fund)	Notes
U.S. Large Stocks	12%	VG S&P 500 Index (VFINX)	Growth
		VG HealthCare Fund (VGHCX)	70% U.S., 30% Foreign
		VG Windsor II Value (VWNFX)	Active Value Fund
		VG Selected Value (VASVX)	50% Large, 50% Small
		DFA High BtM (DFBMX)*	Enhanced Value Index
		VG Value Index Fund (VIVAX)*	Value Index
U.S. Small Stocks	8.5%	VG Tax-Managed Small (VTMSX)*	Blend of Value and Growth
		VG Small Value Index (VISVX)*	Value
		DFA U.S. Small (DFSCX)*	U.S. Micro Cap; smallest 4%
		DFA U.S. Small Value (DFSVX)*	Value among smallest 8%
International Large Stocks	5%	VG Pacific Index (VPACX)*	Mostly Japan and Australia
		VG Europe Index (VEURX)*	Europe Index
		VG Tax-Managed Int'l (VTMGX)	Blend of Value and Growth
		DFA International Large (DFALX)	Blend, Active Mgmt., low fee
		DFA International Value (DFIVX)	Value, strong compared to DFALX
International Small Stocks	10%	VG International Explorer (VINEX)	Growth
		DFA International Small (DFISX)	Blend
		DFA International Small Value (DISVX)	Value
Emerging Market Stocks	6.5%	VG Emerging Market Index* (VEIEX)	Index
		Emerging Markets Small (DEMSX)	Small Blend
		Emerging Markets Value (DFEVX)	Value
		DFA Emerging Markets Large (DFEMX)	Large Blend

Bonds

Asset Class	%	Funds (* Denotes index fund)	Notes
Short-Term/ Money Market	4%	VG Short-Term Corporate (VFSTX)	Some credit and interest risk
		VG Prime Money (VMMXX)	Money Market
		VG State Tax-Exempt Money Market	If available for your state
Long-Term U.S. Treasury Bonds	4%	U.S. Treasury I-Bonds	Up to $30,000 per year
		VG TIPS Fund (VIPSX)	Hold in IRA
		U.S. Treasuries	Buy through Treasury Direct
U.S. Medium-Term	10%	VG Intermediate Bond Index (VBIIX)*	Corporate
		VG Convertible Securities (VCVSX)	Currently Closed
		CDs	Pentagon Federal, Bank rate
International Medium-Term Bonds	12%	Fidelity New Markets (FNMIX)	Emerging Markets Debt
		DFA Global 2-Year Bond (DFGFX)	Hedged for U.S.D. investors
		PIMCO Foreign Bond (PFUIX)	5-Year Unhedged
		PIMCO Foreign Bond (PFORX)	5-Year Hedged
		T. Rowe Price Int'l Bond (RPIBX)*	Tracks MS International Bond Index
		American Century Int'l Bond (BEGBX) *	Tracks Index, partially hedged
		PIMCO Emerging Markets Bond (PEBIX)	Lower fee than FNMIX
High-Yield Bonds	4%	VG High Yield Corporate (VWEHX)	Higher quality than index
GNMA Mortgage Bonds	5%	VG GNMA Fund (VFIIX)	

Other			
Asset Class	**%**	**Funds (* Denotes index fund)**	**Notes**
Oil & Gas	3%	VG Energy Fund (VGENX)	Broad energy equities
		FBR Natural Gas Index (GASFX)*	For natural gas
		Private investments in oil & gas partnerships	
Market-Neutral	2%	Oppenheimer-Tremont Hedge Fund Index *	
		Rydex SPHINX	See "Descriptions of the Asset Classes," below.
		Other Hedge Fund Investments	Beware high fees in all cases
		Master Limited Partnerships	See "Descriptions of the Asset Classes," below, for examples
Commodities	4%	Oppenheimer Real Assets (QRAAX)*	1.4% fee, overweight Oil
		PIMCO Commodities Fund (PCRIX)*	Preferred
		Physical holdings of Gold	Unique timberland REIT
		Plum Creek Timber REIT (PCL)	
Real Estate	5%	VG REIT Index (VGSIX) *	
		International REITs such as (EGLRX)	
		Private investments in rental property	
Private Equity	5%	Direct illiquid investments in companies and new ventures	See "Descriptions of the Asset Classes," below, for details and examples
		Limited partnership shares in private equity pools/funds	
		Ownership or silent partner in franchise	
		Investments in illiquid public companies	
		Business Development Corporations	

Descriptions of the Asset Classes

Here is a brief description of each of the 16 asset classes that make up the Rational Investing Portfolio. The portfolio is made up of roughly 40% stocks, 40% bonds, and 20% other asset classes to provide broad diversification, good return, and modest volatility.

Stocks

Large U.S. Stocks

Large U.S. Stocks make up a big proportion of the world's stock markets and should be well represented in your portfolio. By favoring value stocks, you put historical returns on your side, as these shares have tended to outperform the average large stock over time.

This was first shown by Eugene Fama of the University of Chicago and DFA and Kenneth French, now at Dartmouth, in their widely cited Three-Factor Model documenting the persistence of premiums for owning high book-to-market or value stocks. Over the years, this disquieting theory that provides a sound theoretical rationale for bad companies' stocks outperforming good companies' stocks has withstood sustained assault, and with minor modifications, still stands.

Use it to add value stocks to equity holdings, gaining a slight performance edge and reducing overall risk or volatility.

Small U.S Stocks

The small-company premium has also been documented by Fama and French as part of their Three-Factor Model. Small companies can still be quite large by most people's standards: They are the smallest 20% of the NYSE firms, sometimes referred to as the CRSP Deciles #9 and #10, as well as smaller publicly traded firms. Even smaller private companies are covered in the Venture Capital/Private Equity segment of the "Other" portion of the Rational Investing Portfolio.

Small companies seem less attractive, less well-known, and more subject to financial fluctuations from external market and competitive conditions. This generally keeps their prices lower for a given dollar of earnings, but as these companies grow or move into favor, they can produce an outsized return for investors.

Whether a small company's shareholder is generously or merely adequately compensated for the additional risk taken on, Rational Investors like the fact that small—and especially small value—stock returns are less correlated with the overall market, reducing volatility in the overall portfolio.

International Stocks: Large, Small, and Emerging Market

Some 60% of the world's equity assets are non-U.S. stocks. The Rational Investing portfolio allocates roughly 45% of equity holdings in International Stocks (21.5% of the overall portfolio) which is aggressive by most Americans' standards but is still less than a true market weighting.

Owning International Stocks gives a portfolio exposure to a different set of risks and thus continues to give diversification benefits.

New studies confirm the traditional wisdom: Over the long run, International Stocks do indeed provide reduced volatility in returns. International Small Company Stocks and Emerging Market Stocks tend to be particularly volatile and less correlated with U.S. stocks, with periods of great performance offset by periods of abysmal performance. Over time, though, the growth in these economies provides not only risk reduction, but strong returns.

Bonds

Short-Term Bonds/Money Market

This is the typical money market fund into which cash is swept or left while awaiting investing, spending, or rebalancing. An alternative that might have slightly higher yield would be Vanguard's Short-Term Investment grade Corporate Bond fund.

Long-Term U.S. Treasury Bonds

For this asset class, buy Treasury Bonds or inflation-adjusted I-Bonds directly through Treasury Direct at www.treasurydirect.gov, buy a

U.S. Treasury bond mutual fund, or buy Treasury Inflation-Protected Securities (TIPS).

For a short while in the late 1990s, TIPS offered a 4% real rate of return that could have given investors a chance to effectively lock in their Safe Withdrawal Rate at no risk. (See Chapter 4 for more on the Safe Withdrawal Rate.) And in retrospect, this could have argued for a massive allocation to TIPS. However, for all the planning and obsession over the 4% Safe Withdrawal Rate, it is designed to keep investors approximately 90% safe. So in the majority of real-world scenarios, a portfolio will do even better than simply keeping up with inflation and allowing the safe withdrawal amount.

Thus, a long-term TIPS-only strategy, while producing 20 or 30 years of carefree time in which you need not think about your portfolio and guarding against the small risk of underperforming, guarantees no real growth either.

Today the point is moot, since TIPS yields are under 2%—far below what most would consider a reasonable Safe Withdrawal Rate. However, if real interest rates rise in the future, the debate will resurface.

One final negative about TIPS: They are taxed on the inflation-appreciation component in their redemption value each year. Thus, if you hold TIPS outside a Roth IRA, you will owe taxes on the inflation-adjustment either annually (for taxable accounts) or whenever you withdraw (from a traditional IRA).

Medium-Term U.S. Bonds

Financial researchers Eugene Fama and David Plecha have shown that the slightly higher yield from long-maturity bonds is not fair compensation for their much higher volatility and risk when interest rates change. Also, medium-term bonds are less correlated with equities than longer term bonds.

By sticking with a blend of two-year and five-year average maturity bonds you can capture the bulk of the yield while still ensuring reasonable protection from rising interest rates. Some investors prefer three-year to six-year CDs instead of bonds in this portion of their portfolio.

International Medium-Term Bonds

Like international stocks, two-year and five-year international bonds give assets held in currencies other than the dollar, which adds to diversification. DFA hedges currency risk in its bond funds, which costs money and takes away this currency diversification benefit. But both PIMCO and American Century offer International Bond funds that are not hedged.

In general, bonds serve to dampen volatility from equity returns, but don't add much to long-term returns.

GNMA Mortgage Bonds

GNMA Bonds are issued by the Government National Mortgage Association, an agency of the U.S. government, and as such are considered to have creditworthiness comparable to U.S. Treasuries. These bonds are less risky than Fannie Mae or Freddy Mac bonds.

Investors' funds have been lent directly to GNMA, which pays a coupon and returns principal and is not affected by individual mortgagees repaying their loans or prepaying their mortgages. GNMA yields tend to be about 0.5% higher than comparable Treasury Bonds.

High-Yield Bonds

This category of fixed income investment bears special mention for two reasons. First, it comes with high annual interest payments. And second, returns tend to be countercyclical, less correlated with other bonds. During periods of rising interest rates, the high-yield market generally does not fall as quickly as other bonds of similar maturity. Likewise, it will not prosper during periods of falling interest rates, but is rather tied to the perceived fortunes of the stock market.

Its uniqueness makes it attractive—and fortunately, Vanguard has a good low-cost fund: High Yield Corporate (VWEHX). This fund will move differently from other high-yield funds in that it invests in only the highest quality high-yield bonds, and thus underperforms the high-yield index in the good years. But it has nowhere near the credit risk and defaults in the tough years—and there are tough years in the high-yield bond segment. Hold high-yield in tax advantaged accounts if possible to reduce taxable income.

Other

Oil and Gas

Energy markets, driven by the prices for oil and gas, are not highly correlated with other asset classes and as such have a place in your portfolio. Ideally, you might be able to directly own partnership shares in an oil or gas producer, lock yourself in for ten or 20 years, and reap a steady, high return. Certainly many investors have been able to follow this script. Unfortunately, others have ended up with dry holes or fast-talking operators who made investor money disappear into thin air. Investigate carefully before buying.

If you don't have access to this type of investment, there are alternatives. In particular, the FBR Gas Index (GASFX) is a mutual fund that gives you pure exposure to the natural gas market which is underrepresented in the commodities indexes relative to its importance in the economy—and the Vanguard Energy Fund (VGENX) can give you focused exposure, albeit via stocks, to the oil and related energy markets.

Market-Neutral Hedge Funds

The hedge fund industry has taken off in recent years among institutional and individual investors alike. Hedge funds tend to attract great fund managers due in no small part to the lure of up to 20% of the profits they make from managing them. The "Market-Neutral" moniker is a catchall for a number of different hedge fund strategies that use esoteric methods to seek profits uncorrelated to stock and bond markets. Several investment strategies are generally grouped under this heading—including index arbitrage, convertible-warrant hedging, merger arbitrage, interest rate arbitrage, Long-Short strategies, and others.

Rather than invest directly in a single hedge fund, you may want to invest in one of the new variety of funds of hedge funds. If you are an accredited investor and can stomach the 1.95% fees on top of the fees the hedge funds themselves charge, then you can invest in the Rydex SPHINX fund of hedge funds that tracks the S&P Hedge Fund Index. Alternately, the Oppenheimer-Tremont unit of CSFB has now lowered to a $50,000 minimum on its Market-Neutral fund of funds. With a 1.96% fee and 5% profit-sharing bonus and a 2.5% load, it is still a bit of a toss-up whether this will be good for investors—and there is little history to go on.

You might also consider investing in Master Limited Partnerships for this part of your portfolio. Often they own pipelines, but are generally not correlated with the oil and gas markets themselves. Possible new funds include Energy Income & Growth (FEN), Fiduciary/Claymore (FMO), Kayne Anderson (KYN), and Tortoise Energy (TYG).

In general, don't invest in hedge funds that simply offer a manager who is talented at picking stocks and bonds. At these fees, you should get something more esoteric than that.

Commodities

It is reasonable to ask whether commodities belong in your portfolio. Traditionally considered too risky for retirees, asset allocators have given them much attention lately due to their occasional high returns and consistently low correlation to equity and bond markets. But until recently, investors who wanted commodities exposure had to either buy stocks in natural resources firms (which would then tend to correlate more closely with stock markets), or invest in futures (complex, high risk, and by nature short-term and high-maintenance).

Both PIMCO and Oppenheimer began offering a unique vehicle a few years ago that directly purchases commodities contracts and Treasury Bonds in the correct proportions to track an index of commodities: the DJ/AIG Commodity Index, or the Goldman Sachs Commodity Index. Although the retail versions of these funds carry loads and high fees, there are ways, through Vanguard and other fund supermarkets, to get into the low-fee, no-load institutional versions of these funds. That brings your fees down within range to consider, though the Oppenheimer fund's fee, QRAAX, is still 1.5% per year; the PIMCO fund's fee, PCRIX, is half that.

A timberland REIT, Plum Creek Timber (PCL), may also offer a way to invest in this high-performing and relatively uncorrelated-to-equities asset class. Timberland is difficult to invest in any other way short of buying into timberland limited partnerships—nearly as difficult and expensive for individuals as buying actual land and arranging to have it managed and harvested.

You may also wish to hold physical stocks of gold coins for the ultimate time-tested safety asset. Precious metals funds are also available with unusual, and for some investors, attractive counter cyclicality and risk reward profiles. Over the long run, these tend to be poor investments, though they do react well as short-term hedges that can be psychologically comforting during market turmoil.

Commercial Real Estate

Direct investment in real estate has been a cornerstone in many early retiree and other wealthy investors' portfolios. If you don't want to make the effort to become a landlord directly, you might try to learn—perhaps from an accountant or financial planner—about becoming part of a limited partnership that invests in commercial real estate such as mini-malls or medical services buildings.

These investments, highly illiquid, have tended to do well for investors through good and bad economic times, but they are hard to find. Until such an opportunity comes along, you can invest in REITs. These are usually best held in your tax-advantaged accounts, since they do tend to throw off relatively large amounts of taxable income. Vanguard's REIT index fund (VGSIX) is simple and inexpensive. International REITs are starting to form, such as Alpine International (EGLRX), that give further diversification into overseas real estate markets.

Beware of viewing the purchase of a second home as a "real estate investment," however. Unless you gain rental income from it on a par with other rental investments, this is an expense, not an asset. Merely hoping for a capital gain does not convert a second home into an investment.

Venture Capital/Private Equity

Investing in small, private firms less correlated with the public stock markets helps add resiliency to your portfolio. A few Private Equity funds have recently gone public and you can now buy into them as easily as buying an ordinary share of any stock or fund, though they remain expensive and unproven investments.

If you are an accredited investor—defined as $1 million of net worth for a couple or $300,000 of annual income for a couple during the past two years—you can try to become a limited partner in a venture capital fund. Alternately, you can make independent angel investments or work with small firms to gain stock or options in their firms as partial payment for your services. A private investment in a small public company (PIPE) could give you the type of preferred stock that big investors tend to favor with more protections than the public common shareholders.

While you wait to be able to assemble these deals, you might choose to invest this allocation in the smallest cap NASDAQ stocks—including pink sheet or OTC NASDAQ stocks. Compared to the effort you will undertake to select and invest in a single private equity deal, the risk and illiquidity you face in a small OTC NASDAQ stock is minor. You may even be able to meet management or get to know the company if it is local, as you would expect to do in any private equity deal in which you invest.

How to Use the CD-ROM

F iles mentioned in this book are included on a CD-ROM in the back of the book. This CD-ROM, which can be used with Windows computers, installs files that you use with software programs that are already installed on your computer. It is not a standalone software program. Please read this appendix and the README.TXT file included on the CD-ROM for instructions on using the Forms CD.

Note to Mac users: This CD-ROM and its files should also work on Macintosh computers. Please note, however, that Nolo cannot provide technical support for non-Windows users.

How to View the README File

If you do not know how to view the file README.TXT, insert the CD-ROM into your computer's CD-ROM drive and follow these instructions.

- Windows 2000, XP, and Vista: (1) On your PC's desktop, double click the My Computer icon; (2) double click the icon for the CD-ROM drive into which the CD-ROM was inserted; (3) double click the file README.TXT.

- Macintosh: (1) On your Mac desktop, double click the icon for the CD-ROM that you inserted and (2) double click the file README.TXT.

While the README file is open, print it out by using the Print command in the File menu.

Three different types of files are on the CD-ROM:

- Financial planning spreadsheets in Microsoft Excel format (XLS), which you can use with Microsoft's Excel or another spreadsheet program that can read XLS files (see "Using the Financial Planning Spreadsheets," below),

- MP3 audio files that you can listen to using your computer's media or MP3 player (see "Listening to the Audio Files," below), and

- PDF files that can be viewed only with Adobe Acrobat Reader 4.0 or higher (see "Printing PDF Files," below). These forms are designed to be printed out and filled in by hand or with a typewriter.

See the end of this appendix for a list of forms, their file names, and their file formats.

Listening Without Installing

If you don't want to copy 41 MB of audio files to your hard disc, you can "play" the CD on your computer. For details, see "Playing the Audio Files Without Installing," below.

Installing the Files Onto Your Computer

Before you can do anything with the files on the CD-ROM, you need to install them onto your hard disk. In accordance with U.S. copyright laws, remember that copies of the CD-ROM and its files are for your personal use only.

Insert the CD and do the following:

Windows 2000, XP, and Vista Users

Follow the instructions that appear on the screen. (If nothing happens when you insert the CD-ROM, then (1) double click the My Computer icon; (2) double click the icon for the CD-ROM drive into which the CD-ROM was inserted; (3) double click the file WELCOME.EXE.)

By default, all the files are installed to the \Retirement Plan Resources folder in the \Program Files folder of your computer. A folder called "Retirement Plan Resources" is added to the "Programs" folder of the Start menu.

Macintosh Users

Step 1: If the "Retirement Plan CD" window is not open, open it by double clicking the "Retirement Plan CD" icon.

Step 2: Select the "Retirement Plan Resources" folder icon.

Step 3: Drag and drop the folder icon onto the icon of your hard disk.

Using the Financial Planning Spreadsheets

This section concerns the files for the financial planning spreadsheets that can be opened and completed with Microsoft's Excel or another spreadsheet program that "understands" XLS files.

These spreadsheets are in Microsoft's Excel format. These files have the extension ".XLS." For example, the Cash Tracking Worksheet discussed in Chapter 2 is one of the tabs in the file Chapter 2 Spreadsheets.xls. All files and their filenames are listed below.

To complete a financial planning spreadsheet you must: (1) open the file in a spreadsheet program that is compatible with XLS files; (2) fill in the needed fields; (3) print it out; (4) rename and save your revised file.

The following are general instructions. However, each spreadsheet program uses different commands to open, format, save, and print documents. Please read your spreadsheet program's manual for specific instructions on performing these tasks.

Step 1: Opening a File

There are three ways to open the spreadsheet files included on the CD-ROM after you have installed them onto your computer.

Windows users can open a file by selecting its "shortcut" as follows: (1) Click the Windows "Start" button; (2) open the "Programs" folder; (3) open the "Retirement Plan Resources" subfolder; (4) click on the shortcut to the spreadsheet you want to work with.

Both Windows and Macintosh users can open a file directly by double clicking on it. Use My Computer or Windows Explorer (Windows 2000, Vista, or XP) or the Finder (Macintosh) to go to the folder in which you installed or copied the CD-ROM's files. Then, double click on the specific file you want to open.

You can also open a file from within your spreadsheet program. To do this, you must first start your spreadsheet program. Then, go to the File menu and choose the Open command. This opens a dialog box where you will tell the program (1) the type of file you want to open (*.XLS); (2) the location and name of the file (you will need to navigate through the directory tree to get to the folder on your hard disk where the CD's files have been installed).

If these directions are unclear you will need to look through the manual for your spreadsheet program—Nolo's technical support department will not be able to help you with the use of your spreadsheet program.

Where Are the Files Installed?

Windows Users
- XLS files are installed by default to a folder named \Retirement Plan Resources in the \Program Files folder of your computer.

Macintosh Users
- XLS files are located in the "Retirement Plan Resources" folder.

Step 2: Entering Information Into the Spreadsheet

Fill in the appropriate information according to the instructions and sample spreadsheets in the book. As you fill in these spreadsheets, numeric calculations are performed automatically.

Step 3: Printing Out the Spreadsheet

Use your spreadsheet program's "Print" command to print out your document.

Step 4: Saving Your Spreadsheet

After filling in the form, use the "Save As" command to save and rename the file. Because all the files are "read-only", you will not be able to use the "Save" command. This is for your protection. If you save the file without renaming it, you will overwrite the original financial planning spreadsheet, and you will not be able to create a new document with this file without recopying the original file from the CD-ROM.

Using Print-Only Files

Electronic copies of useful files are included on the CD-ROM in Adobe Acrobat PDF format. You must have the Adobe Reader installed on your computer to use these files. Adobe Reader is available for all types of Windows and Macintosh systems. If you don't already have this software, you can download it for free at www.adobe.com.

All files, their file names, and their file formats are listed at the end of this appendix.

These files cannot be filled out using your computer. To create your document using these files, you must: (1) open the file; (2) print it out; (3) complete it by hand or typewriter.

Step 1: Opening PDF Files

PDF files can be opened one of three ways. Windows users can open a file by selecting its "shortcut" as follows: (1) Click the Windows "Start" button; (2) open the "Programs" folder; (3) open the "Retirement Plan Resources" subfolder; (4) click the shortcut to the form you want to work with.

Both Windows and Macintosh users can open a file directly by double clicking it. Use My Computer or Windows Explorer (Windows 2000, XP, or Vista) or the Finder (Macintosh) to go to the folder you created and copied the CD-ROM's files to. Then, double click the specific file you want to open.

You can also open a PDF file from within Adobe Reader. To do this, you must first start Reader. Then, go to the File menu and choose the Open command. This opens a dialog box where you will tell the program the location and name of the file. (You will need to navigate through the directory tree to get to the folder on your hard disk where the CD's files have been installed).

Where Are the PDF Files Installed?

Windows Users
- PDF files are installed by default to a folder named \Retirement Plan Resources in the \Program Files folder of your computer.

Macintosh Users
- PDF files are located in the "Retirement Plan Resources" folder.

Step 2: Printing PDF files

Choose Print from the Adobe Reader File menu. This will open the Print dialog box. In the "Print Range" section of the Print dialog box, select the appropriate print range, then click OK.

Step 3: Filling in PDF files

The PDF files cannot be filled out using your computer. To create your document using one of these files, you must first print it out (see Step 2, above), and then complete it by hand or typewriter.

Listening to the Audio Files

This section explains how to use your computer's media player to listen to the audio files. All audio files are in MP3 format. (Most computers come with a media player that plays MP3 files.) For example, "Interview with Bob Clyatt" is on the file ClyattInterview.mp3. At the end of this appendix, you'll see a list of the audio files and their file names.

You can listen to files that you have installed on your computer, or you can listen without having installed the files to your hard disk (see "Playing the Audio Files Without Installing," below).

Please keep in mind that these are general instructions—because every media player is unique, these steps may not mirror the steps you need to follow to use your player.

Please do not contact Nolo's technical support if you are having difficulty using your media player.

Listening to Audio Files You've Installed on Your Computer

There are two ways to listen to the audio files that you have installed on your computer.

Windows users can open a file by selecting its "shortcut" as follows: (1) Click the Windows "Start" button; (2) open the "Programs" folder; (3) open the "Retirement Plan Resources" subfolder; (4) open the "Audio" subfolder; (5) click the shortcut to the audio segment you want to hear.

Both Windows and Macintosh users can open a file directly by double clicking it. Use My Computer or Windows Explorer (Windows 2000, XP, and Vista) or the Finder (Macintosh) to go to the folder in which you installed or copied the CD-ROM's files. Then, double click the MP3 file you want to hear.

Where Are the Audio Files Installed?

Windows Users
- MP3 files are installed by default to a folder named "Audio" within the \ Retirement Plan Resources folder in the \Program Files

Macintosh Users
- MP3 files are located in the "Audio" folder in the "Retirement Plan Resources" folder.

Playing the Audio Files Without Installing

If you don't want to copy 41 MB of audio files to your hard disk, you can "play" the CD on your computer. Here's how:

Window users

Step 1: Insert the Forms CD to view the "Welcome to Retirement Resources CD" window. (If nothing happens when you insert the Forms CD-ROM, double click the My Computer icon, double click the icon for the CD-ROM drive into which the Forms CD-ROM was inserted, and double click the file WELCOME.EXE.)

Step 2: Click "Listen to Audio."

Mac users

Step 1: Insert the Forms CD. If the "Retirement Resources CD" window does not open, open it by double clicking the "Retirement Resources CD" icon.

Step 2: Open the "Audio" folder by double clicking the "Audio" icon.

Step 3: Double click the audio file you want to hear.

List of Files Included on the CD-ROM

The following spreadsheet files are in Microsoft Excel Format (XLS):

File Name	Worksheets Included in File
Ch2Spreadsheets.xls	Cash Tracking Worksheet
	Track Your Spending: Annual Expenses
	Track Your Spending: Month One Expenses
	Track Your Spending: Month Two Expenses
	Track Your Spending: Total Expenses
	Early Retirement Spending
	Total Savings Over Time
	Savings, Income, and Expenses
	Snapshot of Annual Finances in Retirement
	Buying vs. Leasing a Car
Ch3Spreadsheets.xls	Target Asset Allocation: Step 1—List Assets
	Target Asset Allocation: Step 2—Review Asset Allocation
	Target Asset Allocation: Step 3—Plan Transactions
	Portfolio Management Fees
Ch4Spreadsheets.xls	Safe Withdrawal Calculation
	Potential Revenue from Part-Time Work
	Long-Term Planning: Effects of Withdrawals
Ch5Spreadsheets.xls	Your Income
	Your Adjustments
	Your Deductions
	Your Tax Credits
SampleSpreadsheets.xls	Early Retirement Spending
	Total Savings Over Time
	Savings, Income, and Expenses
	Snapshot of Annual Expenses in Retirement
	Target Asset Allocation: Step 1—List Assets
	Target Asset Allocation: Step 2—Review Asset Allocation
	Target Asset Allocation: Step 3—Plan Transactions
	Long-Term Planning: Effects of Withdrawals

The following files are in portable document format (PDF):

File Name	Worksheet
VanguardQuestionnaire.pdf	Vanguard Risk Assessment Questionnaire
SemiRetirement.pdf	Is Semi-Retirement Right for You
Creativity.pdf	Get Going: Accessing Your Creativity
StrategicPlanning.pdf	Strategic Planning for Your Life
Wheel.pdf	Exploring the Nine Dimensions of Your Life: The Wheel

The following files are Audio (MP3):

File Name	Contents
ClyattInterview.mp3	Interview with Bob Clyatt
SholarInterview.mp3	Interview with Bill Sholar

Index

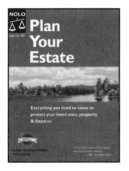

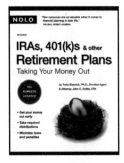

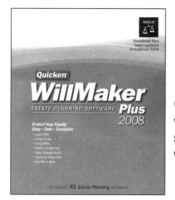

Get the Latest in the Law

Nolo's Legal Updater

We'll send you an email whenever a new edition of your book is published!
Sign up at **www.nolo.com/legalupdater**.

Updates at Nolo.com

Check **www.nolo.com/update** to find recent changes in the law that
affect the current edition of your book.

Nolo Customer Service

To make sure that this edition of the book is the most recent one, call us at
800-728-3555 and ask one of our friendly customer service representatives
(7:00 am to 6:00 pm PST, weekdays only). Or find out at **www.nolo.com**.

Complete the Registration & Comment Card ...

... and we'll do the work for you! Just indicate your preferences below:

Registration & Comment Card

NAME		DATE

ADDRESS

CITY	STATE	ZIP

PHONE	EMAIL

COMMENTS

WAS THIS BOOK EASY TO USE?   (VERY EASY)   5   4   3   2   1   (VERY DIFFICULT)

☐ Yes, you can quote me in future Nolo promotional materials. *Please include phone number above.*

☐ Yes, send me **Nolo's Legal Updater** via email when a new edition of this book is available.

Yes, I want to sign up for the following email newsletters:

☐ **NoloBriefs** (monthly)
☐ **Nolo's Special Offer** (monthly)
☐ **Nolo's BizBriefs** (monthly)
☐ **Every Landlord's Quarterly** (four times a year)

☐ Yes, you can give my contact info to carefully selected
partners whose products may be of interest to me.

RECW 1.0

NOLO

Nolo
950 Parker Street
Berkeley, CA 94710-9867
www.nolo.com

YOUR LEGAL COMPANION